GENDER, FAMILIES, AND ELDER CARE

OTHER RECENT VOLUMES IN THE SAGE FOCUS EDITIONS

GENDER, FAMILIES, AND ELDER CARE

Jeffrey W. Dwyer
Raymond T. Coward
editors

SAGE PUBLICATIONS
The International Professional Publishers
Newbury Park   London   New Delhi

For information address:

SAGE Publications, Inc.
2455 Teller Road
Newbury Park, California 91320

SAGE Publications Ltd.
6 Bonhill Street
London EC2A 4PU
United Kingdom

SAGE Publications India Pvt. Ltd.
M-32 Market
Greater Kailash I
New Delhi 110 048 India

Printed in the United States of America

Library of Congress Cataloging-in-Publication Data

Main entry under title:

Gender, families, and elder care / Jeffrey W. Dwyer, Raymond T.
  Coward, editors.
        p. cm. — (Sage focus editions ; 138)
    Includes bibliographical references and index.
    ISBN 0-8039-3932-9. — ISBN 0-8039-3933-7 (pbk.)
      1. Aged—Care—United States. 2. Caregivers—United States.
  3. Sex role—United States. 4. Aged—United States—Family
  relationships. I. Dwyer, Jeffrey W. II. Coward, Raymond T.
  HV1461.G45   1992
  362.6—dc20   91-40695

92 93 94 10 9 8 7 6 5 4 3 2 1

Sage Production Editor: Diane S. Foster

To the women in our lives who have taught us so much about family and caregiving—through their actions, comportment, and integrity.

Judith Lynn Blazek Dwyer
Amanda Elizabeth Dwyer
Eva Ryan Ebley
Carrie E. Ebley Coward
Carrie E. Coward Morris
Andrea Sushok Coward
Rosalyn Green Coward
Gail Beavers Coward
Carrie Elizabeth Coward

Contents

PART III: Theory and Research

PART IV: Implications for Policy and Practice

Acknowledgments

It would not have been possible to contemplate, plan, and complete this project without the support, input, and assistance of many individuals. Collectively, the authors, our colleagues in family and aging research, the staff of the Center for Health Policy Research at the University of Florida, and our families have made this book better as a result of their advice and encouragement. As is often the case, however, there are several individuals who have made very specific contributions that we would like to recognize.

First and foremost, we are indebted to the prominent scholars who have contributed chapters to this volume. Their task was not an easy one. Each author was asked to write on a very specific issue, meet a tight writing schedule, conform to a specific set of format and style guidelines, and endure our requests for outlines and drafts of their chapters well before their final manuscripts were due. Their hard work, diligence, patience, and professionalism made it possible for us to integrate each chapter into a broader framework that, we believe, makes a significant contribution to the literature. We hope that they are pleased with the result. In addition, their commitment as individuals to the issues discussed in this volume is evidenced by the fact that each author has agreed to forgo all royalties so that a donation can be made to a selected nonprofit organization that provides services to elders. We are grateful for, and proud of, their beneficence in that regard.

Second, in November 1989, we met with several prominent scholars at the annual meetings of the Gerontological Society of America and the National

Council on Family Relations. They provided critical feedback on a preliminary prospectus that we had developed describing this project. Their critique and advice helped to shape the focus, content, and structure of the book in its formative stages. Specifically, in addition to some of the people who were subsequently asked to contribute chapters, we appreciate the involvement in that process of Karen Altergott, Timothy H. Brubaker, Marjorie Cantor, and Anne Martin-Matthews. We would also like to thank Mitch Allen, executive editor of Sage Publications, for his support, accessibility, and patience throughout the course of this project.

Third, we have benefited significantly from the efforts of our colleagues at the Center for Health Policy Research (CHPR) at the University of Florida. Specifically, we would like to thank our friend and colleague, Michael K. Miller, director of the CHPR, for creating an environment that facilitates and encourages all types of intellectual contributions. In addition, Christine Bono-Boyett, Linda Kain, Dan Nissen, and Riccardo Nuzzo have provided various kinds of assistance throughout the development of this project. Finally, this book would not have been possible without the assistance of Amy Coenen and Claydell Horne. They were responsible for all aspects of preparing the final manuscript, and we sincerely appreciate their commitment and good-natured attitude throughout.

Finally, our wives (Judith Blazek Dwyer and Andrea Sushok Coward) and children (Amanda Elizabeth Dwyer, Ryan Wells Coward, and Carrie Elizabeth Coward) have attributed our working evenings and weekends, the delayed chores around the house, and other related repercussions of our work over the last few months to "the book." Now that it is complete, we'll have to find another excuse. Yet it is their love for us and their support for our work that makes it possible for us to pursue intensely our interest in issues that we believe are important.

In spite of all of the support, advice, and encouragement we have received during the development of this book, undoubtedly errors remain. For those we take full responsibility.

—Jeffrey W. Dwyer
Raymond T. Coward

Introduction

Despite the proliferation of research on caregiving issues in recent years and the frequency with which gender is included in caregiving analyses, to date the gendered nature of family caregiving has not been clearly articulated. The idea for this book evolved from a series of discussions in which we became mindful of two important realities about family caregiving research: First, gender plays a central role in understanding family care of the elderly; second, no comprehensive resource existed that dealt with this issue. This book was conceived in light of our belief that a more complete appreciation of the significance of gender in the social context of caregiving will improve theory, research, policy, and practice related to impaired elders and their family relations.

We envisioned a volume that would consolidate and synthesize the widespread, multidisciplinary research that addresses the gender/family/aging nexus. Moreover, it was important that the book benefit researchers and practitioners, as well as students interested in family, aging, and women's issues. The optimal way to produce such a volume, we decided, was to capitalize on the existing knowledge and expertise of a selected group of scholars. The result is a compendium of closely linked chapters that inform the ongoing debate regarding the equitable distribution of responsibility for elder care.

The book was conceptualized and organized to meet three specific goals:

- to identify the fundamental demographic, conceptual, social, and economic factors that influence the association between gender and family care of the elderly
- to provide comprehensive literature reviews of gender issues within the three major types of family relationships that provide care to frail elders (spouses, adult children, and siblings)
- to examine the gender/family/aging nexus from the perspective of theory, research, policy, and practice, and to consider the implications of the gendered nature of family caregiving for the future in these areas

The Structure of the Book

With these goals in mind, we have separated the book into four parts. Part I, Perspectives on Gender and Family Caregiving, contains three chapters designed to provide an introductory overview of gender in the social context of family caregiving. Chapter 1 sets the stage for the issues discussed in this volume by focusing on the sociohistorical role of the family in caring for frail elders, defining important concepts in family caregiving research, and exploring future trends that may affect the gendered nature of family care for the elderly. These topics are important because they help to explain why a better understanding of the association between gender and family caregiving is essential if we are to develop an effective system of long-term care services that are sensitive to the needs of elders and caregivers—both women and men.

Following a brief overview of age and gender differences in the United States, Chapter 2 explores the demography of family caregiving from a gender perspective, using data from the 1982 National Long-Term Care Survey. Gender differences among both caregivers and care recipients are explored, with specific distributions provided by the age and marital status of the elder. The data presented in this chapter provide a detailed picture of the involvement of men and women of various relationship types in the care of older family members.

Finally, Chapter 3 reviews the conceptual perspectives that have been used in recent years to explain the gendered nature of family care for the elderly. Specifically, the author describes three frameworks that have informed previous research in this area (e.g., psychological/individual, sociological, and feminist) and reviews the strengths and weaknesses of these approaches. The purpose of the chapter, therefore, is not to "break new ground," but to provide a clear understanding of the conceptual perspectives that have guided much of the research in this area. Together, the three chapters in Part I provide essential background information for understanding many of the issues and ideas that are addressed in subsequent chapters.

Part II, The Structure of Caregiving Relationships, includes three chapters that focus on the family members who most frequently provide care to impaired elders: spouses, adult children, and siblings. The intent of each of these chapters is to provide a comprehensive review of the caregiving literature related to a specific type of family relationship. The authors focus on six common themes: the stress and burden associated with providing care, reciprocity between caregiver and care recipient, the level of impairment of the care receiver, the tasks performed and the hours of care provided by the caregiver, the interaction between family members and the formal service sector, and the affection and life satisfaction of the caregiver and the care recipient. In addition, each author examines issues in elder care that are unique to the particular relationship being addressed.

Part III, Theory and Research, includes four chapters that, together, provide an agenda for the development of future theory and research on gender and family care of the elderly. Specifically, Chapter 7 focuses on the obligation felt by children to care for their parents—that is, filial responsibility. The large body of literature that has been written on this topic over several decades is synthesized in this chapter, and conceptual and methodological issues are discussed. Chapter 8 complements the preceding chapter by also focusing on the adult child-parent relationship. The author argues that differences in the provision of elder care by adult sons and daughters are a special case of gender differences in broader domains of family behavior (i.e., the domestic division of labor, nurturance in family role behavior, and kinship relations). Moreover, theoretical propositions are advanced that summarize what is known about the adult child-parent caregiving relationship and place elder care in this broader context. Possible directions for future theory development are also discussed.

The two chapters in Part III that focus on research are also complementary. Chapter 9 addresses methodological difficulties in the study of gender and family caregiving by reviewing seven deficiencies in the current literature: the underrepresentation of men, small sample sizes, the focus on primary caregivers to the exclusion of other roles, reporting biases in mental health effects, the lack of longitudinal research, the failure of quantitative research to predict mental health effects for male caregivers, and the relative absence of qualitative research. Recommendations are offered for resolving each of these deficiencies. Following the specific emphasis on methodological issues in the previous chapter, Chapter 10 establishes an agenda for future research that both describes how a knowledge base should be built and identifies specific aspects of the gender/family/aging nexus that have the greatest potential for enhancing our understanding of the gendered nature of family care for frail elders.

Finally, Part IV, Implications for Policy and Practice, is designed to consider the inferences of the information and data reviewed in the other sections of the book for policy and practice. Collectively, the three chapters in Part IV offer an agenda for the future that is built on understanding the dynamics of the gendered nature of family care for the elderly and the development of gender-sensitive aging and family policies that can be implemented successfully in the practice environment.

In Chapter 11, employment, family caregiving, and employer-based policies regarding elder care are addressed. Specifically, the chapter discusses the influence of employment on caregiving behaviors and the effect of caregiving on employee performance. This is a specific area of social policy that deserves increased attention because of the large number of family caregivers who are employed outside the home. Moreover, for reasons discussed in this chapter, the need for employer-based family care policies will increase in the coming decades.

While Chapter 11 has a specific emphasis on employment, Chapter 12 provides a more general look at gender inequities in other areas of social policy related to family caregiving. The chapter describes structural gender inequities in elder care that interact with inadequate community care policies to perpetuate the provision of elder care by unpaid female family members. In addition to discussing the impact of specific policies that affect both caregivers and care receivers, the chapter advances suggestions for future policy development.

Finally, Chapter 13 examines the implications of the gendered nature of family care for practitioners who work with elders and their families. After briefly addressing the impact of research on the practice environment, this chapter focuses on the gender-sensitive assessment of elder family care units and the targeting of clinical support. In addition, intervention strategies that may be influenced by gendered norms and expectations are discussed, as well as guidelines for gender-sensitive interventions. Finally, the author identifies five areas of gender-friendly research that would benefit practitioners by establishing a basis for developing successful practice models to support both men and women in their elder-care responsibilities.

Cautions and Limitations

Like most efforts of this kind, this product is not perfect; indeed, no one is more acutely aware of that fact than we are. Not all relevant issues related to gender and family care of the elderly are adequately covered in this volume—there were simply too many issues and we had a limited amount of space.

Perhaps the most obvious shortcoming is the absence of a specific chapter that examines the influence of culture in shaping gendered behavior and, therefore, the structural form of family care for the elderly. Although there are frequent references in various chapters to the effect that culture has on defining what help is to be given and who is to provide it, as well as a "call" for more research on the topic in Chapter 10, these treatments are clearly insufficient. Indeed, an adequate discussion of the influence of culture on the gender/family/aging nexus might well require an entire book. Hence, while we acknowledge the lack of a specific emphasis on culture in this volume, we have attempted to underscore its importance throughout the book.

Similarly, although we have endeavored to orchestrate the individual chapters in this volume into a cohesive whole, we did not manipulate the unique deductions or opinions of the authors. As a result, because the contributors to this book are from a variety of disciplinary backgrounds and have a wide range of experience in dealing with the issues discussed in this volume, there were bound to be differences of opinion about certain issues even though everyone was working from essentially the same corpus of information. For example, what is referred to as the "psychological/individual" perspective in Chapter 3 is called the "psychoanalytic" perspective in others. We have made no attempt to rectify these differences; rather, we believe that they underscore the range of thought about the issues being discussed and highlight the need to conduct further research to achieve greater consensus on these continuing controversies.

Despite these shortcomings, we are pleased with the final product. It brings together for the first time a large body of research and information that is focused exclusively on the critical role of gender in understanding the patterns of family caregiving to older persons in our society. We hope that you will find it a useful resource in your quest to understand this phenomenon better.

PART I

Perspectives on Gender and Family Caregiving

1

Gender, Family, and Long-Term Care of the Elderly

JEFFREY W. DWYER
RAYMOND T. COWARD

Current projections of the disabled elderly population indicate that by the middle of the twenty-first century there will be more older Americans in need of long-term care assistance than there were people over age 65 prior to 1960 (U.S. Bureau of the Census, 1989; U.S. Senate, Special Committee on Aging, 1987). One consequence of this expected growth in the long-term care population is that policymakers, concerned with rising social and health care costs, have "discovered the 'family' as an untapped resource" (Horowitz, 1985a, p. 200) and a less expensive alternative to government-supported programs (Abel, 1986; Callahan, 1988). Family gerontologists have responded to this increased attention by focusing their research on the role of the family in providing assistance to frail older people and the effects that caregiving has on family members (Abel, 1990a; Brody & Brody, 1989; Mancini & Blieszner, 1989).

During the 1980s, one of the most consistent findings that emerged from this literature was that aging policies based on informal family care exacerbated the already disadvantaged position of women by not accounting for the unobserved health, social, and economic costs associated with elder care (Osterbusch, Keigher, Miller, & Linsk, 1987; see also Chapter 12, this volume). As a result, it is now apparent that long-term care and familial responsibility for the aged must be considered within a framework that recognizes the centrality of gender in the social context of family caregiving.

In this chapter our goal is to orient the reader to the problem of gender inequality in family caregiving and to the issues that will be addressed in subsequent chapters. We begin by discussing three empirical generalizations that underscore the importance of gender as a differentiating characteristic in the social context of family caregiving. Second, we examine the socio-historical role of the family in caring for frail and disabled elders. Next, we address three questions that focus on the fundamental elements of family caregiving and have gender as a central component: What is family caregiving? Who needs family caregiving? Who provides family caregiving? Finally, we briefly explore social trends that are likely to affect the gendered nature of family caregiving in the future.

Gender, Family, and Long-Term Care: Empirical Generalizations

Empirical generalizations are "first-order abstractions that describe actual events in the empirical world" (Turner, 1982, p. 219). As such, they are established findings that should become the basis for developing more general propositions and axioms that *explain* these regularities (Homans, 1974). Although the conceptual and theoretical development of the family caregiving literature is limited (Finley, 1989; see also Chapters 3 and 8, this volume), the empirical evidence supports three generalizations that address the role of the family and of gender in providing long-term care to disabled elders.

- The family is the primary source of long-term care assistance for the aged.

The magnitude of care provided by family members is substantial. Approximately 80% of disabled elders live in the community (U.S. Senate, Special Committee on Aging, 1987), and three out of four community-dwelling frail elders receive all of their support from family and friends (Scanlon, 1988). Stone, Cafferata, and Sangl (1987) have reported, for example, that relatives provide between 3.5 and 5.1 hours of care each day, and perform between 7 and 10 caregiving tasks, depending on their relationship to the frail elder. The significance of such care cannot be understated.

Elders who have received family assistance typically enter nursing homes at greater levels of impairment (Barney, 1977) and, while living in the community, use fewer home-based formal services (Ward, Sherman, & La Gory, 1984) than their counterparts without such support. Paringer (1983) has estimated that the cost of replacing the care currently provided "free" by family members would be $9.6 billion.

• A majority of the caregiving assistance attributed to the family is provided by women.

A wealth of evidence now supports the generalization that families rarely provide caregiving assistance—women do (Brody, 1981; Cantor, 1983; Horowitz, 1985b; Stoller, 1983). Wives are more likely to be caregivers than are husbands (Barusch & Spaid, 1989; Tennstedt, McKinlay, & Sullivan, 1989), daughters are more likely to provide care than are sons (Coward & Dwyer, 1990; Dwyer & Coward, 1991), and sisters are more likely to provide care than are brothers (Matthews & Rosner, 1988). Indeed, among the unmarried frail elderly who remain in the community, 80% are cared for by women (Soldo & Myllyluoma, 1983). Hence, although elder care is a relatively new form of family labor (Finley, 1989), it is a "family responsibility" dominated by women.

• Most elderly people in need of long-term care are women.

For largely demographic reasons, most older people in need of long-term care are women (Abramovitz, 1988). As a result, vague references to the "frail elderly" in caregiving research mask the fact that, among those in need of caregiving assistance, "the poor and solitary are very likely to be women" (Goldscheider, 1990, p. 535). There are currently 68 men to every 100 women over age 65, and the ratio of women to men over age 85 (the so-called oldest-old) is greater than 2:1 (National Research Council, 1988).

As we approach the twenty-first century, the importance of these three empirical realities cannot be minimized. The demographic and economic projections of the elderly population with which we are confronted (see Chapter 2, this volume) only highlight the need for a better understanding of the gendered nature of family caregiving.

Gender and Family Caregiving in Sociohistorical Perspective

As is often the case when exploring complex social phenomena, such as family caregiving, misinterpretations of the past and misunderstandings about the present can lead to policies that have deleterious consequences for specific groups of people. In this context, it has been argued that "the family" benefits from government intervention only when its needs are consistent with those of individuals or are coincident with the resolution of other social or economic crises (Schorr, 1968). Yet, the converse is also true: "The family" can be imperiled when it is viewed as a solution to societal problems.

Although it was once believed that the elderly were isolated and abandoned, we now know that, with few exceptions, the family has always provided long-term caregiving support (Brody & Brody, 1989; Shanas, 1979a). There is also little debate over the assertion that women have historically been the "caregivers" within families (Dwyer & Seccombe, 1991). In light of the ample empirical and intellectual support for these generalizations, it is reasonable to ask why the long-term care/family/gender nexus has become, at the close of the twentieth century, the subject of such widespread debate that hundreds of published articles now address one or more related topics under the rubric of family caregiving (see, for example, the reference list for this volume). It is our contention that a range of social, historical, demographic, and economic factors have converged to place increased emphasis on the gendered nature of family caregiving.

Family Caregiving for Dependent Elders Was Not Always a Significant Social, Family, or Gender Issue

Although we have come to accept "the proposition that it is women's role to provide the day-to-day care of the old" (Brody, 1986, p. 198), it is important to remember that the emphasis placed on family care of the elderly has not always been the same as it is today. In the mid-nineteenth century, for example, people over age 65 accounted for approximately 2.1% of the population, and this figure had risen to only 4.1% by 1900 (Moroney, 1980). Therefore, even though providing care for a spouse and children was a responsibility associated with women, this obligation rarely included meeting the needs of frail, older, family members (Haber, 1983). In addition, although women now substantially outnumber men among those over age 65 (Soldo & Agree, 1988), in 1900 the ratio was 98 women per 100 men over 65; the number of elderly women did not exceed the number of older men until approximately 1940 (U.S. Bureau of the Census, 1975). As a result, while middle-aged couples today typically have at least two parents alive, more than half in 1900 had no surviving parents (Uhlenberg, 1980) and those who were alive were no more likely to be mothers than fathers.

We have also been socialized to think that there is an unalterable connection between being old and being sick (Stahl & Feller, 1990) and that dependent elders have historically been cared for in the context of an extended family system. In 1900, however, "many old people had patterns of daily activity indistinguishable from the rest of the adult population" (Dahlin, 1980, p. 106), because retirement had not yet emerged as a viable option. Most people over age 65 expected to live vigorous lives until they died. In addition, although many older people lived with their children, the elders were usually the heads of these households, rather than dependents, and they were equally likely to live with married daughters as with sons (Dahlin, 1980). The aged at the turn of the century also maintained relatively high social status because they still retained economic control of their holdings (primarily through the inheritance of land). This social status, however, was not without a price. According to D. H. Fischer (1978), many elderly people received respect, honor, and veneration from their family members, but without affection, devotion, and love. Nevertheless, providing family care to frail elders was an infrequent phenomenon, and gender was not a significant distinguishing characteristic of the caregiving environment.

Public Acceptance of Financial Responsibility for Disabled Elders and the Emergence of Women as the Primary Family Caregivers

As industrialization took hold during the early twentieth century, employment opportunities for the aged declined and aging came to be viewed as a social problem that could be solved through societal intervention. By the 1930s, although old-age pensions were becoming more common, the elderly were among the poorest groups in the United States, and support for the dependent aged "increasingly shifted to the public sector" (Axinn & Stern, 1985, p. 654). It was during this period that the public accepted financial responsibility for the disabled elderly, absolving family members of similar obligations (D. H. Fischer, 1978). These changes were manifested in the growth of a human services bureaucracy between 1930 and 1960 that, among other major functions, sought to relieve families of some of the responsibilities associated with the care of impaired older family members.

According to many family researchers, the structural isolation of the elderly and their loss of function in society were among the costs of shifting from an extended to a nuclear family system in order to meet the specialized needs of a modern industrial society (Parsons, 1944). Much of the gerontology literature prior to the 1960s was predicated on the belief that premodern families were "closer, warmer, and stronger than the 'isolated' nuclear family with its 'isolated elderly' of the modern era" (Goldscheider, 1990, p. 533). The assertion that the elderly were isolated was based, in part, on data showing that nursing home admissions had risen substantially since 1930 (Doty, 1986)—an outcome that presumably reflected the shifting of responsibility for disabled elders from the private to the public sector. Further analysis revealed, however, that this trend was largely a function of the lesser use of mental institutions as placements for the elderly and the rise in the proportion of the older population that was over age 75 (the most frequent users of institutional services), rather than overt neglect on the part of the family (Doty, 1986). Today, the irony of the myth of the isolated elderly is that adult child caregivers "provide more care and more difficult care to more parents over much longer periods of time than they did in the good old days" (Brody, 1985, p. 21).

Although the family was absolved of much of the financial responsibility for the disabled elderly who were in institutions, many older people still required some form of caregiving assistance. The ideology of "separate spheres" that emerged during this period associated caregiving values with the home and women and exonerated men, who worked for profit in the marketplace, from caregiving obligations (Hooyman, 1990). Although caregiving was valued as a function of daily family life (Ehrenreich, 1983), it was devalued in an industrializing society that defined work in terms of output and wages rather than nurturance and maintenance (Bernard, 1983). According to Hooyman (1990), "The ideology of separate spheres took two competing philosophies—the old one of community, responsibility, and duty, and the new one of individualism—and resolved the conflict along the lines of gender: women would nurture, men would achieve; women would be the carers, men the breadwinners" (p. 228).

The Limits of Government and Increased Familial Responsibility for the Care of Frail Elders

By the mid-1960s, family gerontologists had begun to establish that older people were not isolated or abandoned, but an integral part of a modified extended family system (Litwak, 1965). Research demonstrated that elders participated in an ongoing series of exchanges with other family members and that, in addition to socializing children, a primary function of the family was to provide security for adults in later life (Sussman, 1965). For a time this system, in which the public provided financial support and the family provided caregiving assistance, was sufficient. However, once expenditures for the disabled elderly outstripped the perceived ability of government to provide the necessary economic resources, public officials turned to the family to assume a greater portion of the caregiving burden.

The economic decline of the late 1970s forced governments to realize the limits of their resources and to renege on many of the "promises" they had made in the 1960s. One manifestation of these economic realities was a search for new mechanisms to fulfill government responsibilities to older citizens. During this same period, family gerontologists were busy establishing the preeminent role of the family as a resource for disabled older family members. The simultaneous recognition of the need for inexpensive long-term care alternatives and the active involvement of family members in providing elder care furnished some policymakers with a justification for the drastic cuts that were made in government programs in the early 1980s. Subsequently, however, families came to be viewed not simply as one among several long-term care options, but as a cost-containment resource capable "of absorbing an even greater proportion of the care than they do now" (Horowitz, 1985a, p. 230). This evolution in the emphasis placed on family caregiving has fueled an ongoing debate between those who urge the development of public policies supportive of family care and those who wish to place even greater responsibilities on the family as a means to deal with the rising costs associated with the care of disabled elderly people.

In light of the overwhelming evidence concerning the predominant role of wives and daughters in caregiving, the public policy emphasis on families that prevailed in the 1980s placed the burden of elder care squarely on women. According to Hooyman (1990), "The current public policy option of transferring caregiving work from the public to the private sphere is apparently based on the erroneous assumption that informal structures for providing care (e.g., the family) are underutilized and simply need to be activated" (p. 223). Yet this emphasis occurred at a time when rising divorce rates, increased female labor force participation, and other factors associated with the "gender revolution" of the last three decades made women less able than ever to fulfill such responsibilities without significant consequences (Goldscheider, 1990).

"A decade of investigation suggests that while families are the preeminent and often the only source of community-based long-term care for impaired aged, the well-being of family caregivers is compromised in the process" (Noelker, 1990, p. 189). As a result, family gerontologists, in an effort to influence family and aging policies, focused a great deal of attention during the 1980s on the negative consequences of caregiving for family members. Although the family caregiving literature has established that caregiving does have deleterious effects on caregivers and care receivers alike, "the homogenization of such crucial variables as type of relationship, sex, health, and work status" (Cantor, 1983, p. 597) obscures important differences in the social context of caregiving. Perhaps the most important and most frequently cited of these "obscured variables" is gender. Although the language of caregiving emphasizes the role of the family, Horowitz (1985b) has argued that "when the needs of an older parent grow, the sex of the adult child is one of the most important and consistent predictors of caregiving involvement" (p. 612).

Gender and Family Caregiving

The fundamental elements of all family caregiving research are embodied in three questions: What is family caregiving? Who needs family caregiving? Who provides family caregiving? The answers to these questions, however, vary widely in the caregiving literature. Indeed, the lack of clarity about these questions has limited the comparability of results and has obscured the role that gender plays in caregiving by focusing attention on broad categories of people (e.g., family caregivers, spouses, adult children) rather than on the characteristics of individuals who provide and receive care (e.g., daughters, sons, mothers, fathers).

What Is Family Caregiving?

One of the first quandaries faced by researchers in this area is defining the phenomenon of interest, that is, family caregiving. Some have suggested that *caregiving* refers to care provided to an elderly person who has some degree of physical, mental, or emotional impairment that limits his or her independence and necessitates ongoing assistance (Horowitz, 1985a). From this perspective, family caregiving begins in earnest when an older person becomes sufficiently impaired (physically or mentally) to require assistance in order to function effectively in a noninstitutionalized setting and a family member begins to provide or facilitate such care. Yet caregiving can also be conceived of as a lifelong series of interactions between the caregiver and the care recipient. In this context, caregiving is a more diffuse phenomenon that exists over a number of years and evolves, only during periods of increased impairment, into the type of caregiving typically addressed in the aging context.

Doty (1986) has argued that caregiving is motivated by three factors: love and affection, a desire to reciprocate for past assistance, and "a more generalized societal norm of spousal or filial responsibility" (p. 46). Hence a distinction may be made between caregivers who care *about* and those who care *for* impaired elders (Lewis & Meredith, 1988). The former do so out of love and affection, while the latter perform out of a sense of obligation (Hooyman, 1990).

Until now, many family gerontologists have resolved the dilemma of identifying what caregiving is by relying on a fixed set of tasks that they have decided are indicative of caregiving. These tasks usually coincide with the activity of daily living (ADL) and instrumental activity of daily living (IADL) impairments experienced by disabled elders. ADLs are personal care tasks (e.g., bathing, toileting, eating, and dressing), and IADL tasks consist of responsibilities such as shopping, cooking, and transportation that typically require lower levels of emotional, physical, and time commitments. Family caregiving from a task perspective, then, occurs when there are "relatives and friends who help impaired persons with such tasks" (Abel, 1990a, p. 140).

Despite the frequency with which task-centered definitions of caregiving are used, recent research suggests that the association of ADL and IADL tasks with caregiving differs by gender and family position (i.e., spouse versus adult child) and, therefore, may not accurately reflect the contributions of some family members. For example, data from the National Survey of Informal Caregivers show that, among spouse caregivers, husbands report providing more hours of care and helping with more caregiving tasks than do wives. In explaining this finding, Dwyer and Seccombe (1991) argue that men and women define *caregiving* differently. Specifically, wives fail to acknowledge many of the tasks they perform in the caregiving environment as caregiving per se because they are responsibilities that women have performed throughout their lives (e.g., preparing meals, housework, laundry). Husbands typically do not struggle with this distinction. Rather, they readily classify the performance of such tasks as caregiving because usually they become responsible for them only when their spouses become disabled. Sons and daughters also differentially associate certain ADL and IADL tasks with caregiving, although not in ways consistent with those of wives and husbands (Dwyer & Seccombe, 1991). In addition, elderly care recipients have strong gender-related feelings about what constitutes family caregiving and who should provide such care (Matthews & Rosner, 1988). As a result, defining caregiving in terms of tasks is problematic because of the interaction between tasks and gender.

The emphasis placed on specific tasks in recent years has made it easier to recognize that informal care is "socially necessary work and has an important place in the long-term care system" (Abel, 1990a, p. 141). Yet not all tasks are typically measured in caregiving research. Sons are less likely to perform "hands-on" tasks (Montgomery & Kamo, 1989), for example, but are much more likely to perform male-oriented tasks such as home mainte- nance and car repair (Coward, 1987). In addition, wives usually provide more help with meals and laundry than do husbands, while husbands provide greater assistance with transportation and handiwork (Markides, Boldt, & Ray, 1986; Young & Kahana, 1989). As a result, although caregiving is associated with the provision of assistance in the form of tasks, the lack of specificity, both conceptually and methodologically, about which tasks con- stitute family caregiving makes it difficult to assess accurately the gendered nature of the caregiving environment.

Who Needs Family Caregiving?

People over age 65 who require caregiving assistance are typically referred to as *frail elders*. Defining this population is essential because the size of the frail elderly population is inextricably tied to level of impairment, which, in turn, is associated with differential levels of involvement of males and females. Specifically, as the needs of elders shift from assistance with IADLs to assistance with ADLs, daughters are more likely to provide care than are sons (Dwyer & Coward, 1991; Montgomery & Kamo, 1989).

Three definitions of the frail elderly have been predominant in the care- giving literature. In early caregiving research the phrase *frail elderly* referred to elders who had levels of impairment comparable to the institutionalized elderly, but were still living in the community (Shanas, 1979b). This criterion included approximately 10% of the elderly population, primarily individuals who were bed- or housebound and required a substantial amount of in-home care (Horowitz, 1985a). It also reflected the emphasis by policymakers on family support as a low-cost alternative to institutionalization by focusing on the economic costs of these long-term care options (Comptroller General of the United States, 1977). In their efforts to show that families were an integral part of the long-term care system, however, family gerontologists inadvertently exaggerated this comparison by failing to include the non-economic costs of providing care (e.g., stress and burden) to elders who were unable to function independently (Abel, 1990a). This comparison with the institutionalized population also failed to acknowledge the wide range of help provided by family members to older, but less disabled, persons.

A similarly restrictive definition of the frail elderly focused solely on ADL disabilities, because they are significant predictors of an array of service use ranging from physician services to nursing homes (Wiener, Hanley, Clark, & Van Nostrand, 1990). Although estimates of the number of elders who experience at least one ADL impairment vary from 5% to 8.1%, depending on the national survey data used (Wiener et al., 1990), this definition includes elders who require ongoing assistance with personal care needs such as bathing, toileting, and eating, but may not require institutionalization. Like the previous definition, however, it emphasizes levels of impairment that are likely to require nonfamily formal (paid) assistance.

Most family caregiving researchers, however, define the frail elderly as those people over age 65 who experience at least one ADL *or* IADL functional impairment. According to Horowitz (1985a), it is "this broader definition which is most relevant, defining the conditions under which reciprocal family exchanges begin to shift and the move is made into a caregiving relationship" (p. 195). Results from the National Long-Term Care Survey indicate, for example, that approximately 20% of the elderly population is "frail" using the combined ADL/IADL criterion (Macken, 1986). Data from the Supplement on Aging of the 1984 National Health Interview Survey, however, suggest that 32.7% of the elderly population conforms to this definition (Coward, Cutler, & Mullens, 1990). Hence, although this definition is more inclusive, estimation problems are also present in this context.

Perhaps more problematic is the fact that different researchers and surveys use different types of impairments in constructing ADL and IADL indices (see Chapter 9 in this volume for a more comprehensive discussion of the methodological deficiencies of research in this area). These measures are not, as they are often assumed to be, unvarying lists of specific functioning disabilities. Consequently, using such indices as a basis for identifying "impaired elders" may bias our assessment of "who needs family care."

Who Provides Family Caregiving?

It is difficult to characterize the "family" in family caregiving just as it has become problematic to describe the family at all stages in the life course.

High divorce rates, residential independence, and increased female labor force participation have combined to affect both the caregiving ability of family members and the potential of elders to receive assistance in old age (Goldscheider, 1990). For most people, however, although "fictive family" (e.g., neighbors, friends) may emerge to provide assistance to older people when it is needed and "blood relatives" are not available (Gubrium & Buckholdt, 1982), the "family" in caregiving research usually refers to individuals, or groups of individuals, who are related by blood or marriage. Specifically, most elderly people who require caregiving assistance receive help from spouses or adult children (including in-laws).

In most instances, one individual, the primary caregiver, provides nearly all of the caregiving assistance attributed to the family (Cantor, 1983; Sangl, 1985). The likelihood of being a primary caregiver follows a hierarchical pattern (Horowitz, 1985a). If a spouse is available and his or her health permits it, he or she is most likely to be the primary caregiver (Stoller & Earl, 1983). In the absence of a spouse, an adult child usually assumes caregiving responsibilities (Stoller, 1983). Lacking a spouse or adult child, other family members (e.g., siblings) typically provide care (Johnson, 1983). Although family caregiving is generally viewed as a specific activity, the role of family caregiver becomes a significant social role, with accompanying norms and expectations, "particularly when individuals assume *primary* responsibility for the care of an elderly relative" (Suitor & Pillemer, 1990, p. 311).

The focus on a primary caregiver, however, obscures the fact that, in many instances, men do provide assistance to frail elders. There is evidence, for example, that men help with different tasks (Coward, 1987; Matthews & Rosner, 1988), fulfill different roles (Montgomery & Kamo, 1989; Stoller, 1990), and define the context of caregiving differently (Dwyer & Seccombe, 1991) than women and that these dissimilarities have not been addressed adequately in family caregiving research (see also Chapter 9, this volume). Yet sons typically become primary caregivers only when no female siblings are available (Coward & Dwyer, 1990; Horowitz, 1985b; Stoller, 1983) and husbands who provide care are much more likely to receive some type of formal assistance (Horowitz, 1985a).

Finally, results from a recent study of male caregivers involved in caregiver support groups indicate "that there is an identifiable group of husbands, sons, grandsons, brothers, and other men who are deeply involved in providing primary care for an elderly relative, usually a woman" (Kaye & Applegate, 1990a, p. 139). These men were engaged in a wide range of caregiving tasks, used varying levels of family and formal assistance, and expressed relatively low levels of burden (Kaye & Applegate, 1990a). Although the unique character of the sampling frame used in the research (e.g., caregiver support groups) reduces the generalizability of the findings, the results serve to remind us that men do provide care.

Factors That May Affect the Gendered Nature of Family Caregiving in the Future

A number of authors have argued that American families are changing and that those changes have the potential to affect the future care of older persons by family members (Brubaker, 1985a; Cicirelli, 1981; Goldscheider, 1990; Mancini & Blieszner, 1989). In this section we briefly discuss four of these changes.

Declining Family Size

The proportion of families with only one child has been increasing, while the number of two-child families has remained approximately the same and the number of large families has declined dramatically (U.S. Bureau of the Census, 1990). In 1970, 20.2% of all American families had three or more children; by 1988, only 9.9% of families fit this description (U.S. Bureau of the Census, 1990). This change is significant because there is some evidence that there is a caregiving "advantage" to having more children. Lee, Dwyer, and Coward (1990), for example, have demonstrated that the number of children is a significant predictor of an elder coresiding with a child or having a child living nearby. Although coresidence is not necessary, some degree of physical proximity is required if a child is to provide ongoing caregiving assistance (Finley, Roberts, & Banahan, 1988). As a result, a decline in the number of children a person has upon entering old age may have an impact on the pattern of care that person receives (see Chapter 5 in this volume for a more detailed discussion of this issue).

Increased Female Labor Force Participation

The participation of women in the labor market has increased dramatically during the last half of the twentieth century. Among women ages 25 to 54, for example, "more than 7 of 10 . . . are now in the labor force, up from 3 of 10 four decades earlier" (Shank, 1988, p. 3). Perhaps more important, it is projected that by the year 2000, 76.5% of women 45 to 54 and 49% of women 55 to 64, those women most likely to provide care to impaired parents, will be in the labor force. Clearly, as Shank (1988) has argued, "labor market activity is now the norm for women, and high participation rates are evident in nearly all demographic groups" (p. 6). Moreover, women's employment is not part-time employment intended to add discretionary money to the family income. Rather, in 1986, 78% of all employed women between the ages of 25 and 54 worked full-time. (See Chapter 11 in this volume for a more complete discussion of these employment trends and their potential impact on family care of the elderly.)

Divorce Rates

Although divorce rates in the United States have leveled off, current rates are still very high compared with previous decades (Martin & Bumpass, 1989; Reiss & Lee, 1988), and it is estimated that approximately 55% of those born from 1946 to 1960 (the so-called baby boomers) will experience divorce (Norton & Moorman, 1987). Among the elderly, divorce eliminates one primary source of care—a spouse. The divorce of an adult child may also alter the probability that he or she will be able to provide care to an impaired parent. This trend has gender implications because women bear the economic brunt of divorce (Weitzman, 1985), although the future costs of divorce may actually have the greatest long-term consequences for older men. Goldscheider (1990) has argued that "in old age, as employment-based resources become less central and as family relationships based on marriage and parenthood grow in importance, it is males who are at risk" (p. 533).

Longer Life Expectancy

The growth in the numbers of elders reaching very old ages is problematic because the highest rates of disability and impairment are found among the oldest-old (Manton & Soldo, 1985; see also Chapter 2, this volume). Moreover, at higher levels of impairment, elders are more likely to be receiving care and assistance from family members (Coward et al., 1990). Thus parent care will increasingly become a normative life event (Brody, 1985). In addition, there will be an expansion in the number of adult children who will be old themselves when they are caring for a frail parent. In 1980, there were a quarter million elders living in households with elders from a generation preceding them (e.g., a parent, parent-in-law) (Coward, Cutler, & Schmidt, 1989), and this number will surely rise in the coming years.

Conclusion

The gendered nature of family caregiving has implications for theory, research, policy, and practice. Theory about family caregiving will continue to be underdeveloped until efforts are made to place elder care in a broader conceptual framework that emphasizes gender. Caregiving research, on the other hand, must become more focused and must approach gender as one of the fundamental elements of a system of relationships that affect the social context of caregiving. In addition, aging and family policy will not be consistent with the needs of caregivers and frail elders unless policymakers begin to develop, implement, and support gender-sensitive initiatives. Finally, from a practice perspective, service providers, in their development and administration of caregiving assistance programs designed to maximize care provided to older persons, should understand fully the differences between men and women in attitudes toward, resources for, and expectations of caregiving.

2

Demographic Perspectives on Gender and Family Caregiving

RAYMOND T. COWARD
CLAYDELL HORNE
JEFFREY W. DWYER

At least three characteristics of previous research on the demography of family caregiving have inhibited our understanding of the gendered nature of family care. First, many of the earliest studies in this area did not even report the gender of the caregiver; rather, they focused on the relative participation of different types of family members (i.e., spouses versus adult children). As a consequence, although those studies provided information about the comparative participation of various family members, they offered no insight into the role of gender as a factor in determining who gives or receives caregiving assistance. Second, in research where gender was introduced, many investigators narrowed their focus to a single type of family member (e.g., adult children or, specifically, sons versus daughters). As a result, although such studies helped to focus our attention on gender differences, they did little to inform us about inequalities or disparities that transcended specific types of familial relationships. Finally, much of the early work on the demography of family caregiving was based on local or regional samples, which made it difficult to generalize the findings to national trends. Thus, although there is general agreement that it is an important element in caregiving, there is still a great deal that we do not know about gender (both of the caregiver and of the care recipient) and the demography of family care for the elderly.

In this chapter we will explore the composition of the helping networks described by frail elders as a function of the gender of the elder. Our data source is a large, nationally representative sample of impaired elders. First, however, we will review gender differences in the recent demographic transformations that have occurred in the age structure of the population of the United States and the potential implications of those changes for the long-term family care of elders.

Age and Gender Differences
in the Population of the United States

The number of elderly persons in the United States who may need family care has risen dramatically during the twentieth century as the age structure of our population has undergone astonishing transformations. As age increases, persons are more likely to experience physical disabilities and limitations in their functional abilities (Coroni-Huntley et al., 1985; Kane, Ouslander, & Abrass, 1989; Macken, 1986; Manton & Soldo, 1985). Moreover, as age and disabilities increase, elders are more apt to be receiving aid from family caregivers (Coward, 1987; Coward, Cutler, & Mullens, 1990; Stone, Cafferata, & Sangl, 1987). Thus the "graying" of U.S. society has significant implications for the aging family and for family caregiving.

Increases in the Number and Proportion
of Elderly Persons

Both the number of elders living in our society and the proportion of the population that is elderly have increased since the turn of the century. In 1900 there were 3.1 million persons 65 years of age or older in the United States (Atchley, 1988). By 1990, however, estimates indicated that the elderly population had grown to 31.6 million (U.S. Bureau of the Census, 1989). Moreover, as a proportion of total population, the elderly have increased from 4.1% in 1900 to 12.6% in 1990. By the year 2040, demographers have estimated that persons 65 years of age and older will account for one in five Americans (21.6%), or more than 66 million persons (National Research Council, 1988).

The growth of the elderly population, however, has not been uniform across the full spectrum of persons who are over the age of 65. That is, the number of elders aged 85 years and older (the so-called oldest-old) has grown at a significantly faster rate than other age categories of elders. Specifically, Rosenwaike (1985) has noted that "between the 1960 and 1980 censuses, the oldest-old increased by 141 percent in the United States, a rate far in excess of that of all persons 65 and over (54 percent), or that of the total population (26 percent)" (p. 188). Perhaps as important as the rapid expansion of the oldest-old population that occurred in the past is the growth of this group of elders, which is expected to continue, unparalleled, for the next 50 years. Middle series projections estimate that, by the year 2040, there will be approximately 12.8 million persons over the age of 85 years in the United States (Rosenwaike, 1985).

Shifts in the Gender Structure of the Aged Population

As the age structure and life expectancies of the population in the United States have shifted, significant gender differences have emerged. As recently as 1930, for example, the population aged 65 years and older was composed of approximately equal numbers of males and females (Pegels, 1988; Treas, 1977). But by 1987, there were only 68.4 males for every 100 females (U.S. Bureau of the Census, 1989), and this ratio is predicted to continue to decline, although more slowly than in the past, into the first two decades of the next century (National Research Council, 1988). By the year 2040, it is estimated that there will be 12.6 million more women than men aged 65 and older.

The expanding group of elders aged 85 years and older has also become increasingly more female in its composition. In 1940 there were 75.0 men aged 85 and older for every 100 females of the same age; by 1980 this ratio had decreased to 43.7/100, and it is predicted that the disparity will increase through the early decades of the twenty-first century (Binstock & Shanas, 1985; Rosenwaike, 1985).

The Need for Long-Term Family Care

The dramatic increases in the number of persons aged 65 years and older, coupled with the critical differentials that exist by age and gender, have significant implications for family caregiving. For example, although increased life expectancy has added more years of healthy living for many Americans, it has also increased the number of persons in our society with chronic illnesses, functional impairments, and health-related disabilities.

Among the elderly, the proportion of persons experiencing difficulty performing activities of daily living increases steadily with advanced age. For example, data from the Supplement on Aging of the 1984 National Health Interview Survey indicate that 17.1% of young-old respondents (age 65-74) report difficulty performing one or more personal care activities, but the rate rises incrementally for the older age groups—27.8% for those 75-84 and 48.8% for those 85 and older (U.S. Senate, Special Committee on Aging, 1988a). Not only does the prospect of disability increase with age, but the probability of experiencing multiple impairments also escalates notably after age 75 (Macken, 1986).

Finally, because females have higher rates of disability than do males (Kane et al., 1989; Manton & Soldo, 1985), the increasing proportion of the aged population that is female represents a greater potential need for personal care assistance. Figure 2.1 illustrates that among various age groups of elders, females uniformly have higher rates of disability than their male counterparts. For example, Manton and Soldo (1985) have estimated that in 1980 there were 40.6% more females than males over the age of 85 who had difficulty performing five or six ADLs.

The Gender Composition of Helping Networks

Most Americans are now well aware that only a small fraction of elders live in nursing homes or other institutionalized settings at any one point in time. Less well understood, perhaps, is the fact that only one out of five *disabled* elders lives in an institution (U.S. Senate, Special Committee on Aging, 1988b). Stated differently, 80% of *disabled* elders are living in some kind of noninstitutional setting in the community (e.g., their own homes, the homes of adult children, or rented rooms or apartments). For those elders who are living in the community, there is ample evidence that family members represent the largest source of support and assistance when help is needed (Branch & Jette, 1983; Brody, 1985; Brubaker, 1985a; Litwak, 1985; Mancini, 1989a; Mancini & Blieszner, 1989; Sauer & Coward, 1985; Stephens & Christianson, 1986; Stoller & Earl, 1983). Indeed, estimates suggest that between 75% and 80% of all help received by elders living in the community comes from informal support systems—primarily family members (Coward, 1987; Stone et al., 1987). But who are these caregivers? And, given the focus of this book, are there differences by gender in the networks surrounding elders?

Percent of Persons With Disability

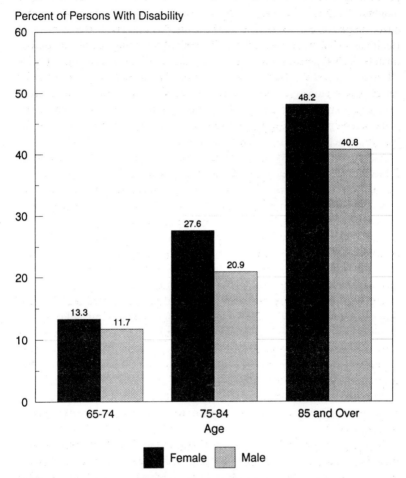

Figure 2.1. Disability (IADL and ADL) by Gender, 1982 Long-Term Care Survey Data

Soldo and Manton (1985). Reprinted by permission.

The 1982 National Long-Term Care Survey

In order to produce a detailed description of gender differences in family caregiving, we used data from the 1982 National Long-Term Care Survey (NLTCS) (a set of interviews with elders who reported having problems performing at least one ADL *or* IADL task for a period of at least three months). The NLTCS is a nationally representative sample of noninstitutionalized impaired elderly people in the United States (U.S. Department of Health and Human Services, 1984). The initial screening sample of approximately 36,000 persons was drawn from the Medicare enrollment files for all 50 states and the District of Columbia. The sample was stratified by geographic region, age, race, and reason for Medicare entitlement in order to ensure proportional representation of the groups of interest. Each person in the screening sample was contacted by telephone to determine if he or she had, or expected to have, problems performing any ADLs or IADLs.

As a result of this screening, 6,393 persons, representing a population of 5.1 million people (Macken, 1986), or approximately 17% of all people over age 65, were determined to have long-term problems with at least one ADL or IADL task. The sample does not represent, therefore, a simple random sample of elders living in community settings. Rather, it is a more select sample that focuses on those with impairments (as defined by difficulty performing ADL and IADL tasks). As a consequence, it does not include help received by more able elders and help received with tasks that are considered less essential to maintaining an independent life-style.

The final sample that we used in our analysis comprised 5,273 of the original sample of 6,393 (82.5% of the original sample). Some elders were eliminated from our analysis because at the time their personal interviews were conducted (as opposed to the telephone screening), they did not report impairments with either ADL or IADL tasks (508 persons, or 7.9%). Other respondents were eliminated because they either had missing data on one or more of the key variables included in the analysis or reported not receiving help from any source (formal or informal) with the tasks under investigation (612, or 9.6%).

By using the most refined codes available in the NLTCS, we were able to identify 10 categories describing the relationship between the caregiver and the care recipient: spouse, parent, sibling, adult child, child-in-law, other relative, friend, hired help, person from a helping agency, and other nonrelative. In all but the last three categories, we were able to distinguish male from female caregivers. Thus in the parent category we were able to demarcate fathers from mothers, and among siblings we were able to differentiate brothers from sisters. To our knowledge, a description of gender differences in the caregiving networks of elders with this amount of detail has not been published previously in the family caregiving literature.

**Gender Comparisons of
the Use of Different Caregivers**

Table 2.1 presents the percentages of elders who were receiving help from individuals in the various relationship categories. The data are presented for the total sample and then by the gender of the elder. Since many elders were receiving help from persons in more than one relationship category, the column percentages in Table 2.1 (and in subsequent tables) do not sum to 100. In addition, within some of the relationship categories, elders could have been receiving assistance from more than one person of that relationship at the same time (e.g., elders could have been receiving help from more than one daughter simultaneously). The figures in the tables, however, represent the proportion of elders in each category who indicated that they were receiving help from at least one person of that relationship type, *not* the total number of persons in that category who were providing care. For example, in the row representing sons in Table 2.1, the figure 18.2 represents the percentage of all elders who reported receiving help from sons (959/5,273 = 18.2%). The number in the *n* column, 959, is the number of elders who reported receipt of help from sons, *not* the number of sons who were helping parents (actually, these 959 elders reported 1,138 sons who were providing care).

From the columns for the total sample, we are able to determine that the largest proportion of elders reported receiving help from daughters (34.0%) and wives (23.6%). The next most frequently mentioned relationships, in descending order, were sons (18.2%), hired help (15.1%), husbands (14.1%), and persons from social service agencies (13.0%). All of the remaining categories had less than 10% of the elders reporting care from that source. Although nearly twice as many elders reported receiving help from daughters-in-law compared with sons-in-law (8.0% and 4.6%, respectively), both were relatively minor actors in the overall composition of the helping networks. Thus, although a wide range of different persons were reported as caregivers, certain sources were much more apt to be reported as providing care—namely, spouses (primarily wives), adult children (primarily daughters), and formal caregivers (either hired help or persons from social service agencies). Collectively, these three categories accounted for more than two-thirds of all the help received.

The receipt of help by impaired elders from their mothers or fathers was a rare occurrence. In this large sample of elders ($N = 5,273$), only 10 persons (less than 1%) mentioned their parents as a source of help. In contrast, the

Table 2.1 The Relationship of the Caregiver to the Elderly Care Recipient by the Gender of the Care Recipient

Relationship of Caregiver to Elder	Total Care Recipients (N = 5,273)		Male Care Recipients (N = 1,839)		Female Care Recipients (N = 3,434)	
	%	n	%	n	%	n
Husband	14.1	743	—	—	21.6	743
Wife	23.6	1,246	67.8	1,246	—	—
Father	0.0	4	0.0	1	0.0	3
Mother	0.0	6	0.0	2	0.0	4
Brother	1.6	87	1.7	31	1.6	56
Sister	4.9	258	3.5	64	5.7	194
Son	18.2	959	15.0	275	19.9	684
Daughter	34.0	1,791	20.5	377	41.2	1,414
Son-in-law	4.6	241	2.7	50	5.6	191
Daughter-in-law	8.0	422	4.8	89	9.7	333
Other male relative	8.0	421	6.0	110	9.1	311
Other female relative	4.3	754	8.5	156	17.4	598
Male friend	3.8	202	4.0	73	3.8	129
Female friend	9.8	516	4.9	90	12.4	426
Hired help	15.1	796	10.3	190	17.7	606
Person from social service agency	13.0	687	10.2	188	14.5	499
Other nonrelative	5.1	270	4.4	81	5.5	189

SOURCE: 1982 National Long-Term Care Survey (U.S. Department of Health and Human Services, 1984).
NOTE: The figures in percentage columns represent the percentages of elders in each category who reported receiving help from persons of that particular relationship. Because elders could report the receipt of help from more than one person, the column totals do not sum to 100%. The figures in the n columns represent the exact numbers of elders reporting the receipt of help from someone of that relationship.

next smallest category of helper was siblings, where 345 of the elders (6.5% of the total sample) reported receipt of help from that source.

Differences by the gender of the elder. Table 2.1 also contains comparisons by the gender of the elder. In these columns we can observe some significant differences in the distribution of the caregiver types by the gender of the elder.

Older males appear to be highly dependent on their wives as sources of assistance. Two of three older males (67.8%) reported receiving help from wives, while only about one in five (21.6%) of the impaired older females reported receipt of help from a husband. At the same time, fewer older males than females reported the receipt of help from adult children (either sons or daughters). However, in the helping networks of males, the ratio of elders receiving help from sons to elders receiving help from daughters (1:1.4) was not as great as that observed in the helping networks of female care recipients (1:2.1). Finally, approximately one in ten of the older male care recipients reported hiring help (10.3%), and a similar number acknowledged receiving help from formal service providers (10.2%); both of these figures were smaller than among their female counterparts.

In contrast, the helping networks of older females were less dependent upon spouses and, as a consequence, were more diverse in their composition. A higher percentage of older females (contrasted with males) reported receiving help from most of the other relationship categories—daughters, sons, sisters, sons-in-law, daughters-in-law, both male and female "other" relatives, female friends, and both categories of formal providers (hired help and persons from social service agencies). However, the most significant shift between males and females, after the decrease in dependency on spouses, was the increased dependency on daughters. Indeed, the relative dependency on spouses and daughters seemed to reverse itself between male and female elders. That is, among older males, wives were the most frequently mentioned source of support, followed by daughters (67.8% and 20.5%, respectively). In contrast, among older women, daughters were the most frequently mentioned source of support, followed by husbands (41.2% and 21.6%, respectively). Sons occupied the third most frequently mentioned position in both networks.

Differences by gender and the age of the elder. Table 2.2 presents comparisons of the percentages of elders reporting receipt of help from various relationship categories by age. Elders are grouped into three commonly used age categories: 65-74 years of age (40.1% of the sample), 75-84 (40.2%), and 85 and older (19.7%). Within each age category, the patterns for male care recipients are distinguished from those for female care recipients.

Perhaps the most striking difference between the comparisons by age categories in Table 2.2 is the decline in the percentage of elders dependent upon spouses and the parallel increase in the percentage receiving help from adult children. These two trends were apparent among both male and female care recipients; however, there were significant differences observed by the gender of the care recipient. For example, although there was a steady decline

Table 2.2 The Relationship of the Caregiver to the Elderly Care Recipient by the Age and Gender of the Care Recipient

				Age of Recipient					
			65–74			75–84			85+
Relationship of Caregiver to Elder	Total (N = 2,115)	Males (N = 880)	Females (N = 1,235)	Total (N = 2,121)	Males (N = 689)	Females (N = 1,432)	Total (N = 1,037)	Males (N = 270)	Females (N = 767)
Husband	14.1	—	37.9	11.4	—	16.9	3.2	—	4.3
Wife	31.9	76.7	—	21.5	66.2	—	11.1	42.6	—
Father	0.0	0.0	0.0	0.0	0.0	0.0	0.0	0.0	0.0
Mother	0.0	0.0	0.0	0.0	0.0	0.0	0.0	0.0	0.0
Brother	1.8	1.6	1.9	2.1	2.5	2.0	0.5	0.0	0.7
Sister	6.2	3.9	7.8	4.8	3.5	5.5	2.5	2.2	2.7
Son	14.4	11.6	16.4	18.7	14.8	20.6	24.8	26.3	24.3
Daughter	25.0	15.2	32.0	36.4	21.5	43.5	47.4	35.2	51.6
Son-in-law	2.6	2.2	2.9	4.8	2.2	6.1	8.1	5.9	8.9
Daughter-in-law	5.0	2.2	7.0	9.1	6.4	10.3	12.1	9.6	12.9
Other male relative	7.0	5.2	8.3	8.1	6.1	9.1	9.6	8.2	10.2
Other female relative	11.8	6.6	15.5	15.5	9.0	18.6	17.1	13.3	18.4
Male friend	3.5	3.6	3.4	3.9	4.6	3.6	4.3	3.3	4.7
Female friend	7.6	3.6	10.5	11.3	5.1	14.3	11.2	8.5	12.1
Hired help	11.9	7.5	15.1	16.4	12.1	18.5	18.9	15.2	20.2
Person from social service agency	11.1	7.7	13.4	13.9	12.2	14.7	15.3	13.3	16.0
Other nonrelative	4.8	4.4	5.0	4.5	3.3	5.0	7.1	7.0	7.2

SOURCE: 1982 National Long-Term Care Survey (U.S. Department of Health and Human Services, 1984).
NOTE: The figures in this table represent the percentages of elders in each category who reported receiving help from persons of that particular relationship. Because elders could report the receipt of help from more than one person, the column totals do not sum to 100%.

with age in the proportion of elders reporting help from spouses, in all age categories a greater percentage of elders reported wives than husbands as helpers. Among the oldest-old (those 85 and older), these differences were quite dramatic. Nearly half of the men of that age (42.6%) reported receiving help from wives, whereas only 1 in 23 of the women that age (4.3%) was receiving help from a husband. Indeed, the highest proportion of women reporting help from husbands (37.9% of women age 65-74) was less than the smallest proportion of men reporting receiving help from wives (42.6% among the oldest category of men).

Similarly, there were two significant differences by gender in the pattern of care received from adult children. First, with one exception, a greater proportion of female than male care recipients received help from adult children—both sons and daughters (the one exception was that a slightly higher percentage of males over the age of 85 years reported help from sons than did females that age—26.3% versus 24.3%). Second, daughters, as opposed to sons, were mentioned as a source of help by a greater proportion of elders (both fathers and mothers) at all ages. Thus, across all age groups, mothers were more likely than fathers to receive help from both sons and daughters (with one exception), and both fathers and mothers were more likely to report help from daughters than from sons. Finally, there is one additional trend worth mentioning. At all ages, sons appeared to play a more prominent role in the networks of fathers compared with those of mothers. Specifically, the *difference* between the percentage of males reporting help from sons compared with help from daughters in all three age groups (3.6%, 6.7%, and 8.9%, respectively) was *smaller* than the same ratio among female recipients of care (15.6%, 22.9%, and 27.3%, respectively). Although daughters were the more frequently mentioned adult child caregivers in *all* comparisons, the involvement of sons was more pronounced in the network of fathers.

Gender differences were also apparent among daughters-in-law and sons-in-law. Specifically, at all age levels, more elders reported receiving help from daughters-in-law than from sons-in-law, although, as mentioned previously, children-in-law were infrequently named as helpers. Also, a higher percentage of mothers than fathers reported help from both daughters-in-law and sons-in-law across all age categories.

Age and gender differences were also observed in the use of "other relatives" and friends. As age increased, a greater proportion of persons reported the use of male and female "other relatives" and male and female friends. Among both types of helpers, however, females were a more frequently mentioned source of help than males across all age groups and among both male and female care recipients. In addition, with two exceptions, female care recipients had higher proportional use of both of these sources of support than did males across all age groups. The exceptions were in the use of male friends among persons 65-74 and 75-84, where the percentages of males reporting receipt of help were higher than those of females (3.6% to 3.4% and 4.6% to 3.6%, respectively).

Finally, a higher proportion of persons in the older age categories reported receipt of help from formal service providers—both hired help and persons from social service agencies. However, the magnitude of the increases in these categories were not nearly as great as the increases observed across age categories in the increasing proportion of elders reporting help received from daughters and sons, or the decline in the percentage reporting receipt of help from spouses. Higher proportions of females than males were observed receiving help from formal service providers among all age categories. However, the discrepancy between male and female care recipients was smallest among the oldest age categories.

Differences by gender and marital status of the elder. Table 2.3 presents comparisons of the percentages of elders reporting receipt of help from various relationship categories by the marital status of the elder. Elders are grouped into four marital status categories: married (2,245 persons, or 42.6% of the sample), widowed (2,506 persons, or 47.5%); divorced or separated (236 persons, or 4.5%), and never married (258 persons, or 4.9%). Within each marital status category, the network patterns of male and female care recipients are presented separately.

These data confirm the notion that spouses, when available, are the "first line of defense." Although older men were more likely to be receiving help from spouses than were older women, a high degree of spousal helping was observed among both groups (93.2% of males received help from spouses, as did 80.9% of females). This high prevalence suggests the strength and commitment of marital partners to provide aid and assistance to each other in times of need (see Chapter 4 in this volume for a more complete discussion of patterns of spousal helping).

Among married persons, after spouses, all other sources of formal or informal support were relatively infrequent. Indeed, no other relationship was mentioned by more than 20% of the sample. The pattern of queuing of these other helpers, however, reflected a familiar motif, with daughters the most mentioned after spouses (19.2%), then sons (11.6%), followed closely by formal service providers (11.8% hired help and 10.2% received help from social service agencies). As in both of the earlier tables, in Table 2.3 we see a smaller difference between the proportion of elders receiving help from

Table 2.3 The Relationship of the Caregiver to the Elderly Care Recipient by the Marital Status and Gender of the Care Recipient

	Marital Status of Care Recipient											
	Married			Widowed			Divorced or Separated			Never Married		
Relationship of Caregiver to Elder	Total (N = 2,245)	Males (N = 1,331)	Females (N = 914)	Total (N = 2,506)	Males (N = 320)	Females (N = 2,186)	Total (N = 236)	Males (N = 90)	Females (N = 146)	Total (N = 258)	Males (N = 91)	Females (N = 167)
Husband	32.9	—	80.9	—	—	—	0.0	0.0	0.0	—	—	—
Wife	55.3	93.2	—	—	—	—	0.0	1.1	0.0	—	—	—
Father	0.0	0.0	0.0	—	—	—	0.0	0.0	0.0	0.0	0.0	0.0
Mother	0.0	0.0	0.0	—	—	—	0.0	0.0	0.0	0.0	0.0	0.0
Brother	0.5	0.5	0.6	1.5	2.2	1.4	1.3	2.2	0.7	13.2	16.5	11.4
Sister	1.5	0.5	3.1	4.7	4.1	4.8	10.6	13.3	8.9	31.8	36.3	29.3
Son	11.6	12.3	10.5	25.2	30.3	24.5	22.9	13.3	28.8	1.6	1.1	1.8
Daughter	19.2	16.2	23.7	50.5	43.4	51.6	33.1	22.2	39.7	2.7	1.1	3.6
Son-in-law	2.0	1.7	2.3	7.5	7.5	7.5	2.5	2.2	2.7	1.2	0.0	1.8
Daughter-in-law	2.9	2.0	4.2	13.0	15.9	12.5	11.9	11.1	12.3	0.4	0.0	0.6
Other male relative	3.7	3.6	3.7	10.9	11.9	10.8	9.3	10.0	8.9	16.3	15.4	16.8
Other female relative	5.9	4.6	7.8	20.2	18.8	20.4	17.0	10.0	21.2	27.1	27.5	27.0
Male friend	2.2	2.7	1.4	4.6	5.0	4.5	8.1	12.2	5.5	7.4	11.0	5.4
Female friend	3.6	2.1	5.7	14.1	12.2	14.4	15.7	14.4	16.4	16.3	9.9	19.8
Hired help	11.8	8.2	17.0	17.0	15.3	17.3	17.4	16.7	17.8	22.9	18.7	25.2
Person from social service agency	10.2	9.2	11.5	14.9	10.9	15.7	15.3	12.2	17.1	17.4	17.9	17.4
Other nonrelative	2.9	2.6	3.4	5.8	6.6	5.7	9.3	13.3	6.9	13.6	13.2	13.8

SOURCE: 1982 National Long-Term Care Survey (U.S. Department of Health and Human Services, 1984).
NOTE: The figures in this table represent the percentages of elders in each category who reported receiving help from persons of that particular relationship. Because elders could report the receipt of help from more than one person, the column totals do not sum to 100%.

sons versus daughters when they are helping fathers as opposed to mothers. In both situations, daughters were more prominent. However, among fathers, the difference between the proportion receiving help from sons and daughters was smaller (1:1.3) than observed among mothers (1:2.3).

Among the formerly married (widowed or divorced/separated), daughters were the primary source of help. Daughters were mentioned as helpers most frequently by both male and female recipients and by both widowed and divorced/separated persons. Sons were the second most frequently mentioned helpers, with the exception of divorced/separated male elders. Besides daughters, who provided the most care, there was a great diversity of care reported. Hired help (16.7%) and female friends (14.4%) were followed by a cluster of five other relationships that all appeared with about the same frequency: sons (13.3%), sisters (13.3%), nonrelatives (13.3%), male friends (12.2%), and persons from social service agencies (12.2%). Both categories of the formerly married (i.e., widowed and divorced/separated) were more apt to report help received from formal service providers than were elders who were married. And, as observed previously, the rate of use of formal service providers was consistently higher among female than among male care recipients.

One other observation is worth mentioning. Both categories of the formerly married, but especially the widowed, reported rates of help received from "other relatives" (both males and females) that were considerably higher than among married care recipients. For example, whereas only 7.8% of married females reported receiving help from a female "other relative," 20.4% of widowed females and 21.2% of divorced/separated females reported receiving help from persons in that category.

Among the never married, a completely different pattern of help emerged. In this group, the highest percentage of elders named sisters (31.8%) as helpers—a relationship that was seldom mentioned by elders in the other marital categories. Sisters were consistently the most frequently mentioned helpers among both never-married male and never-married female care recipients. The second highest percentage of elders in this group named other female relatives as helpers (27.1%). Again, this pattern held for both male and female care recipients. Compared with other marital status groups, the never-married group also reported the highest percentage of elders who were dependent on other male relatives (16.3%), female friends (16.3%), nonrelatives (13.6%), and brothers (13.2%). The relative use of male relatives and nonrelatives was very similar between male and female care recipients, but for the other two categories (female friends and brothers) there were significant differences between the two groups. Specifically, never-married males reported a greater use of brothers than did never-married females (16.5% versus 11.4%), whereas never-married females reported a greater use of female friends than did never-married males (19.8% versus 9.9%). Finally, the never married also reported the greatest percentages of any of the marital status categories in their use of formal providers—either hired help (22.9%) or persons from social service agencies (17.4%). Although the frequency of use of formal service providers was highest among females (as it had been in the comparisons presented in Tables 2.1 and 2.2), there was actually very little difference between never-married males and females in their use of this source of support.

Collectively, the data in Table 2.3 form three distinct patterns. Married elders were highly dependent on spouses, with children a distant second. The formerly married, in contrast, were most apt to be dependent on adult children (primarily daughters), with other female relatives and formal service providers as secondary sources. Finally, the never married reported a diverse set of helpers, with particularly high use of sisters, other female relatives, and formal service providers.

Summary of the Data Analysis

From this analysis of data from the 1982 National Long-Term Care Survey (U.S. Department of Health and Human Services, 1984), a number of general patterns have emerged that describe gender differences in the caregiving networks that surround impaired elders. Specifically, the following generalizations are derived from the data in Tables 2.1, 2.2, and 2.3:

- Across elders in all age, gender, and marital status categories, wives and daughters were the most frequently mentioned providers of care.
- Across almost all age and marital status categories, females were more apt than males to be receiving help from both adult children and formal service providers.
- There were significant differences among groups of elders in their use of formal service providers, ranging from a low of 7.5% (among male care recipients aged 65-74) to a high of 25.2% (among never-married females who were receiving care).
- Older men were highly dependent on their wives as sources of support, whereas older females had more diverse helping networks.
- Among the oldest-old, elders were less apt to be dependent on spouses and more likely to depend on adult children. In addition, higher proportions of the elders in the older age categories reported the use of formal service providers.

- If impaired elders had marital partners available, it was very likely that they were receiving help from their spouses—regardless of whether they were male or female.
- There were significant differences in the composition of the helping networks as a function of marital status. Married elders (both males and females) were highly dependent on spouses, with children a distant second. The formerly married were most dependent on adult daughters, with sons frequently the second most mentioned source of support. However, the formerly married also reported the frequent use of other female relatives and formal service providers as secondary sources. The never married reported a diverse set of helpers, with particularly high use of sisters, other female relatives, and formal service providers.
- Although daughters, compared with sons, were mentioned as helpers by a higher percentage of both fathers and mothers, sons were a more prominent source of help for fathers than for mothers.

Final Comments

The demographic description presented in this chapter of those who provide care to the elderly reinforces the proposition that gender is a central element in analyzing family care of the elderly. Women are usually the recipients of care; they are also most often the providers of care. This pattern can be explained in part by demographic realities—women live longer than men (and thus are more apt to experience physical and mental impairments and, as a consequence, are more likely to find themselves in need of family care) and tend to marry older men (and thus are much more apt to find themselves caring for impaired spouses in the later part of their lives). However, even taking into account these two important demographic differences between men and women, still only a portion of the gender variation in family care of the elderly appears to be explained. Beyond demography, other psychological, sociological, economic, and political forces are at work that, in combination, lead to the gender-differentiated patterns of care that have been repeatedly observed.

3

Conceptual Perspectives on Gender and Family Caregiving

ALEXIS J. WALKER

Caregiving is women's work (Abel, 1986). This is true of both informal caregiving (i.e., that provided by family members) and formal caregiving (e.g., that provided by paid nurses and social workers). The rise in women's participation in the paid labor force has not altered the fact that the majority of care is provided by women (Brody & Schoonover, 1986; Thompson & Walker, 1989; see also Chapter 11, this volume). The caregiving literature has demonstrated convincingly that women provide more care and a greater variety of care to the elderly than do men. What accounts for these differences? How can we explain the dominance of women in the caregiving domain?

This chapter represents an attempt to answer these questions. In it, the psychological, sociological, and feminist perspectives that have been employed to explain the prominence of women in caregiving to the elderly are outlined. Each perspective acknowledges a gendered system of family caregiving, yet each asserts different explanations for it. The major tenets of each view are presented, and their weaknesses are identified as well. The chapter concludes with a discussion of the ways in which the three frameworks have been employed in the caregiving literature and a call to move research beyond a gender difference approach.

AUTHOR'S NOTE: Work on this chapter was supported by National Institute on Aging Grant No. AG06766. I am grateful to Linda Thompson, Jeffrey W. Dwyer, and Raymond T. Coward for their helpful comments.

34

Psychological/Individual Perspectives

It has been postulated that women, through their connection to others, are simply more caring and nurturant than men (Abel, 1986; Gilligan, 1982; Noddings, 1984). Indeed, taking care of others is associated not only with women, but with the places wherein close ties with women are found: home, family, and the "caring professions" (Finch & Groves, 1983; Graham, 1983). Hence, from psychological/individual perspectives, women's caregiving is motivated by their attachment to care receivers or by the fact that caregiving is central to the identity of women (Graham, 1983).

Caregiving as Central to Women's Identity

The most well-known proponent of the belief that caregiving is inherent in the identity of women is Nancy Chodorow. From a psychoanalytic framework, Chodorow (1978) has argued that mothering is reproduced in this society (i.e., mothers beget mothers who beget mothers) in such a way that caregiving becomes identified with women. Indeed, she has argued that a woman's empathic personality is produced by families. In Chodorow's view, the psychological foundation for parenting occurs during infancy; that is, individuals remember the unique intimacy they shared as infants with their mothers and hope to re-create it. This early experience leads to individual expectations of mothers as having "unique capacities for sacrifice, caring, and mothering" (p. 83).

Because they were raised primarily by women and not men, "girls come to experience themselves as less separate than boys, as having more permeable ego boundaries . . . [and they] come to define themselves more in relation to others" (Chodorow, 1978, p. 93). The lack of separation means that girls remain part of the mother-child relationship longer than do boys. Thus girls include empathy in their self-definition, while boys do not. The personality of girls, therefore, is based on the retention and continuity of external relationships:

> Women's mothering . . . produces psychological self-definition and capacities appropriate to mothering in women, and curtails and inhibits these capacities and this self-definition in men. The early experience of being cared for by a woman produces a fundamental structure of expectations in women and men concerning mothers' lack of separate interests from their infants and total concern for their infants' welfare. Daughters grow up identifying with these mothers, about whom they have such expectations. This set of expectations is generalized to the assumption that women naturally take care of children of all ages and the belief that

women's "maternal" qualities can and should be extended to the nonmothering work that they do. (Chodorow, 1978, p. 208)

Gilligan's (1982) view of gender as a basis for moral behavior is grounded in Chodorow's work. That is, it arises from the assumption that women have empathic personalities and define themselves in relation to others. Gilligan extends Chodorow's argument, however, concluding that women have an ethic of care that reflects both their "sensitivity to others" and the assumption that women have "responsibility for caregiving" (p. 16). Indeed, a significant aspect of women's moral development, in Gilligan's view, is that women struggle over the conflict between their own needs and the needs of others.

In both of these models, women are caregivers. It is central to their identity. Men, on the other hand, come to define themselves in other ways—as the recipients of care or as instrumental agents (e.g., those who write checks for formal services), but not as hands-on caregivers. Others disagree that caregiving is a basic personality characteristic of women. They suggest, instead, that women's connections to others form the basis of caring labor.

Attachment as a Motivation for Caregiving

For some, attachment to care recipients is seen as a central motivator of caregiving by women (Graham, 1983). While men also are emotionally connected to care recipients, they appear to express their attachment primarily in ways other than caregiving (e.g., by the provision of economic support).

There is considerable evidence that women have stronger emotional ties with their family members than do men (Markides, Boldt, & Ray, 1986). The relationship between mothers and daughters is seen as particularly compelling (Abel, 1986; Hagestad, 1982). Because of the similar roles they occupy, mothers and adult daughters engage in many of the same activities (e.g., housekeeping) and have similar responsibilities (e.g., taking care of family members who are ill) (Hess & Waring, 1978b). These similar roles result in great potential for shared activities as well as the frequent exchange of aid (Kivett, 1988). To account for gender differences in intergenerational relationships, Troll (1987) has suggested that men emphasize "horizontal" ties (i.e., to spouses) while women emphasize "vertical" ties (i.e., to parents and children). The stronger vertical attachments of women may explain why daughters are more likely to be caregivers to elderly parents than are sons. That is, in the face of a needy loved one, a woman may feel no choice but to respond by providing care (Finch & Groves, 1983).

In a random-digit dialing survey of adults in a southern city, Finley, Roberts, and Banahan (1988) found that, although daughters and sons had similar levels of affection for their aging parents, affection motivated daughters, but not sons, to feel obligated to care for mothers and fathers. That is, among daughters, emotional closeness to parents predicted a sense of obligation to provide care to them, but for men affection was not a significant predictor of filial obligation. These authors conclude that the process of developing a sense of filial obligation differs for women and men. Specifically, they argue that there is an emotional component to filial obligation for women.

The popular literature seems to reflect the idea that women are more attached to family members—that there is a unique relationship between a daughter and her aging parent, for example. A recent self-help book for caregiving daughters (Norris, 1988) has a chapter aimed at helping men to deal with the situation of having a wife or sister caring for an aging parent. In it, Stafford (1988) offers the following advice to husbands and brothers of caregivers:

> Try to imagine what your wife or sister is going through. . . . Don't tell her to do less because perhaps she can't. You see, she's not trying to help, she's trying to please. She's not only trying to be a caregiver, she's trying to be a daughter. . . . You can't help more because you're already acceptable in your parents' eyes. You can't do more because *you* can't be a daughter. (p. 181)

In sum, psychological/individual perspectives suggest that women are, naturally, nurturers and caregivers. In particular, both their identity and their attachment to loved ones conspire to create nurturing beings. Men are seen as having a fundamentally different identity and as responding to attachment through labor force participation, that is, by supporting family members economically.

Weaknesses of the Psychological Approach

The psychological approach to the gendered nature of family caregiving can be challenged. The fact is that many women are not nurturant, and many men are (McHale & Huston, 1984; Wiesenfeld, Whitman, & Malatesta, 1984). Indeed, there is considerable variability within the two groups in the capacity for nurturance. Not all women feel prepared and eager to care for small children or elders, and some men respond enthusiastically to such demands. Recent research also suggests that women are no more likely to experience feelings of filial obligation than are men (e.g., Finley et al., 1988; see also Chapter 7, this volume).

In addition, prevailing definitions of closeness or attachment may be biased. In emphasizing concepts such as nurturance, there is considerable evidence of the attachments formed by women but little evidence of the emotional connections involving men. Moreover, Cancian (1986) has argued that the dominant cultural definitions of love stress tenderness and emotional expressiveness, qualities usually associated with women, whereas practical activities designed to help others, usually associated with men, are not defined as love.

Finally, because caregivers, especially women, report negative feelings while giving care (Barusch & Spaid, 1989), we cannot assume that caregiving and positive feelings toward care receivers are necessarily linked (Dressel & Clark, 1990). In general, the psychological/individual perspectives of gender and caregiving reify caring as it exists in our culture (Graham, 1983); that is, they legitimate the existing, gendered pattern of caregiving.

Sociological Perspectives

Sociological theorists have suggested that both socialization and social structure contribute to the gendered nature of care. These explanations are explored in the sections that follow.

Socialization

Sociologists posit that individuals are trained or socialized into roles that define caregiving as women's responsibility. Parsons and Bales (1955) have described role differentiation that occurred as a result of industrialization. They distinguish between complementary "instrumental" and "expressive" tasks, thus differentiating the role of women from that of men (Dressel & Clark, 1990). Men were responsible for the connection between families and the cruel, cold outside world. That is, they were the family breadwinners and they mediated between their families and other social institutions. Women were responsible for nurturing family members. That is, they took care of family members' socioemotional needs. Parsons and Bales, and others, view the labor of women and men as dichotomous in ways other than their differential assignment to expressive and instrumental tasks. Other dichotomies include the dominant roles individuals should occupy (i.e., women should be caregivers and men should be paid workers) and the locations of these roles and tasks (i.e., women should function primarily in the home and men primarily in the public sphere) (Dressel & Clark, 1990). Thus ideas about the location, nature, and principal giver of care define caregiving in a gendered way. Children are exposed to these gender dichotomies and learn gendered behavior, in part, through the process of socialization. Through socialization, attitudes and behaviors consistent with gender differences are internalized.

Social Structure

Age stratification. Society is organized in such a way that women do most of the caregiving. For example, the age stratification of the population, higher mortality rates for men, and the phenomenon of women typically marrying men older than themselves have led to the greater incidence of women caregivers (Horowitz, 1985b). The vast majority of elderly men are married, and the vast majority of elderly women are widowed (see Chapter 2, this volume). Health problems, and concomitant needs for care, increase with age. Therefore, most dependent elderly men receive care from their wives (Spitze & Logan, 1989; Stone, Cafferata, & Sangl, 1987). Most dependent elderly women are widowed; thus they receive care from children, usually their daughters (Stone et al., 1987). Consequently, age stratification results in a greater incidence of women caregivers (Fine, 1985).

Gendered nature of paid work. Some argue that women are more likely to be caregivers, in part, because they are less likely than men to be employed (Horowitz, 1985b). Not only do women participate in the paid labor force at lower rates than men, they are also more likely to be employed seasonally or part-time (Ferber, 1982; Moen & Dempster-McClain, 1987). While employed women make sizable and important contributions to their household incomes, among married couples husbands still contribute a greater proportion than do wives (Spitze, 1988). Thus when a family has two incomes it is usually more dependent on the income of the man. It is no surprise, then, that daughters are more likely than sons to reduce their commitment to paid work as a result of caregiving (U.S. House of Representatives, Select Committee on Aging, 1987). This occurs because, compared with employed men, employed women may leave the paid labor force at lower economic cost to their families.

In sum, sociological perspectives argue that social expectations impel women into, and propel men away from, caregiving. Women are seen as having been socialized for the expressive tasks that are believed to constitute caregiving, while men have been socialized for instrumental responsibilities. In addition, the smaller number of elderly men and greater number of elderly women make it likely that more women and fewer men will give care. Finally, the differential distribution of women and men in the paid labor force makes it more likely that women will be the caregivers within a family.

Weaknesses of the Sociological Approach

The sociological perspective also may be challenged. It may be true that caregiving tasks are specialized activities with which women have more experience than men. However, there is a fundamental argument against the socialization perspective. In almost every category of caregiving help, women provide more help than do men (Finley, 1989). Even in some of the tasks typically associated with men (e.g., financial management, heavy chores), women do as much caregiving as men (Horowitz, 1985b; Stoller, 1990). Thus, in the case of caregiving to the elderly, "masculine" or instrumental tasks are not systematically performed by men. All of the tasks associated with caregiving (e.g., personal care, meal preparation, bureaucratic mediation, household maintenance) must be learned. Skills such as cooking and giving personal care are not maturational in nature—as are motor and cognitive skills—for either women or men. All people must learn such skills as how to clean house or how to bathe a dependent person, and both women and men have demonstrated the ability to learn such tasks (Stone et al., 1987). For example, while fathers in two-parent families have limited involvement in child-care tasks, single-parent fathers have been shown to perform the same child-care tasks as mothers (Risman, 1987). Moreover, many husbands and sons perform caregiving tasks for their wives and parents (Stone et al., 1987).

Regarding the role of differential participation in the labor market, some women do leave the paid work force to give care to aging family members (Brody, 1985), but most do not. In addition, the differences in work status between women and men are not sufficient to account for the existing gender differences in caregiving (Finley, 1989). Finally, employed women parallel their nonemployed peers in caregiving behavior (Brody & Schoonover, 1986; Finley, 1989; Matthews, Werkner, & Delaney, 1989). That is, participation in the labor market does not prevent women from caregiving; it seems only to prevent men.

Feminist Perspectives

Feminist theorists call attention to the work that women do. Indeed, the current escalating interest in family caregiving may be due, in part, to the value placed by feminist scholars on women's labor. Feminists argue that women do the caregiving in society because of the dominant ideology of caregiving, the low value placed on the work of women, social disregard for the costs of caregiving to women, and lack of government support for meeting the needs of its citizens (Abel, 1986; Daniels, 1987; Finch & Groves, 1983; Graham, 1983; Ungerson, 1983). Feminists also argue that we are a long way from understanding family caregiving. While there have been many quantitative studies of caregiving, qualitative work is needed to explore the subjective experience of caregiving for the caregiver (Abel, 1990b). Such work would illuminate the nature of the experience for both women and men.

Ideology of Caregiving

The ideology behind the term *caregiving* suggests its equation with women and with home and family life (Finch & Groves, 1983). The very use of the word *care* implies intimacy and connection, not just the meeting of physical needs (Graham, 1983). In a feminist view, caregiving is less a natural expression of a woman's personality or feelings toward others than a reflection of her place in the broader social system (Graham, 1983).

The ideology of what women "should" be doing is reinforced by the perception that paid or formal care is inferior to care provided by family members (i.e., women) (Glazer, 1990). Indeed, family members know that formal caregiving is not really "care" because it lacks the commitment and affection that define caregiving by mothers, wives, and daughters (Glazer, 1990; Graham, 1983).

The Low Value of Women's Work

The unpaid labor associated with families and performed primarily by women is not defined as work (Daniels, 1987). Unpaid work in our culture—that is, women's work—is invisible. Even women do not see some of their activities as work. In general, according to Daniels (1987), there is a

resistance to conceptualizing interpersonal activities as work [that] comes from the expectation that emotional interpersonal gestures are natural expressions that come spontaneously. . . . My argument is that, whatever their natural propensity [women] are trained in these skills. In consequence, women are more likely to be able to do this job. Their practice comes from weaving the fabric together in their friendships, families, and work settings. The skill at this weaving comes from attending to the background comforts that make interaction pleasanter, from watching out for hesitances, likes, and dislikes of others in the social setting and trying to accommodate them. Once these behaviors become habitual, women are just "naturally" better at this work. Of course, social life would run more smoothly if every able-bodied person attended to those matters, rotating some tasks around or shifting them from one to another as context permitted. (p. 410)

In other words, society sees caregiving as psychological rather than as a product of the political and economic systems in which we reside (Aronson, 1985).

Social Disregard for the Costs of Caregiving

Society considers the unpaid labor of women "low cost" to individuals, to families, and to communities, because not all costs of this labor are assessed (Glazer, 1990). For example, we do not include among the costs of caregiving those financial losses incurred by women who have reduced or terminated their involvement in paid work because of caregiving; lost contributions to retirement plans, including Social Security; lost potential for financial equity in interpersonal relationships (Aronson, 1985); or lost taxes to federal and local governments. In other words, women sacrifice their financial independence to meet their perceived social obligation to be unpaid caregivers (Finch & Groves, 1983). Such costs are borne disproportionately by minority and low-income women (Glazer, 1990).

In addition to financial costs, there are psychological costs as well. For example, women caregivers report significantly greater burdens from caregiving than do men (Barusch & Spaid, 1989). In addition, women have been shown to be more depressed by caregiving (Gallagher, Rose, Rivers, Lovett, & Thompson, 1989; Pruchno & Resch, 1989; Young & Kahana, 1989). Thus it is inaccurate to consider the unpaid caregiving labor of women to be "low cost."

Inadequate Government Support

Two related factors are the high cost and limited availability of paid caregiving. When caregiving is neither available nor affordable, the responsibility falls to family members, typically women (Abel, 1986; Glazer, 1990).

Local, state, and federal governments do not provide sufficient support to help meet the care needs of the elderly (Aronson, 1985; Glazer, 1990; Ungerson, 1983; Walker, 1983). What government does not provide, families—women—must; that is, the burden of elder care is seen as residing in families rather than with the state (Abel, 1986). In addition, the state allocates services in such a way as to increase the proportion of unpaid women caregivers. For example, in England, isolated individuals often receive formal help, while individuals with family members, particularly daughters, do not (Ungerson, 1983). Similarly, in the United States, the establishment of diagnostic related groups (DRGs) has resulted in individuals being released from hospitalization while they still require intensive care (Glazer, 1990). Thus health care costs have been diverted from the government and/or private insurance to family caregivers, primarily women. Finally, there are insufficient facilities and programs to meet the needs of elderly care receivers (Abel, 1986). Thus many families have no choice but to provide their own care. As long as alternatives are neither viable nor available, caregiving will continue to be provided by the informal sector—that is, by women (Finch & Groves, 1983; Walker, 1983).

In sum, according to feminist perspectives, the dominant ideology defines caregiving as women's work. Such work lacks value in our society, in part because women do it. While women experience significant and extensive costs through their caring labor, there is a social disregard for those costs. While there is disagreement over the degree to which the care of older people is a personal, familial, or societal responsibility, the costs of elder care are being borne increasingly by women (Glazer, 1990).

Weaknesses of the Feminist Approach

While most feminists agree that the dominant ideology of society contributes to women's prominence in caregiving, that women's caregiving labor is neither highly valued nor adequately compensated, and that the lack of government support for meeting the needs of citizens compels women to give care, among feminists there are differing opinions as to how caregiving itself should be viewed.

Abel and Nelson (1990) claim that two views inform most feminist perspectives on women's caregiving. The first emphasizes the nature of caring labor. Feminists who embrace this perspective see caregiving as oppressive. In this paradigm, the repetitive, boring, and alienating nature of caregiving is believed to contribute to women's secondary status in the labor market. If women were not compelled to do this work, they could contribute more to the economic support of their families and themselves. This negative view is bolstered by the literature suggesting that caregiving is a "burden" (e.g., Brody, 1985; Brody, Hoffman, Kleban, & Schoonover, 1989; Cantor, 1983).

The alternative perspective emphasizes the positive side of caregiving (Abel & Nelson, 1990). In this approach, caregiving women are believed to be engaging in fulfilling and meaningful work that has its foundation in reciprocity. Ruddick's (1989) philosophy of "attentive love" characterizes this view. She believes that mothering (which can be carried out by both men and women) is a response to the three demands of a child: the demand to have one's life preserved, the demand to develop and grow, and the demand to develop into a being that would be acceptable in the mother's community. The act of responding to these demands, in Ruddick's view, leads to a certain way of thinking, attentive love. Ruddick proposes that, because of its responsiveness to the needs of vulnerable beings, attentive love can be the basis for world peace. Such a perspective celebrates women and their behavior.

For Abel and Nelson (1990), neither of these approaches is adequate. While the negative view highlights the fact that caregiving is work (i.e., work is not found only within the paid labor market) and separates sentimentality from caregiving, it ignores the social connections that are integral to it. On the other hand, the positive view is insensitive to the ways in which social structure is re-created within families and is vulnerable to exploitation; that is, it can be used to justify the inferior position of women in society.

Abel and Nelson (1990) and Fisher and Tronto (1990) demand a more complex view of caregiving. In Abel's (1986) view, caregiving is both a profound personal experience and an oppressive social institution. Caregiving can contribute to a person's sense of connection, yet it can also interfere with the activities that contribute to a sense of competence in adulthood and to economic independence (Abel, 1986). Caregiving can reflect concern and affection, but it can also reflect fear and obligation (Abel, 1986).

A feminist perspective explicating the importance of power has been developed by di Leonardo (1987). Her contribution is focused on women and the labor of kinkeeping, but her analysis could be expanded easily to family caregiving. Some have suggested that women's unpaid work interferes with their access to the paid labor market (di Leonardo, 1987), but that the labor market also discriminates against women such that unpaid work continues to be the province of women. Di Leonardo extends her argument to the individual level by contending that unpaid labor provides potential satisfaction and power for women not available to them in paid work. Through kin work, women create obligations in children and in men and accumulate power over other women. In other words, kin work (and caregiving) provides for women a place to acquire satisfaction and power.

Other feminists would caution, however, about the potential danger of focusing exclusively on the positive outcomes of caregiving for women, as such a focus may contribute to maintaining women's subordinate social status (Abel & Nelson, 1990). As the examples given here show, feminists have yet to develop a completely satisfactory perspective on caregiving.

Use of Frameworks in the Literature

Few studies of family caregiving have focused attention on the role of gender. Although recently researchers have begun to look across types of caregivers (i.e., spouses, daughters), many continue to aggregate across caregiver categories in their analyses.

Most of the studies that have focused on gender have simply described rates and/or the extent of caregiving for wives versus husbands and/or daughters versus sons (Horowitz, 1985b; Stone et al., 1987). Others have identified gender differences in caregiving, associating these differences with demographic variables (e.g., employment status), but have not offered explanations for them (Stoller, 1983). Most research has relied on psychological (B. Miller, 1987; Stoller, 1990) and/or sociological (Coward & Dwyer, 1990; Montgomery & Kamo, 1989; Stoller, 1990) perspectives to account for the differences in behavior between women and men. As already indicated, such approaches ignore the ideology of caregiving as women's work, its invisible nature, and the lack of available, affordable alternatives.

While it is important to document and describe caring labor, the gender difference approach tends to reify the immutably distinct nature of women and men. Typically, in such an approach, caregiving by women is defined as normative and men's performance is compared to it (Crawford & Maracek, 1989). This strategy of identifying gender differences understates both the diversity within gender and the similarities between women and men. As recent research has shown, not all sisters approach caregiving in the same way, and some brothers are like some sisters in their caregiving behavior (Matthews & Rosner, 1988). The difference approach also neglects the role of social relations in constructing gendered behavior (Crawford & Maracek, 1989; Fine, 1985). For example, research has revealed that power differences are more influential than gender in explaining interpersonal communication patterns (Howard, Blumstein, & Schwartz, 1986). In addition, recent work postulating a microstructural approach (Risman & Schwartz, 1989) argues convincingly that gendered behavior emerges from social conditions.

One recent study by Finley (1989) employed a feminist perspective to illuminate the gendered nature of family caregiving. Finley disputes both psychological and sociological rationales for the greater caring labor of women. Her data demonstrate that neither psychological (i.e., attitudes of filial obligation) nor sociological (i.e., specialization of tasks, available time, amount of conflict with other roles) perspectives are sufficient to explain the gender difference in caregiving. She concludes that, since psychological and sociological explanations do not account for the difference, the social value of men's work must; that is, men's contributions in society are valued more than are women's.

Clearly, additional work is needed to explicate the gendered nature of family caregiving. To date, the data suggest that psychological, sociological, and feminist perspectives are inadequate to explain what women and men do as caregivers. Research that focuses on the ways in which context creates gendered behavior offers great potential for providing an understanding of the gendered nature of care.

PART II

The Structure of Caregiving Relationships

4

Gender Differences in the Experiences of Caregiving Spouses

ELEANOR PALO STOLLER

Spouses are the first line of defense for elders in coping with disease and disability (Brubaker, 1985b; Horowitz, 1985a; Shanas, 1980). Spouses handle a broader range of tasks, provide more hours of assistance (Tennstedt, McKinlay, & Sullivan, 1989), and are more likely to provide personal care than are other caregivers (Stone, Cafferata, & Sangl, 1987). Furthermore, compared with other family members, when husbands and wives are primary caregivers, their efforts are less likely to be supplemented with help from other informal caregivers or from formal services (Tennstedt et al., 1989). In comparison with other caregivers, spouses tolerate greater disability for a longer time, with fewer mediating resources and at greater personal cost (Hess & Soldo, 1985; Horowitz, 1985a). Doty (1986) also contends that spouses exhibit "a strong tendency to maintain caregiving whatever the social/emotional costs and stop only when deterioration of their own health physically prevents them from providing the services" (p. 51). Troll, Miller, and Atchley (1979) explain this greater commitment by asserting that spouses view the provision of care as a normative expectation of marriage. Husbands and wives have less discretion regarding caregiving responsibilities, since caring for an impaired partner is seen as part of the marriage contract (Miller & Montgomery, 1990).

Husbands and wives are the most dependable caregivers (Fischer & Hoffman, 1984), and the absence of a spouse is a crucial predictor of institutional placement (Health Care Financing Administration, 1981). The institutionalization rate of married elderly is about half that of either the never married or the previously married, even at the extremes of old age and disability (Hess & Soldo, 1985). Wives, especially, often feel that placing a husband in a nursing home is a violation of their marriage vows (Fradkin & Liberti, 1987), and husbands are less likely to be institutionalized than are wives (Fischer & Hoffman, 1984). Indeed, the British wives interviewed by Oliver (1983) frequently equated institutionalization with divorce.

Data from the National Long-Term Care Survey confirm the importance of spouses as providers of care; in that study's sample, 35.5% of all people providing care to disabled elderly were spouses (Stone et al., 1987). Husbands and wives are also more likely than other helpers to handle caregiving responsibilities on their own. In the National Long-Term Care Survey, some 60% of the wives were sole caregivers, and an additional 37.6% were primary caregivers who received some help. Among husbands, 55.4% were sole caregivers and an additional 41.9% were primary caregivers with additional help. Only 2% of wives and 3% of husbands were classified as secondary caregivers. In contrast, 29.6% of daughters, 52.5% of sons, 49.8% of other female helpers, and 73.5% of other male helpers were considered secondary caregivers (Stone et al., 1987). Furthermore, as Tennstedt and her colleagues (1989) have demonstrated, the contributions of secondary caregivers are lowest when the primary caregiver is a spouse.

This chapter examines the experiences of husbands and wives caring for disabled partners. The first section summarizes research contrasting spouses with other caregivers. The second section explores similarities and differences in the caregiving experiences of husbands and wives. Special attention is given to the ways in which gender structures the meaning and consequences of the role of caregiver. The chapter concludes with a summary of shortcomings in the available literature and offers suggestions for future research.

The Experiences of Spouses as Caregivers

Although spouses provide a higher level of help over a longer period of time than do other caregivers, several investigators have reported that spouses also experience less role conflict and lower levels of burden (Johnson & Catalano, 1983; Young & Kahana, 1989). Spouse caregivers are less likely to encounter competing demands from other roles, since most are out of the labor force and have completed child-rearing obligations (Hess & Soldo, 1985). Other researchers, however, report that spouse caregivers experience higher levels of burden than other caregivers (Cantor, 1983; George & Gwyther, 1986).

Caregiver burden includes emotional, social, economic, and physical dimensions. Emotional stress for spouse caregivers emerges both from concern over their partners' health and safety and from a need to redefine long-term patterns of roles and responsibilities (Horowitz, 1985a). The illness or disability of a spouse also undermines the other partner's basis of self-identity. As Silverman (1987) explains, "Marriage provides each partner with a way of framing and focusing their daily life, with a personal identity and with a place in society" (p. 72). The disability of a spouse, particularly when it entails cognitive impairment, removes this source of support. Spouse caregivers sometimes experience guilt about feelings of anger and resentment directed at a partner whose disability has interrupted plans for the couple's retirement. Guilt can also arise when the healthy partner begins to dislike a spouse whose personality has changed as a result of illness (Hooyman & Lustbader, 1986).

Closely related to emotional strains are the time demands and restrictions on personal freedom imposed by caregiving responsibilities. As Horowitz (1985a) points out, "Caregiving activities often require extensive adjustments in previous daily schedules. Disruption of domestic routines, decreased personal time, less time for social and leisure activities, inability to take vacations, rearrangement of work schedules, and restricted mobility are all common indicators of this pervasive problem" (p. 209). Restrictions on social activities can undermine support networks and contribute to the isolation of caregivers. B. Miller (1987) attributes restrictions on social life to a variety of factors, including self-withdrawal by the caregiver, lack of time or available in-home help, declines in invitations from friends, and problematic public behavior of the care recipient. Both the husband and wife caregivers in her sample complained that, while they still considered themselves a couple, friends began to respond to them as two individuals, one healthy and one impaired. Some spouses may restrict social activities because they "feel that enjoying their own mobility while their partners suffer illness and confinement is contrary to the meaning of marriage" (Hooyman & Lustbader, 1986, p. 31).

Financial strains are usually described by spouse caregivers as less severe than social or emotional pressures. While this is true for other caregivers as well, spouses, who must draw from shared economic resources, report financial hardship more often than do other caregivers (Hooyman & Lustbader, 1986; Rimmer, 1983). Inadequate third-party reimbursement for nursing home care creates a strong incentive for home care of spouses, who risk impoverishment if their partners are institutionalized. While concern with financial resources is less significant than emotional commitment for most couples, worry about spending down assets adds to the strain of caregiving.

Caring for a frail adult involves hard physical labor, which can negatively affect the caregiver's health. The spouses of the most severely impaired elderly are usually old themselves and face caregiving responsibilities with diminishing physical resources. Several studies have documented the preponderance of health problems suffered by spouse caregivers in comparison with other caregivers (Cantor, 1983; Johnson & Catalano, 1983), and in comparison with age peers in the general population (Pruchno & Potashnik, 1989; Satariano, Minkler, & Langhauser, 1984). In fact, declines in the health status of spouse caregivers constitute a major antecedent to the institutionalization of care recipients (Doty, 1986).

The focus on caregiver burden in the empirical literature has overshadowed the positive consequences of helping an ill or impaired spouse. While caring for a husband or wife contributes to physical, emotional, and financial strain, it can also produce some benefits. Couples can be drawn closer together through the expression of love for each other and through the fulfillment of the marital commitment to care for the partner "in sickness and in health" (Haug, 1985; Montgomery, Gonyea, & Hooyman, 1985). The tangible contributions of caregiving can also provide an opportunity to express gratitude for years of devotion and support earlier in the marriage. Caregivers also receive satisfaction from an awareness that their efforts alleviate the negative consequences of illness or disability and contribute to the other person's quality of life.

Comparisons of Caregiving Husbands and Wives

Most research comparing the experiences of spouses with the experiences of other caregivers makes it difficult to disentangle the impact of the relationship of the caregiver to the care recipient from the impact of the gender of the caregiver (Young & Kahana, 1989). Men and women occupy distinct roles in American society and encounter different structural barriers in fulfilling these roles. While the task structure facing caregiving husbands may be similar to that facing caregiving wives, the gender of the spouse caregiver has a significant impact on the meanings and consequences of the caregiving role.

Most studies of caregiver burden report that husbands experience lower levels of burden than do wives (Barusch & Spaid, 1989; Fitting, Rabins, Lucas, & Eastham, 1986; Horowitz, 1985a; Pruchno & Resch, 1989). At the same time, married women are more likely to be institutionalized than are married men, so, as Fischer and Hoffman (1984) conclude, husbands may not be quite as dependable as wives in providing long-term care. Hess and Soldo (1985) interpret this apparent discrepancy as evidence that husbands and wives have different tolerance thresholds or "tipping points" at which the demands of the caregiving task overwhelm their capacity. The next section explores similarities and differences in the caregiving experiences of husbands and wives, including the meaning of care and the impact of caring on the division of labor, social support networks, and financial resources.

The Meaning of Care

Caring for an impaired spouse has a different meaning for a husband than it has for a wife. Psychoanalytic feminist theorists emphasize the greater emotional significance of caregiving for women than for men (see Chapter 3, this volume). Theorists working within this perspective argue that the internalization of an injunction to care and concern for others rather than self are central elements in understanding feminine identity (Gilligan, 1982; Graham, 1983). Women's capacity for empathy and intimacy, which contrasts with men's separateness and rigid ego boundaries, is rooted in the social fact that women do the mothering in our society (Chodorow, 1978). Because women feel strongly connected to others, they frequently judge themselves according to an ethic of responsibility to people close to them (Gilligan, 1982). As a result, wives tend to focus on changes in the marital relationship brought about by their husbands' infirmities, whereas husbands focus more on specific tasks (B. Miller, 1987). Wives are also more likely than husbands "to feel submerged in caregiving [and to] experience emotional closeness and connectedness with the recipient of care" (Abel, 1990a, p. 142). B. Miller (1987) illustrates the empathy and personal responsibility described by these theorists. The wives in her qualitative study devised strategies for supporting their husbands' sense of control, even as the wives assumed escalating responsibilities for task management and decision making. Because they felt responsible for their husbands' safety, they were less willing than were caregiving husbands to leave their impaired spouses alone. At the same time, they were concerned that their husbands would feel "demeaned by the babysitting connotation of not being able to stay alone" (p. 450) and devised various explanations for the presence of paid respite workers.

This difference in the psychological significance of caring may explain why women have more trouble setting limits on their caregiving and suffer more distress when they cannot relieve their husbands' suffering (George & Gwyther, 1986; B. Miller, 1989; Zarit, Reever, & Bach-Peterson, 1980; Zarit, Todd, & Zarit, 1986). In contrast, men are likely to feel less guilty than women about not doing enough or to feel less personal responsibility for their wives' well-being (Robinson & Thurnher, 1979). As Abel (1990b) has argued, this interpretation is consistent with feminist analyses that women respond to difficulties by seeking to absorb the costs themselves.

In contrast to predictions by psychoanalytic feminist theory, Pruchno and Resch (1989) report that the husbands they studied were more highly invested in the caregiver role than were the wives. They interpret this difference within the context of reciprocity, explaining that husbands expressed "a greater sense than did the wives that the care they currently provided to their spouses was due to them" (p. 163). Spitze and Logan (1989) also hypothesize that women's contributions to their families throughout the life cycle are more visible than men's financial contributions, so "an older women may be seen as more deserving of physical and emotional support due to norms of reciprocity" (p. 108). From this perspective, caring is an opportunity for husbands to reciprocate for years of nurturing and support.

Another approach to understanding the meanings husbands and wives attribute to caring emphasizes the degree of continuity with previous roles. Several writers have argued that caring for an ill or disabled spouse is more "natural" for women and more consistent with their previous roles. As Pruchno and Resch (1989) contend:

> The current generation of caregiving wives was raised during a time when, from an early age, females were socialized to be more family oriented and nurturant. It may be expected that these women would view caregiving as a continuation of earlier responsibilities, whereas men, socialized to focus on the external world, would view demands as foreign. (p. 159)

On the other hand, by the time wives assume caregiving responsibilities for their husbands, their children are usually independent. Adopting the role of caregiver is less a continuation than a return to earlier responsibilities. This resumption "conflicts with the decisions many women are making to take more control of their lives and not be locked into traditional roles" (Zarit et al., 1986, p. 260). Having raised their children and, perhaps, cared for their older parents, they "approached their later years with the hopes of leaving the caregiving role behind. Now they felt saddled with yet another caregiving demand, and many resented it" (Pruchno & Resch, 1989, p. 164). Fitting et al. (1986) cite this discontinuity in caregiving responsibilities among women as an explanation for their finding that wives are more likely than husbands to experience deterioration in their relationships with their spouses.

Other researchers disagree with the argument that caregiving represents a continuation of women's gender-linked responsibilities. Brubaker (1985b) contends that traditional sex role differences become blurred in old age, with women developing a more instrumental orientation and men becoming more expressive and nurturant. His argument is consistent with Guttman's (1987) notion of "reclaimed powers," which hypothesizes that during the postparental years, women become more assertive and instrumental whereas men become more nurturant and expressive.

B. Miller (1987) also has viewed caregiving in later life as associated more closely with the male role than with the female role, although for different reasons. Focusing on the instrumental aspect of the role, she assumes that being in charge of another adult is an extension of the traditionally male role of authority figure. In contrast, women have had little preparation for assuming authority over adult men.

> The males' assumption of authority over their wives was presented as a natural extension from their authoritative role in the family. . . . For wives, assuming an authority position over another adult, especially a man who had probably been the authority figure in the marriage, was one of the hardest aspects of the caregiving role. . . . Most saw the shift in authority relationships as a burden with heavy personal costs. (B. Miller, 1987, p. 449)

The Impact of Caring on the Division of Labor

The frailty of an older spouse introduces constraints on the couple's division of household labor. The consequences of these constraints depend upon the extent and range of incapacity experienced by each spouse and by the couple's division of labor prior to the onset of disability.

Most of the current cohort of elderly people exhibit traditional attitudes regarding gender roles, characterized by a sex-segregated division of labor. Unfortunately, as Ross (1987) has pointed out, we do not have longitudinal data showing changes in the division of household labor over time, so we lack information regarding task arrangements of current cohorts of elderly at earlier points in the life cycle. This makes it difficult to disentangle the impact of life-course changes from cohort effects. Some insights can be gained, however, by reviewing current material on the gender division of labor.

The division of household labor literature demonstrates that the cultural assignment of domestic production has not changed in response to women's increased labor force production over the last 40 years. Women who work for wages spend fewer hours in housework, although the total workweek is longer (Hartman, 1980). Women with higher incomes can reduce their work loads by delegating tasks to hired help or by purchasing market equivalents. Nevertheless, they retain responsibility for most domestic tasks, with husbands' contributions typically viewed as "helping." Tasks performed by husbands are characterized by clearly defined boundaries (e.g., mowing the lawn), flexible scheduling and an element of discretion as to when the tasks will be done (e.g., doing household repairs and handling finances), and greater leisure components (e.g., playing with children) (Meissner, 1977). As a result, husbands have more control over their time, whereas women's work is more likely to lock them into a rigid schedule (Hochschild, 1989).

Several investigators have found that husbands increase their involvement in household work when they retire, particularly in the more expressive areas of housework, such as cooking, gardening, and home decorating (Coverman & Shelley, 1986; Gordon, Gaitz, & Scott, 1976; Parron & Troll, 1978; Rexroat & Shehan, 1987). Other researchers, however, argue for the continuity of preretirement patterns of task assignment in late-life marriages (Albrecht, Bahr, & Chadwick, 1979; Keith & Schafer, 1986). Brubaker and Kinsel (1988), for example, report that older wives maintain responsibility for cooking meals, washing dishes and clothes, writing letters, and cleaning the house, while older husbands maintain responsibility for yard work, car maintenance, and house repairs. Condie (1989) identifies both patterns among his sample of couples who had celebrated their golden wedding anniversaries:

> Their household division of labor appeared to be structured along traditional lines, with wives doing much more of the cleaning and cooking while men mowed the lawn and fixed things. However, sharing domestic duties was common, and there was a relatively strong degree of interdependence. (p. 155)

A synthesis of these empirical results indicates that, although retired husbands increase somewhat their participation in domestic work, women retain responsibility for household production and continue to bear a greater share of household work. In fact, recent time-budget studies have estimated that retired wives spend 150-300% more time on household tasks than do their husbands (Altergott & Duncan, 1987; Rexroat & Shehan, 1987; Zuzanek, 1987).

Evidence regarding the division of household labor suggests that the impact of the disability of a spouse is gender specific. The incapacity of a husband means that a wife caregiver assumes greater responsibility for male-stereotypic tasks, such as yard work, household repairs, and financial management. However, because wives already perform the majority of domestic production, assuming responsibility for their husbands' tasks has little impact on the total work load of caregiving wives (Rexroat & Shehan, 1987). In contrast, when a wife is disabled, the husband caregiver is faced with the need to assume responsibility for more household chores. This involves more than mastering specific instrumental tasks; it means decreases in autonomy and flexibility of scheduling. Since the wife is almost always responsible for the home, even if she delegates some tasks, the disability of a wife means the couple has lost a manager of domestic production. Furthermore, since women perform a larger share of domestic work, changes in the household division of labor are more dramatic if the wife is the care recipient (Szinovacz, 1989). Szinovacz (1989) has also found that the illness or disability of a wife results in a greater reorganization of household activities than does the illness or disability of a husband. In fact, Brubaker and Kinsel (1988) argue that it is illness rather than retirement that alters preretirement patterns in the way households tasks are divided.

Research on widowhood suggests that mastering new task areas and increasing self-reliance contribute to a sense of mastery and self-esteem (Neale, 1987; Silverman, 1987). Moss, Lawton, Dean, Goodman, and Schneider (1987) argue that caregiving may sometimes present not a burden but a challenge, an opportunity to demonstrate competence and experience a sense of achievement. In a caregiving situation, this potential benefit can be eroded when the dependent spouse is reluctant to give up responsibility. Frustrated watching someone intrude on what has been his or her domain, the disabled spouse may criticize the caregiver's task performance. Disagreements can also emerge around standards of cleanliness or styles of task performance. Hooyman and Lustbader (1986) comment:

> Divergent opinions as to how neatly clothes are to be folded, the way dishes are to be washed, the degree of exactitude necessary to balance a check-book, how carefully a car is to be handled, and the way a garden is to be maintained—all of these can be infuriating to a person who has lost control over areas of life previously managed without interference. (p. 36)

Impact on Social Support Networks

In addition to the impact on the division of household labor, the disability of a spouse also produces gender-specific outcomes on both socioemotional and instrumental support. Elderly husbands and wives assume care responsibilities with different social resources. Older men have more acquaintances but are less likely to have confidants other than their wives (Depner & Ingersoll-Dayton, 1988; Vaux, 1985). They are more likely to rely exclusively on their wives for meeting their needs for empathy, affection, and companionship. In contrast, women are more likely to have developed a wider range of close friendships with other women (Antonucci & Akiyama, 1987; Vaux, 1985). These findings led Noelker and Poulshock (1982) to conclude that when caring for their husbands limits their social activities, wives experience greater losses, while caregiving husbands can more easily adjust to exclusive focus on the marital dyad.

Disability also has gender-specific effects on the couple's social network. The illness of a wife means that the couple has lost the person who traditionally maintained contact within kin networks (Leigh, 1982; Mercier, Paulson, & Morris, 1989). This kinship work has been defined by di Leonardo (1987) as the "conception, maintenance and ritual celebration of cross-household ties, including visits, letters, telephone calls, presents and cards to kin; the organization of holiday gatherings; the creation and maintenance of quasi-kin relations; and decisions to neglect or to intensify particular ties" (p. 442). The work of kinship takes both time and skill. It differs from housework and direct caregiving in that it is harder to substitute hired help. Caregiving husbands, therefore, more frequently experience declines in social contact with family and kin outside the helping network, a handicap encountered less often by caregiving wives (Morgan, 1989; Rosenthal, 1985).

The initial advantages of larger support networks, however, disappear if the husband's escalating care needs isolate the wife caregiver. Fradkin and Liberti (1987) comment:

> Caregivers often talk about being isolated, of losing companionship and social contacts. Family and friends who are upset by seeing changes in the husband tend to stay away. Sons and daughters may also view their mother as the one who always holds things together, and may continue to expect her to hold this role in the family despite the change in circumstances. (p. 200)

Miller and Montgomery (1990) found that wives, who identify more with the caregiver role, are more willing to relinquish competing responsibilities.

Men are not only more likely to continue to pursue their own interests, but they are more willing to leave their dependent wives alone (B. Miller, 1987). The resulting isolation that wives often experience exacerbates tensions in the caregiving situation. As Oliver (1983) explains, "A situation in which neither party contributes any new experiences is claustrophobic in the extreme, and most of the women said that this was the point at which they began to feel like care attendants rather than wives" (p. 82).

Impact on Support to the Caregiver

The assumption that caring is "natural" for women also affects the level of support husbands and wives receive. Wives are more likely than husbands to be sole caregivers (Stone et al., 1987). Caregiving husbands, in contrast, are more likely than caregiving wives to receive supplemental assistance from informal helpers and to incorporate formal services (Stone et al., 1987; Tennstedt et al., 1989; Zarit et al., 1986). Part of this difference can be attributed to wives' more extensive experience in managing caregiving responsibilities or to their reluctance to admit they cannot handle responsibilities that are defined as "natural" for women. But it may also emerge from the invisibility of domestic work performed by women. When men provide assistance, their efforts are more likely to be acknowledged (Guberman, 1988). Hooyman (1989) reports that men are more likely than women to receive attention and praise, "since their caregiving tends to be viewed as an unexpected expression of compassion compared to an expected duty for women" (p. 9). In contrast, wives' caregiving efforts are expected and unnoticed. As one 73-year-old wife explained, "People tell me that he deserves all the care I can give him, because he's such a nice person and was always so good to me. Well, I'm a nice person and have always been good to him. What do I deserve?" (Fradkin & Liberti, 1987, p. 200).

Several writers have suggested that the implicit policies of formal programs also reinforce this gender-based division of labor. Women caring for impaired elderly are often considered less needy than male caregivers, a pattern especially pronounced when wives care for disabled husbands (Blaxter, 1976). Oliver's (1983) review of British studies led her to conclude that the presence of a wife in the home means that a man will be discharged earlier from the hospital and will receive fewer aids, adaptations in the home, and domestic services:

When disability strikes, there is the universal expectation—from the medical profession, social services staff and not the least from the husband himself—that the wife will take on everything that is necessary. . . . By seeing the wife as a person who will always be present, always free to assist and always willing to subjugate her own needs and wishes to her husband's, statutory services can avoid providing nearly all services. (pp. 73, 77)

Impact on Financial Resources

Since out-of-pocket expenses are drawn from a common pool, husbands and wives share equally in these costs of care. However, the financial impact of terminal illness on the surviving spouse's economic status is a cost more often borne by wives, since women live longer and generally marry older men. Husbands who are receiving care are more likely to be distressed over the future financial impact of their illness on their wives, since husbands are more likely than wives to have internalized responsibility for providing economically for their families (Hooyman & Lustbader, 1986).

The economic consequences of caregiving extend beyond direct expenditures. Studies of caregiver burden frequently report that financial strains are less severe than the emotional and social pressures, but Rimmer (1983) has argued that the economic and financial loss to the career has been underestimated because of a short-term focus on loss of current income and the direct costs of extra expenses. Caring also has long-term, indirect effects on economic resources. A key factor in assessing economic costs is the impact of caregiving on labor force participation. According to data from the National Long-Term Care Survey, 10% of wives caring for their husbands and 12% of husbands caring for their wives are employed (Stone et al., 1987). Caregiving responsibilities can discourage labor force participation, particularly for older women (Soldo & Myllyluoma, 1983). For many older women, leaving the work force to care for a husband during his final illness amounts to early retirement, especially given the low probability of reemployment among older workers (Schulz, 1988). Fischer and Hoffman (1984) stress the potentially large financial costs to wives who leave the labor force or retire early to care for elderly relatives, not only in lost wages, but also in the opportunity to develop higher earnings profiles and subsequently greater retirement benefits. These costs are particularly severe for wives whose earlier work histories were interrupted to care for young children and/or their own elderly parents. Furthermore, these long-term economic costs to careers may be ultimately shared by the public in terms of losses of current tax contributions and future increased costs of public assistance to an impoverished elderly population (Horowitz, 1985a).

Questions for Future Research

This review of the literature on the experiences of husbands and wives as caregivers has documented both consistent findings and unanswered questions. While descriptions of differences in the experiences of husband and wife caregivers are available in the family caregiving literature, consensus has not yet emerged regarding explanations for these differences. For example, most investigators report that husbands caring for wives report lower levels of burden and stress than do wives caring for husbands, even when controlling for the level of care required. Is this because of women's internalized injunction to care and their less rigid ego boundaries, as hypothesized by psychoanalytic theorists? Is it because caregiving coincides with older men's reclaimed powers of nurturance and expressiveness? Do husbands feel less burden because they receive more assistance from both formal and informal sources and because their efforts are more likely to be recognized? Does caring for an impaired wife provide a husband an opportunity to reciprocate and express gratitude for the years of instrumental and emotional support he received earlier in the marriage? Or, as Horowitz (1989) suggests, does evidence of lower burden emerge in survey research because men are socialized to express an image of competence?

A major shortcoming of the spousal caregiving literature is the focus on white couples. This means that both concepts and measurement techniques reflect the experiences of the dominant group. For example, as this chapter has illustrated, most investigators report that caregiving responsibilities fall on one person, particularly at high levels of disability, and that spouses are the preferred caregivers for elders who are married. Yet Gibson's (1986) research indicates that "older black Americans drew from a more varied pool of informal helpers . . . and were more versatile in interchanging helpers for one another as they approached old age" (p. 95). Her findings suggest that older black couples are less likely to face caregiving responsibilities alone than are older white couples, and that a focus on primary caregivers will underestimate informal resources for blacks more seriously than for whites. For another example, research on the division of domestic labor stresses the stability of the gender-linked allocation of tasks. Yet McAdoo (1986) argues that black couples exhibit greater flexibility in family roles, with parents sharing domestic tasks and child rearing as well as responsibility for earning a living. We need to know more about how this more egalitarian approach to family responsibilities affects the experience of caring for a frail elderly spouse. Expanding the focus of research involves more than simply recruiting black couples into studies of spousal caregiving. As J. Jackson (1989) reminds us, we need to examine the extent to which our basic constructs and measurement instruments reflect differences in the experiences and subjective meanings of caregiving within ethnic communities.

We also need to know more about the impact of social class and economic resources on the coping strategies used by spouse caregivers. It is frequently assumed that older people prefer informal assistance and rely on formal help only as a last resort, when informal help is unavailable or when their needs exceed the resources of informal helping networks. Several researchers have suggested that using paid help can also be a way of minimizing the detrimental psychological consequences of needing and receiving care and of avoiding dependence on one's children (Lee, 1985a; Shenk, 1987). This may be especially true of affluent elderly, who not only have more resources with which to hire help but for whom reliance on paid help has been a way of life (Ostrander, 1984). However, we need to know more about the extent to which reliance on spouses and adult children reflects true preference rather than limited alternatives.

Another variable that merits further attention is the nature of the care recipient's disability. Most of the research on caregiver burden has focused on families of dementia patients. Caring for a cognitively intact but physically impaired older person can be less stressful (Brody, 1989). Although the labor is demanding, the damage to the relationship between the caregiver and the care recipient is less extensive. Poulshock and Deimling (1984) conclude that caregiver burden is lower if the recipient has well-preserved social skills. Although, as suggested previously, physical impairment requires spouses to learn new roles and to redefine aspects of their relationship, both partners can participate in this renegotiation. The impaired spouse can continue to handle some of his or her responsibilities. For example, a physically disabled husband can still participate in financial management, and an impaired wife can continue her correspondence with kin. As Treas (1977) has observed, "Older couples can maintain considerable independence in the face of infirmities by nursing one another or reallocating household chores" (p. 487). Such arrangements not only reduce the work load of the caregiving spouse, but also enhance the self-esteem of the care recipient. By sharing work and learning tasks that have been the responsibility of the impaired spouse, both spouses can relieve some anxiety about the ability of the caregiver to manage in the future.

In contrast, caring for a demented elderly family member is one of the most demanding and disruptive types of caregiving (Brody, 1989). Cognitive impairment undermines the relationship between husband and wife more dramatically than does physical impairment. Although care can be less demanding physically, it usually includes substantial supervision (Lund, Pett, & Caserta, 1988; Ory et al., 1985). While help with physical tasks is amenable to planning and scheduling, supervision is an ongoing activity that often leads caregivers to feel isolated and trapped (Caserta, Lund, Wright, & Redburn, 1987). Unlike cognitively intact patients, who can express gratitude for the help they receive, demented care recipients may disrupt care and be uncooperative (Silliman & Sternberg, 1988). Given evidence of wives' greater sense of personal responsibility for their husbands' well-being, differences in degree of burden between physically and cognitively impaired spouses may be more dramatic for wife caregivers. However, any conclusions must be tentative until more is known about the impact of differential diagnoses.

Another issue that merits more study is the effect of the duration of the marriage. Although this variable is rarely mentioned explicitly, the implicit image that emerges from many studies is that of a couple facing illness and disability after many years of marriage. Caring demands are experienced differently when the marriage is more recent. Hooyman and Lustbader (1986) note:

> A late life marriage may occur more for economic convenience and the need for companionship than from a deep love commitment. The healthier spouse would then be left in a bind if the other became ill, with medical bills and limited mobility disrupting the financial and social basis of the marriage. (p. 81)

The increasing number of second and third marriages also raises unanswered questions about spouse caregivers. The age gap between husband and wife increases with subsequent marriages (Atkinson & Glass, 1985; Vera, Berardo, & Berardo, 1985), and younger spouses find caregiving more burdensome (Hooyman & Lustbader, 1986). These findings have led to predictions that middle-aged and young-old wives caring for very old husbands would find caregiving responsibilities particularly burdensome, even if they had been married 20 or 30 years. This hypothesized stress among younger wives is consistent with predictions that stressful events have more negative impacts when they occur "off-time," that is, at unexpected stages of the life cycle (Blau, 1981; Riley, 1986).

Finally, it is important to consider the extent to which our understanding of caregiving is cohort specific. Little more than a decade has passed since Fengler and Goodrich (1979) first called attention to spouse caregivers as "hidden patients." Consequently, most research on elderly spouse caregivers has examined people born during the first quarter of this century. Future cohorts of spouse caregivers will have experienced different historical periods. Two-earner families are increasingly prevalent at all stages of the family life cycle, although changes in the division of domestic labor are occurring more slowly (Hochschild, 1989). More couples are relying on formal help or commercial substitutes for housework and child care. While women still retain responsibility for domestic production, the growing gap between the rich and poor has enabled affluent women to relieve themselves of some aspects of housework and caring for others by becoming managers of domestic work done by other women (Cole, 1986; Hertz, 1988). Care must be taken that the experiences of current cohorts of caregivers do not constrain the research questions posed by investigators in the coming decades.

5

Gender Differences in Patterns of Child-Parent Caregiving Relationships

RHONDA J. V. MONTGOMERY

One of the most significant changes in family roles in recent history has been the assumption by large numbers of adult children of the responsibility for the welfare and direct care of their parents. The relatively recent emergence of the parent-care role as it exists in the United States today is most often attributed to the unprecedented size of the elderly population, especially that segment requiring assistance with household and personal tasks (Pratt & Kethley, 1988; Stone, Cafferata, & Sangl, 1987). Yet the physically determined needs of parents for assistance do not fully account for the now widely documented willingness of adult children to assume caregiving roles to meet these needs (Brody, 1977; Stone et al., 1987). To account more fully for filial responsibility as exercised by adult children, it is useful to focus on the motives of these children. For a full discussion of issues surrounding filial responsibility, the reader is referred to Chapter 7 of this volume. Here a brief discussion is offered to provide a context within which patterns and consequences of caregiving by adult children can be considered.

Sources of Filial Responsibility

Legal Mandates

In his comprehensive review of issues related to filial responsibility, Schorr (1980) emphasizes both the recency of filial responsibility laws and the historical absence of a moral basis for these laws. Until the development of the industrialized states, the obligation to provide elder care stemmed from the control that elders were able to maintain over the family financial base. Bulcroft, Van Leynseele, and Borgatta (1989) note that the "switch to an industrial economy . . . changed the financial base of the family, introducing the possibility of independent access to financial resources by children, and effectively emphasized the possibility of elders becoming destitute in the absence of control of the family financial base" (p. 377). Hence, despite the moral rhetoric in which filial responsibility laws are often couched, these laws, which currently exist in some form in 30 states, emerged not as a result of moral values, but in response to the threat of a growing financial burden that dependent elders posed to an industrial society. Perhaps it is this absence of a moral basis for filial responsibility laws that accounts for the inconsistency among states in the statement of filial responsibility and its capricious enforcement (Bulcroft, Van Leynseele, & Borgatta, 1989). Clearly, such laws do not account for the prevalence of children as caregivers in either historical or modern times.

Affection and Obligation

The persistence of filial responsibility, despite the absence of legal or economic imperatives, has often led researchers and policymakers to focus on affection as the primary source of parent-care responsibilities (Abel, 1986; Jarrett, 1985). Numerous studies have noted the relationship between affection and the felt obligation to provide for parent care (Horowitz, 1985b) as well as the importance of attitudes of obligation as correlates of contact with parents and assistance to parents (Troll, Miller, & Atchley, 1979; Walker, Pratt, Shin, & Jones, 1990). However, there is a growing literature that questions the importance of "affection" as the primary force underlying filial responsibility and/or the performance of caregiving tasks (Abel, 1990b; Gilligan, 1982; Jarrett, 1985; Walker, Pratt, Shin, & Jones, 1989). Repeatedly, it has been shown that there can be emotional closeness between parent and child without contact or aid being given (Lopata, 1979; Shanas, 1979a; Walker et al., 1989).

At the same time, it has been shown that children who do not feel a great amount of affection for their parents are still able and willing to provide needed assistance (Horowitz & Shindleman, 1983; Walker et al., 1989; Walker, Pratt, Shin, & Jones, 1990). Furthermore, there is growing evidence that caregiving is governed by a plurality of motives that encompass both affection and obligation (Walker et al., 1989; Walker, Pratt, Shin, & Jones, 1990). For many children, affection may influence the way in which responsibilities are experienced, but these children frequently provide care simply because parents need care (B. N. Adams, 1968; Anderson, 1984; Leigh, 1982) or because the children perceive few alternatives (Birkel & Jones, 1989; Brody, 1985; Pratt, Schmall, Wright, & Cleland, 1985).

The Prevalence of Daughters and Sons as Caregivers

Although the motives that prompt adult children to care for their frail parents are not well understood, the predominance of adult children among informal caregivers, especially when a spouse is not available, is undisputed when all types and levels of assistance are considered (see Chapter 2, this volume). The prevalence of children as sources of emotional support, assistance with transportation and banking matters, and help with household chores and activities of daily living has been widely documented over the last decade (Brody, 1985; Cicirelli, 1983; Shanas, 1979b; Stone et al., 1987). At the same time, research has shown that as a group, children provide less intensive care and assist over shorter periods of time than do spouses (Johnson, 1983). This difference between spouses and children is most notable for sons.

There is also a significant difference between sons and daughters in their caregiving activities and experience. The greater prevalence of daughters versus sons as caregivers was initially documented by researchers using availability samples of dyads consisting of impaired elders and their primary caregivers. Almost uniformly, these studies have shown that greater numbers of daughters than sons assist their parents with a wide range of tasks and that daughters' predominance is especially strong with respect to direct personal assistance to their impaired parents (Birkel & Jones, 1989; Cantor, 1983; Horowitz, 1985b; Johnson & Catalano, 1983; Jones & Vetter, 1984; Noelker

& Townsend, 1987). Although the consistency of this finding is compelling, the limitations of the samples utilized in these initial studies have recently prompted several researchers to revisit the issue of daughter dominance (Coward & Brubaker, 1989; Coward & Dwyer, 1990; Montgomery & Kamo, 1989).

Findings from a nationally representative sample of impaired elders and their caregivers have confirmed the predominance of daughters as primary caregivers to impaired elders, even when the number and gender distribution of all available children are considered (Stone et al., 1987; Coward & Dwyer, 1990). For example, in their examination of family structure and caregiving, Coward and Dwyer (1990) report that the highest participation rates of sons in care tasks (24.8%) occurred among families with no daughters, rates that were on a par with the lowest participation rates of daughters (24.6%), which occurred among families of mixed-gender networks. Furthermore, when families with single-gender sibling networks (all male or all female children) were compared, the prevalence of sons as caregivers was much lower than the prevalence of daughters as caregivers (6.9% versus 28.0%). This pattern of dominance by daughters as caregivers has also been affirmed by recent studies that used large random samples of elders residing in the community and that included persons who were less impaired than the sample used by Coward and Dwyer (1990) (Hirshorn & Montgomery, in press; Spitze & Logan, 1990b; Stoller & Pugliesi, 1989; Stone et al., 1987).

Differences in the Caregiving Role

Types of Tasks

The bulk of research suggests that daughters are more likely to provide assistance to their parents and that substantial differences exist in the ways sons and daughters engage in and are affected by the caregiving role. As a rule, daughters are more likely than sons to help elders with household chores, especially food preparation and laundry chores, as well as with personal care tasks that require "hands-on" care and daily assistance (Horowitz, 1985b; Matthews & Rosner, 1988; Montgomery & Kamo, 1989; Stoller, 1983, 1990). In contrast, sons are more likely to perform home repair and maintenance tasks (Coward, 1987; O'Bryant & Morgan, 1990; Stoller, 1990). Among the adult children who help their parents, few differences exist between sons and daughters in their assistance with banking and financial management or intermittent tasks such as helping with legal matters (Montgomery & Kamo, 1989; Stoller, 1990). Indicative of the different types of tasks that sons and daughters tend to assume, daughters also spend more hours each week in parent care (Montgomery & Kamo, 1989; Stoller & Earl, 1983).

Caregiving Roles

The differences in the types of tasks that sons and daughters perform are related to the types of caregiving roles that the two sexes tend to assume. Not only are daughters more likely to engage in caregiving tasks, they are also more likely to assume the role of primary caregiver (Abel, 1987; Coward & Dwyer, 1990; Kivett, 1988; Kivett & Atkinson, 1984; Montgomery & Kamo, 1989; Stoller, 1990). As such, they are more likely to provide "routine" care over longer periods of time (Matthews & Rosner, 1988; Montgomery & Kamo, 1989; Stoller, 1990). Sons, in contrast, more often assume supportive roles that require commitments over shorter periods of time and tend to be peripheral helpers within a caregiving network rather than the central actors.

Even when sons assume the role of primary caregiver, they commit less time to caregiving tasks and are less likely to engage in hands-on care than are daughters (Horowitz, 1985b). These sons tend more often to be managers of care rather than direct providers (Montgomery & Kamo, 1989).

Help for the Helpers

As the term *manager* implies, the assumption by a child of the primary caregiver role does not necessarily mean that he or she is directly responsible for all of the care. Many caregivers seek assistance with their caregiving duties from both formal and informal sources (Abel, 1990a; Archbold, 1983; Brody, Johnsen, Fulcomer, & Lang, 1983; Brody & Schoonover, 1986). The extent of this assistance is related to the gender structure of sibling networks, the type and level of disability of the parent, the gender of the primary caregiver, and family history (Coward & Dwyer, 1990; Matthews & Rosner, 1988; Stone et al., 1987).

Matthews and Rosner (1988) have noted that sisters are most likely to serve as a source of "backup" to their siblings who are primary caregivers. As backup caregivers, these sisters provide whatever assistance is asked for or needed and are expected to be available primarily when "routine" caregivers request services. Brothers infrequently assume this backup role, but instead tend to engage in more circumscribed and sporadic assistance. Matthews and Rosner define *circumscribed participation* as help that is "highly predictable but carefully bounded" (p. 189), such as weekly telephone calls or help with banking matters. *Sporadic assistance* is help that is provided by a child at his or her convenience, such as shopping trips or visits that are not scheduled on a regular basis. In short, sisters tend to support primary caregivers by being available to provide whatever services are needed whenever they are needed. In contrast, brothers tend to help their sisters who are serving as primary caregivers not by being potential backup caregivers, but by providing limited assistance when the brothers choose to do so.

The most common form of assistance given to caregivers by other informal providers is help with shopping and errands (Jones & Vetter, 1984). Assistance to the caregiver with the intimate personal care required by severely physically impaired elders is the form that is least likely to be provided by an informal source. However, Birkel and Jones (1989) found that caregivers of persons with dementia were more likely to rely on other household members for help with intimate tasks, while caregivers of nondemented parents were more likely to rely on formal sources of assistance with personal care tasks. They suggest that this divergence may be due to differences in attitudes that family members may hold about bodily contact with cognitively impaired versus alert elders.

In general, elders with the greatest disabilities receive care from larger networks of care providers, including formal and informal sources (Birkel & Jones, 1989; Neighbors & Jackson, 1984; Stoller & Earl, 1983). As the needs of impaired elders become greater, caregivers draw on greater amounts of formal and informal resources (Montgomery, Kosloski, & Borgatta, 1988-1989).

Although there has been no research reported that has directly investigated differences between sons and daughters in seeking and using assistance from either informal or formal sources, several findings from studies of caregivers suggest that daughters are less likely to receive assistance with their efforts. Certainly, the integral role of daughters-in-law in parent care is widely acknowledged, and is not matched by an equal involvement of sons-in-law (Brody & Schoonover, 1986; Kleban, Brody, Schoonover, & Hoffman, 1989; see also Chapter 2, this volume). There is also some evidence that male caregivers, in general, utilize more formal services to enhance their caregiving than do female caregivers (Wright, 1983).

Plausible Reasons for Gender Differences

Numerous explanations have been advanced to account for the observed divergence of caregiving behaviors between sons and daughters. Grounding her work in theoretical models drawn from the family studies literature, Finley (1989) summarizes four possible explanatory models that could account for the observed differences between sons and daughters: the time-available hypothesis, the external-resources hypothesis, the socialization/ ideology hypothesis, and the specialization-of-tasks hypothesis. In addition to these four explanatory models, Montgomery and Kamo (1989) have suggested that cultural taboos may partially account for differences in the caregiving behaviors of sons and daughters.

The Time-Available Hypothesis

The time-available hypothesis contends that competing time and role demands determine the time available for family labor (Berardo, Shehan, & Leslie, 1987; Condran & Bode, 1982; Coverman, 1985; Ross, 1987). It has been suggested that the predominance of daughters as caregivers can be explained as a consequence of competing demands. In particular, it has been argued that large numbers of daughters who are caregivers are not employed outside of the home; therefore, as a group, daughters have a greater amount of time to devote to caregiving. Although this explanation is intuitively attractive, evidence regarding the relationship between employment and the amount of care provided by sons and daughters does not support the viability of this hypothesis. Past research indicates that the employment status of daughters does not substantially affect the amount of care they provide to parents (Matthews & Rosner, 1988; Stoller, 1990). Therefore, the notion that the greater availability of time due to nonemployment of women accounts for their predominance as caregivers is not consistent with the facts.

The time-available hypothesis becomes even less viable in view of data reported by Montgomery and Kamo (1989) drawn from a sample of adult child caregivers. Their results indicate that only 21% of the employed sons reported spending one hour or more per week doing personal care tasks, while 64% of the employed daughters performed at least one hour of personal care per week. Together, the evidence suggests that employment may decrease the amount of direct personal care provided by adult children, but employment per se does not account for the wide discrepancy between sons and daughters in caregiving patterns. It is possible, however, that the greater resources in terms of money and familial power that employment usually affords sons may account for gender differences in parent care.

External-Resources Hypothesis

According to Finley (1989), the external-resources hypothesis asserts that resources obtained externally, such as income and education, determine the power dynamics within the family and, consequently, the division of labor. Those persons having greater resources are able to translate those resources into power in family negotiations and, as a result, spend less time caregiving. If this hypothesis is correct, people who have personal income from employment or other sources would provide less direct care. The evidence to support this hypothesis is mixed. While there is some evidence that employment for daughters (Brody & Schoonover, 1986; Lang & Brody, 1983) and income (Archbold, 1983) are associated with less direct personal care, there is also evidence, as noted previously, that employed women still supply most of the help for their parents. Perhaps employment status is not a good measure of the external resources for women relative to men, given that, in general, the income of women continues to be lower than that of their male counterparts. Hence, even when they are employed, women encounter lower opportunity costs (i.e., smaller losses in income) when assuming caregiving responsibilities than do men (Walker, 1983).

More insight into the viability of the external-resources hypothesis might be gained by a study that looks at the relative incomes of potential male and female caregivers. It is possible that sons assume the same level of responsibility to ensure the care of their parents as do daughters, but that they are able to buy services because of their higher incomes or to delegate the direct care tasks to female relatives (e.g., their sisters or their wives) because of their relative power within the family (Montgomery & Datwyler, 1990).

Socialization/Ideology Hypothesis

Finley (1989) has suggested that the delegation by men of tasks to women may be the result of socialization processes or ideology. According to the socialization/ideology hypothesis, gender role attitudes are learned through the socialization process, and this process in turn influences the division of labor within families (Berardo et al., 1987; Condran & Bode, 1982; Ross, 1987). This division of labor is not necessarily associated with resources or efficiency, but is simply an outcome of attitudes about responsibilities. Hence the differences between men and women in the extent and intensity of parent care may reflect differences in felt obligation resulting from socialization processes. Certainly there is an abundance of evidence that women have traditionally been responsible for kinkeeping tasks (Finch, 1989; Finley, 1989; Troll et al., 1979; see also Chapter 8, this volume), and parent care may well be viewed as one of these tasks. Others have also argued that young women are more apt to feel obligated for parent care because they have been socialized to nurturing roles (Walker, Shin, Jones, & Pratt, 1987; Walker et al., 1989).

Although appealing, the socialization/ideology hypothesis regarding felt obligation is not supported by the literature. Generally, it has been found that sons and daughters share a common sense of obligation to care for the elderly (Brody et al., 1983; Finley, 1989; Finley, Roberts, & Banahan 1988; Montgomery & Kamo, 1989; Roff & Klemmack, 1986). If there is a difference in filial responsibility attitudes between sons and daughters, it is not in the *level* of felt obligation but rather in the *means* considered appropriate to meet that obligation. It is interesting that Matthews and Rosner (1988) conclude that not only do sons feel less obligated than daughters to assume the role of primary caregiver or to provide routine care personally, but their sisters agree with their perspective. In their study of sibling networks, Matthews and Rosner found that daughters did not look to their brothers for routine care or backup care, but instead expected circumscribed or sporadic assistance from them. Whether these expectations reflect differences in norms or are grounded in realism stemming from past experience remains to be studied. In either case, the findings shift our attention from differences in perceived obligation to differences in the means whereby the obligations are met. Although socialization processes may not result in a differential in the obligations felt by sons and daughters, socialization processes may result in task specialization.

Specialization-of-Tasks Hypothesis

The specialization-of-tasks hypothesis suggests that women and men are assigned to different tasks that maximize the well-being of the family as a whole (Becker, 1981; Condran & Bode, 1982; England & Farkas, 1986). As a result of the separation between the workplace and the family caused by industrialization, men have assumed provider roles and women housekeeper roles (Lein, 1979; Slocum & Nye, 1976). Although recent increases in female labor force participation have helped women cut into the provider role, the housekeeper role is still rarely assumed by men. Many studies have found that people tend to endorse egalitarian attitudes, but do not necessarily behave accordingly (Araji, 1977; Hiller & Philliber, 1986; Slocum & Nye, 1976). To the extent that the specialization-of-tasks hypothesis is correct, we would expect sons and daughters to fulfill their responsibilities to their parents in different ways. In families adhering to traditional means of dividing labor, males would work outside the home and females would assume household and caregiving tasks. Hence sons might fulfill their obligation to care for parents by delegating such care to female relatives, including sisters and wives. In families where both men and women are employed, the specialization of tasks may be observed in the types of household tasks and chores that are assumed. It would follow that sons could most efficiently and/or appropriately perform household chores and tasks that have traditionally been performed by males (e.g., financial management and home repairs) because these are the tasks they have learned through socialization and practice. Similarly, women could most efficiently and/or appropriately perform routine household tasks and personal care tasks because these are skills traditionally taught to women.

Again, the evidence in support of this hypothesis is mixed. Although past research indicates that daughters are more involved than sons in providing emotional assistance and assistance with household and personal care tasks, there is no evidence that sons are the primary providers of any type of service with the exception of home repairs (Coward, 1987; Finley, 1989; Horowitz, 1985b; Montgomery & Kamo, 1989; Stoller, 1990). These findings would suggest that sons specialize in the types of tasks they perform, but daughters do not. This conclusion was also reached by Finley (1989), who investigated the relative prevalence of males and females as care managers versus direct providers. Specialization, to the extent that it exists, consists of sons' limiting their caregiving to traditional male tasks; daughters tend to perform all types of tasks.

Cultural Taboos

It is likely that differential patterns of caregiving that have been observed for sons and daughters cannot be accounted for by a single explanation. Rather, several forces may be at work to account for the differences. One such force may be culturally based proscriptions that are associated with gender role socialization (Montgomery & Kamo, 1989). Socialization processes not only *prescribe* behavior for designated identities within a culture, they may also *proscribe* some behaviors. These proscriptions can become societal taboos. In the case of caregiving, it may be that sons are not only socialized to the provider role to the exclusion of the homemaker role, but also come to view certain types of personal care tasks as taboos. Hands-on care for a parent, such as bathing, dressing, and toileting, may be avoided because such intimate contact is viewed as inappropriate or taboo—too closely aligned with behaviors that break societal norms regarding incest. Some support for this interpretation can be gained from the fact that the differences in the types of tasks that sons and daughters perform have not been found to exist between husbands and wives who assume the caregiving role (Montgomery & Borgatta, 1985). Unlike sons, husbands may not be inhibited in their caregiving practices from performing tasks that require intimate bodily contact (Evandrou, Arber, Dale, & Gilbert, 1986; Finch, 1989; Fitting & Rabins, 1985; Lingsom, 1989; Wright, 1983).

Impacts of Caregiving

Burden and Stress

A whole literature has grown up in the past decade that has documented both the physical and the emotional strains or burdens of caregiving (Abel, 1986; George & Gwyther, 1986; Zarit, Reever, & Bach-Peterson, 1980; Zarit, Todd, & Zarit, 1986). Strain is experienced as disruption of daily routines, infringement on time for other activities and relationships, and emotional stress (Chenoweth & Spencer, 1986; Robinson & Thurnher, 1979). However, the caregiving experience is not equally stressful for all caregivers. In fact, several researchers have noted that the remarkable aspect of caregiving is not that caregivers experience stress and burden, but that many do not experience any stress, or at least not high levels of stress. While the findings from past research have not always been consistent, greater burden and stress have been found to be associated with the performance of personal care tasks that require hands-on care, shared households, greater mental impairment or the presence of dementia, disruptive behaviors, impaired social functioning, greater physical impairment, and role conflicts (Deimling & Bass, 1986; Johnson & Catalano, 1983; Montgomery, Gonyea, & Hooyman, 1985; Noelker & Townsend, 1987; Stoller & Pugliesi, 1989). Factors associated with lower levels of burden or stress include higher levels of affection for the care receiver and assistance or support from other sources (Clipp & George, 1990a; George & Gwyther, 1986; Horowitz & Shindleman, 1983).

Given this profile of factors associated with burden and stress, it is not surprising that several researchers have found that daughters report higher levels of burden or stress than do sons (Horowitz, 1985b; Johnson & Catalano, 1983; Montgomery et al., 1985). These studies suggest that the greater investment of time, physical energy, and emotion that characterizes the caregiving experience of daughters relative to sons is accompanied by a greater burden or stress level. Yet other studies report no differences between the burden or stress levels experienced by sons and daughters. Stoller and Pugliesi (1989), who investigated gender differences in parent care for a random sample of elders residing in the community, found no differences between sons and daughters. These investigators suggest that their findings may reflect the relatively good health status of the population they studied, compared with populations of care receivers studied by other researchers. For the most part, the elders in Stoller and Pugliesi's sample did not require the routine hands-on care that frequently characterizes daughters' caregiving experiences.

Montgomery and Kamo (1989) also report no differences between sons and daughters in levels of objective and subjective burden, despite significant differences in the extent and length of caregiving that the two groups of caregivers reported. In that study, however, the recipients of care were substantially impaired and, on the average, sons provided more extensive care than reported in the Stoller and Pugliesi (1989) study and the earlier study by Montgomery et al. (1985). Hence, while there were differences in the levels of care provided by sons and daughters, the sons in this study tended to perform more caregiving tasks than did sons in the earlier studies. This may account, in part, for the different findings regarding subjective burden.

Specifically, differences were observed in the constellation of factors that were associated with caregiver strain in these two groups despite the lack of difference observed in subjective burden. While the amount of subjective burden for sons depended upon their attitudes toward their parents (affection) and toward their caregiving situations (perceived imposition on personal time), the level of subjective burden among daughters was related to both their attitudes and their circumstances. Those daughters with fewer resources and more demands were more likely to be burdened. In particular, for women, employment, the presence of a spouse, and greater numbers of children were associated with greater burden. For sons, neither the extent nor the type of care provided was associated with burden; nor were any of the indicators of other responsibilities found to be associated with burden. Instead, the primary predictor of subjective burden was the level of imposition that sons perceived to be associated with caregiving tasks. Hence, because sons expect to perform fewer tasks, it is quite likely that they feel greater imposition of the caregiving role even when providing less extensive care. In contrast, daughters expect to provide more care; therefore, their level of subjective burden may be lower relative to the extent of care provided.

Montgomery and Kamo's (1989) findings also suggest that the greater burden reported by women versus men in previous studies may be the result, in part, of their greater involvement as caregivers, but may also be due to their perception of the impact that caregiving has on their other life roles.

Role Conflict

The impact of caring for parents on other roles of adult children has been of some interest to researchers and policymakers. In particular, numerous scholars and policymakers have expressed concern that parent-care responsibilities may be reduced or abdicated by women in younger cohorts who are now employed in the work force in greater numbers and who will be employed over longer periods of time than were women in earlier cohorts. In their comparison of working and nonworking daughters, Brody and Schoonover (1986) found that working daughters provided less personal care assistance than did nonworking daughters, but there was little difference between the two groups in the amount of help given with shopping, housekeeping, banking, or transportation tasks. Stone and her colleagues (1987) found that women rearrange work schedules or reduce work hours, but do not limit their caregiver activities. Montgomery and Kamo (1989) also found few differences in the amounts of care provided by working and nonworking daughters. This pattern was not found for sons, where significant differences in the amounts and types of caregiving tasks were observed between employed and nonemployed sons. Employed sons engaged in substantially fewer caregiving tasks. Due to the cross-sectional nature of the study, however, it is not clear whether employment inhibited caregiving or whether caregiving inhibited employment. Given the dominant pattern of full-time employment among men in this society, it is likely that employment is the driving factor, not the caregiving.

Likely reflecting their greater time commitment to caregiving tasks, daughters tend to perceive more role conflict involved in caring for parents than do sons (Finley, 1989). They see the demands of parent care as impinging on the time they need to meet familial and employment obligations. Stoller and Pugliesi (1989) have suggested that less stress arises from conflict among competing loyalties than from the caregiver's sense that she had to assume full responsibility for both the caregiving tasks and any negative effects this care might have on family life, such as reduced time for family leisure activities or reduced help to other family members that a woman might provide in the role of spouse or mother. This greater sense of conflict is also noted by Kleban and his colleagues (1989), who found that wives who were caring for their parents agreed with their husbands on the extent to which family activities were disrupted, but were more likely than their husbands to feel that the relationships within the nuclear family were negatively affected.

Quality of the Dyadic Relationship

A potential outcome of parent care that some researchers have warned against is the erosion of the quality of the relationship between the parent and the adult child (Cicirelli, 1983; Jarrett, 1985). Early work on the exchange of resources between generations suggests that there is greater affection between children and parents when assistance from children is reciprocated in some manner (B. N. Adams, 1968). The dependence of parents in a caregiving relationship may not only prevent parents from reciprocating help, but may also alter the normal downward flow of help from the older generation to the younger that has been widely documented (B. N. Adams, 1968; Anderson, 1984; Finch, 1989). Together with observations about the difficulties that many caregivers encounter when providing care, this shift in exchange patterns has prompted concern for the quality of relationships between children providing care and their impaired elders (Scharlach, 1987).

Walker, Shin, and Bird (1990) specifically investigated the impact of caregiving on mother-daughter relationships. In keeping with recent calls for more attention to potential positive outcomes of caregiving (Abel, 1990a; B. Miller, 1989; Pratt & Kethley, 1988), these investigators found that most mothers and daughters reported no change or positive effects of caregiving on their relationships. A critical factor affecting daughters' judgments of the quality of the relationship was their satisfaction with the caregiving role. Those daughters who were pleased with their role as caregiver also reported better relationships with their parents. Higher incomes were also associated with more positive judgments of the quality of the relationship.

The only work specifically concerned with parent-son relationships that could be located was a study of fathers and sons in rural areas completed by Kivett (1988). Unfortunately, this study provides little insight into the father-son relationship in a caregiving situation because the majority of sons provided very little assistance, even though they were named by the fathers as the children with whom they had the most contact.

Satisfaction with the Caregiving Role

The complexity of the parent-care experience is underscored by the positive relationship that has been found between satisfaction with caregiving and caregiver stress (Archbold, 1983; B. Miller, 1989; Walker, Shin, & Bird, 1990). Past research suggests that those children who are more directly and intensely involved in caregiving are also more satisfied with the role despite their greater burden and stress. Given this pattern, a logical expectation would be that daughters are more satisfied with their caregiving roles than sons because, as a group, they are more involved with direct caregiving. While this hypothesis has not been tested directly, B. Miller's (1989) work, which focused on the relationship between caregiver stress and satisfaction, does provide some support for the hypothesis. Using the National Long-Term Care Survey, Miller was able to categorize 608 children into three types of caregivers. The "emotionally detached" group included those who had both low satisfaction and lower stress, the "cognitively consistent" group included those who had high stress and low satisfaction, and the "committed group" consisted of those who had high stress and high satisfaction. It is noteworthy that sons tended to be more highly clustered in the detached group than were daughters.

Consistent with the patterns that demonstrate an inverse association between socioeconomic status and direct care, Miller (1989) also found that both income and education were negatively associated with higher satisfaction for both sons and daughters. Also, caregivers reporting problems with the affordability or cost of care reported both high stress and high satisfaction.

Although any explanations for the counterintuitive relationship between high stress and high satisfaction are speculative, two have been offered. Miller (1989) has suggested that satisfaction may stem from a feeling of "success of completion." That is to say, satisfaction may stem from a sense of accomplishment that a person may experience when successfully completing a difficult task, such as dealing with highly stressful caregiving tasks. An alternate explanation is that satisfaction may be related to the avoidance of guilt feelings through greater involvement (Noelker & Townsend, 1987).

Future Patterns of Parent Care

Given the rapid demographic, medical, and social changes that are occurring in society today, it is reasonable to question whether the patterns of parent care observed for today's elderly will persist into the future. One certainty about the future that emerges from both demographic studies and projections of future health care needs of the elderly is that large numbers of older persons will continue to need assistance to reside in the community (Schrimper & Clark, 1985). There is little doubt that adult children will be a major source of this help. The questions that arise about the future of parent care center on the intensity of parent care, the relative contributions of sons and daughters to this care, and the relative contributions of family resources versus public resources to meet the growing need for care. Several scholars have suggested that the smaller number of offspring for future cohorts of older persons and significant changes in patterns of employment for women of these future cohorts will combine to alter parent care by future generations of adult children (Brody et al., 1983; Cantor, 1983; Pratt & Kethley, 1988; Stone et al., 1987).

The Prevalence of Children as Caregivers

Some concern has been expressed that the reduced birthrate observed for current cohorts of persons in childbearing ages will result in large proportions of future cohorts of elders who will not have children who can serve as primary caregivers. While there may be some truth to this prediction, the dynamics that appear to operate for different sibling structures would suggest that there is not a one-to-one correspondence between the reduction in number of offspring and the number of parents who will be without children to assist them. Indeed, the size of the sibling network is less a factor in predicting assistance to older parents than is the gender composition of the network (Hirshorn & Montgomery, in press; Matthews & Rosner, 1988; Spitze & Logan, 1990b).

Sibling structures that include at least one daughter are most likely to include a child who provides parent care. The higher prevalence of daughters as primary caregivers (Coward & Dwyer, 1990), daughters' greater assistance with both activities of daily living (ADL) and instrumental activities of daily living (IADL) (Dwyer & Coward, 1991), and the tendency of sons to serve in a helper role rather than a primary caregiver role (Matthews & Rosner, 1988) are facts that combine to suggest that the segment of the frail elderly population that is least likely to have an adult child serving as a primary caregiver is the segment that has only male offspring. Hence changes in birthrates for future cohorts of elderly will affect the prevalence of adult children as caregivers only to the degree that these changes generate an increase in the number of male-only sibling networks. At the same time, this impact will be somewhat mitigated by the fact that sons who are only children and those who come from male-only sibling networks provide greater amounts of care than do sons from mixed sibling structures (Coward & Dwyer, 1990; Hirshorn & Montgomery, in press). In combination, these patterns suggest that the effect of smaller family sizes on the availability of adult children as primary caregivers for future cohorts of elders is not likely to be substantial.

Changes in the Intensity of Care

A second potential cause for a decrease in parent-care activities in the future is a change in the pattern of employment for future cohorts of daughters. This change includes an increase in the proportion of women working as well as greater continuity in women's work lives. Unlike the majority of daughters who are currently caring for their aged parents, future cohorts will have worked throughout their adult lives, with limited interruption for childbearing and child-rearing activities. This means that greater numbers of daughters will be employed when their parents are in need of help. The salaries of these women will also account for a greater proportion of their household incomes. As a result, their comparative costs for leaving the work force will be greater than those for most daughters providing care today. Together with research findings that indicate little movement out of the work force among daughters caring for parents, these patterns of employment for future cohorts suggest a significant increase in employed caregivers. Earlier in this chapter, it was noted that parent care is not imposed by law, nor is it clear that it is a moral obligation. The responsibility for parent care and the way in which this care is to be provided is simply a sense of self-imposed obligation about which little is known, but that remains persistent. Just as women have continued to work while they simultaneously meet the needs of their dependent children, they are likely to continue to work while they meet parent-care responsibilities.

To the extent that current patterns of caregiving behavior among employed daughters are perpetuated, the impact of employment will not alter the number of elders for whom daughters are serving as primary caregivers, but this employment will likely alter the way in which these daughters provide care. Our knowledge of current patterns would suggest that in the future those employed women who have sufficient resources will purchase direct care services for their parents, thereby reducing the number of hours they spend on ADL tasks (Archbold, 1983). Of course, this assumes the availability of such services. There is little evidence to suggest that these women will reduce their caregiving loads by sharing them with brothers or husbands.

The future caregiving patterns of women with middle and lower incomes, who will have worked most of their adult lives and must continue to work to maintain their families, are less predictable. Middle-income women are not widely represented in the current cohort of adult child caregivers, and little is known about their behaviors. Knowledge of the behaviors of lower-income, working women has been limited also, because they have not been well represented in most study samples. It is likely that this growing segment of working women will be most affected by the multiple pressures of work and family responsibilities. It is their options for meeting parent-care needs that bring into focus alternate visions of the future of parent care. In reality, their options are limited. These working women can simply continue to provide all levels of care by stretching physical, emotional, and financial resources, or they can share the responsibilities with other family members or formal service providers.

Shared Care

Every indicator of the division of family labor in the future, whether grounded in theoretical perspectives or empirical observations, points to the continued prevalence of daughters as primary caregivers for their parents. The cumulative results of numerous studies concerned with parent care overwhelmingly demonstrate that parent care, like housework, has been institutionalized as women's work (Finley, 1989). Whether this reality reflects the tendency of a male-dominated society to place greater value on male contributions, as suggested by Finley (1989), or a persistent societal resistance to changes in family structures and roles despite notable changes in other social institutions is not clear. What is clear, however, is that sons are unlikely to alter their parent-care activities. Hence the only options for women to reduce their parent-care tasks are to alter their sense of obligation concerning the way in which care is to be provided and/or to meet their perceived obligations by purchasing services or by shifting responsibility for parent-care tasks to public entities. That is, women must seek a way out of their tasks other than through sharing those tasks with men.

This conclusion has serious implications for both future research and public policy concerned with parent care. In the future, parent care must be studied within the context of changing family structures and roles, and these changes in turn must be studied within the context of other societal institutions (Mancini & Blieszner, 1989). To understand fully the dynamics of parent care and to meet the needs for assistance of our nation's older disabled citizens most adequately, the focus of caregiving research and policy-making should not be on similarities or differences between men and women, or on women and work issues. The focus of future research needs to be on family and work responsibilities. In this larger context, the issues of parent care are refocused from personal troubles and individual solutions to societal problems requiring public resolutions. When the problem becomes one of creating policies and practices that will help or enable families to meet both family care needs and work responsibilities, individuals will no longer need to seek idiosyncratic solutions to a situation that is widely shared. In some ways the issue of parent care could be viewed as parallel to the issue of education in this country. When it comes to educating our youth, individual families are not expected to provide that education directly, even though they contribute to it through taxes and through individual decisions. They may, however, influence where a child receives education. In a similar manner, the policy issue regarding parent care should focus on how we can care for our elderly while at the same time allowing individuals to meet other family and work responsibilities. The solution to obtaining care for our dependent elders should not be the sole responsibility of each individual family; instead, like public education, it should be a publicly shared responsibility for a dependent segment of our population. If change is to come about, it will necessarily entail more creative and compassionate social policy concerning the care of the elderly.

6

Siblings as Caregivers in
Middle and Old Age

VICTOR G. CICIRELLI

In approaching the topic of siblings as caregivers to the elderly, the position of the elderly person in the family system must be examined. The older person is, first of all, a member of his or her family of orientation, consisting of parents and siblings. For individual elders, this family of orientation may be slowly vanishing, except in memory, as its members die. Nevertheless, as long as any siblings remain as fragments of this family of orientation, they may function as real or potential sources of help. Second, the older person may also be a member of his or her family of procreation, consisting of a spouse and adult children. If there is more than one living adult child, this subsystem of middle-aged siblings may function as a source of help for the elderly parent. In this chapter, existing literature will be examined with an emphasis on gender differences in specific areas of caregiving for each of two generations of siblings, the middle-aged and the elderly. Before proceeding to an examination of gender differences in sibling care of the elderly, however, existing theories of gender role development in adulthood should be considered to determine how gender roles might be expressed in sibling caregiving relationships. Although various theorists differ on minor points, the general consensus is that the developmental trend with increasing age in adulthood is toward decreasing gender differences—that is, reduced sex role salience (Bem, 1979; Sinnott, 1986). The resulting roles have been termed "complex" (Loevinger, 1977; Riegel, 1976), "flexible" (Kline, 1975), "transcendent" (Hefner, Rebecca, & Oleshansky, 1975), and "androgynous" (Neugarten, 1968; Neugarten & Gutmann, 1968). Whatever their label, the greater flexibility presumed to be associated with less salient sex roles in later adulthood is held to be associated with more successful aging.

Helping and caregiving roles have traditionally been considered to be largely women's roles, with women taking on most of the expressive and instrumental aspects of care of the elderly (Brody, 1985; Cicirelli, 1981). When men have taken on caregiving tasks, the tasks have tended to be stereotypically male ones, such as home maintenance, financial management, and transportation. These same gender role differences would be expected to apply to siblings acting as caregivers as well. However, if gender roles become less salient with increasing age, then one would expect to find greater gender differences in caregiving behaviors among a group of middle-aged siblings caring for an aging parent than among a group of elderly siblings caring for a member of the sibship.

To date, the caregiving literature includes a relatively sparse offering of studies dealing with siblings as caregivers of elderly family members. The existing literature will be examined in this chapter to determine whether or not gender differences exist and, if so, whether such differences are greater among middle-aged sibling caregivers than among elderly sibling caregivers.

The Nature of Sibling Relationships in the Second Half of the Life Span

The Middle-Aged Sibling Subsystem in the 1990s

A first question is whether a viable system of middle-aged siblings exists in contemporary American families to serve a caregiving function for elderly parents. Most older people do have living children and most have more than one child. Thus a family subsystem consisting of two or more adult children is typically available for the care of an elderly parent.

The developmental tasks of a sibling group over the life span include the care of aging parents during the parents' decline and death (Goetting, 1986). The extent to which each sibling participates in this developmental task, however, is open to question.

The Elderly Sibling Subsystem in the 1990s

The question of whether there is a viable system of elderly siblings available to provide help to one or more of their group is especially pertinent, since attrition of the sibling subsystem due to death is increasingly likely in old age. Demographic data indicate that most older people have at least one living sibling; thus a sibling is potentially available for help in old age.

During old age, the major developmental tasks facing siblings include the mutual exchange of social and instrumental support during the period of decline as well as the provision of caregiving assistance when a sibling is ill (Goetting, 1986). The extent to which elderly siblings carry out these developmental tasks will also be examined in this chapter.

Caregiving Task Performance and Hours of Care

Middle-Aged Siblings

It is a generally accepted truism that care of an elderly parent is the role of one adult daughter, who serves as the "principal caregiver" (see Chapter 5, this volume). This daughter is assumed to be the one to shoulder the entire caregiving burden or the major portion of it. Few studies have examined the contributions of other adult children in the family in a systematic way. However, the studies that have been conducted thus far suggest that recruiting a particular daughter as principal caregiver is only one of several possible types of family caregiving arrangements.

The work of Matthews and her colleagues, for example, has focused on the contributions of the entire middle-aged sibling subsystem to the care of elderly parents (Matthews, 1987, 1988; Matthews, Delaney, & Adamek, 1989; Matthews & Rosner, 1988; Matthews & Sprey, 1989). In looking first at the sharing of responsibility by pairs of sisters in two-child families, Matthews and Rosner (1988) found that pairs of adult sisters tend to share responsibility for tangible help as well as moral support to parents, with the division becoming more equal when both sisters are employed.

In larger families, support is less likely to be shared by all, especially in those families including one or more brothers. For larger families Matthews and Rosner (1988) identify five types of sibling participation in parent care: (a) routine help, in which regular assistance to the parent is incorporated into the child's ongoing schedule of activities; (b) backup help, in which a sibling not routinely involved in care can be counted on for special emotional support or tangible aid when requested by the siblings giving routine help; (c) circumscribed help, in which the help provided to the parent is carefully limited by amount or type; (d) sporadic help, in which occasional assistance to the parent is provided at the child's own convenience; and (e) dissociation, in which the adult child abdicates any responsibility to help the parent. The relative frequencies of these types of help differ widely. In most cases, help from one or more of the adult siblings in these larger families is circumscribed in nature, sporadic, or nonexistent.

However, styles of caregiving participation within the adult child sibship tend to be associated with gender (Matthews & Rosner, 1988). Sisters are more likely to use routine or backup styles of participation, while brothers' help tends to be sporadic or circumscribed, usually limited to typically male areas of expertise. Yet, when families consisting only of brothers were examined in a study by Matthews, Delaney, and Adamek (1989), the brothers appeared willing to cooperate to meet parents' needs for care and to fulfill their filial obligations. Perhaps brothers can and do take over traditionally female caregiving tasks when there are no sisters in the family.

Recent work by Coward and Dwyer (1990) sheds further light on the caregiving contributions of brothers. Information regarding adult children of dependent elders was based on interviews with 683 caregiving sons and daughters obtained in a large national survey. Subjects' sibling networks were subdivided into single-gender networks, mixed-gender networks, and only children to determine the effects of the gender composition of the sibship. Sons from all three types of sibling networks were less likely than were daughters to participate in parent care or to become principal caregivers. However, participating sons from networks where there were no available sisters provided essentially as many hours of care as daughters from networks where there were no brothers available (whether these sons provided the same types of care as did daughters is not reported). Only in the mixed-gender network did daughters provide significantly more hours of care than did sons. Since mixed-gender sibships are far more prevalent than the other types, these findings are not at odds with those of other studies (Matthews & Rosner, 1988; Matthews, Delaney, & Adamek, 1989).

Brody, in studies of the contributions of siblings of caregiving daughters, found considerable support for the daughter as principal caregiver model (Brody, 1990; Brody, Hoffman, Kleban, & Schoonover, 1989; Brody, Kleban, Hoffman, & Schoonover, 1988). Daughters serving as principal caregivers reported that they provided an average of 24 hours of help weekly to the elderly parent (those daughters sharing a residence with the parent were largely responsible for the high average value), while their sisters who lived nearby provided 8 hours of help weekly. In contrast, brothers who lived nearby provided only 4 hours of help. In Brody's work, only help with ADL and IADL tasks was investigated. Siblings' help in other areas was not measured, although some services of other types can be time-consuming and might have lessened the observed gender differences. However, gender differences disappeared when siblings were geographically distant from the parents, mainly because little help was provided by either brothers or sisters.

Cicirelli (1981, 1984), in studies of adult children's help to their elderly parents, also investigated the contributions made by siblings of the adult child who was considered by the elderly parent to be "closest" or from whom the elder first sought help. Two groups of adult children were studied, those who had intact marriages and those who had experienced some form of marital disruption (divorce, widowhood, or remarriage). Adult children with intact marriages reported giving significantly more help to their elderly parents than their siblings, while those with disrupted marriages gave about the same amount of help as did their siblings. In both cases, however, there were gender differences in the types of help provided. When asked to indicate which sibling provided the most help with various types of services, sisters were named more frequently as helpers with homemaking, personal care, home health care, transportation, and psychological support, while brothers were named more frequently as helpers with maintenance, bureaucratic mediation, and protection. Interviewees were also asked about the amount of help with parent care that they anticipated from their siblings at a future time when parents' needs for care were greater. There was little difference in the total amount of help expected from brothers and sisters, but the type of help expected again seemed to fall into traditional masculine and feminine roles.

The findings of the various studies of siblings in the adult child generation show considerable convergence despite the different methods used. The data clearly indicate that there is a great deal more support from siblings than has been generally recognized, particularly in cases where the daughter has experienced marital disruption or is employed. Overall, sisters provide more help than do brothers; sisters have a greater tendency to share help equally; and sisters and brothers tend to provide different types of help, structured according to traditional gender role norms. The literature indicates that sons provide a more limited range of caregiving tasks (or purchase services) and abdicate caregiving roles sooner than do daughters (Brody, 1990; Montgomery & Kamo, 1989), although a recent seven-year study (Stoller, 1990) found no difference in the stability of sons and daughters as caregivers. These conclusions appear to apply to the contributions of all siblings as well as to the principal caregiver.

However, it has been argued that researchers' emphasis on daughters (sisters) as caregivers and their exclusive concern with a limited group of caregiving tasks has led to a lack of recognition of the contributions of sons (brothers) (see Matthews, 1988; Montgomery & Kamo, 1989). That is, the tasks used to assess caregiving are the ones that women traditionally have done. However, these tasks may be required only when the parent is in a stage of advanced frailty; at earlier stages of dependency, other types of assistance are needed. Here brothers and sisters of the adult child generation may make more equal contributions. The more intensive types of care may not be required by all parents or may be needed only for a brief period. Further studies are needed to investigate this question.

Also, studies do not exist that examine brothers' and sisters' contributions to the care of elderly fathers compared with the care of elderly mothers. It may be that gender differences follow a different course with respect to elderly fathers, depending on the degree of impairment and the range of caregiving tasks required.

Elderly Siblings

The help that elderly siblings provide for one another has frequently been overlooked, on the assumption that spouses and adult children are the major caregivers for the frail elderly person. In addition, it is often assumed that siblings are themselves too old or frail to offer any help. Yet it has been recognized for many years that siblings can take on important caregiving functions (e.g., Townsend, 1957). Cases in which an older person has taken on the full care of a frail sibling have been reported in the literature and have been observed by this writer, but a more systematic study of the help exchanged between elderly siblings has been relatively recent.

Cicirelli (1979) found that siblings were mentioned by small percentages of all elderly people as primary sources of help in such areas as psychological support, business dealings, homemaking, protection, and social and recreational activities. If occasional and supplementary help by siblings had been included in the study, their contribution would surely have been greater. Surprisingly, help from siblings became more important among the octogenarians and nonagenarians included in the study. In general, however, siblings were seen as reserve sources of help to be called upon only in crises and special situations. Scott (1983) reports similar low levels of help from siblings, with transportation and care during illness the most prevalent types of help.

Recent work has investigated sibling help in old age more thoroughly. In a two-year longitudinal study, Gold (1986, 1989b) interviewed men and women over age 65 about their sibling relationships. The study excluded those subjects who had never married, had no living siblings, were childless, or were twins in order to eliminate those for whom the sibling relationship might have had unusual salience. Ultimately, data were gathered regarding 80 sibling dyads, with the four gender combinations (women with sisters, women with brothers, men with sisters, and men with brothers) in approximately equal representation. Instrumental support to siblings appeared to go to those siblings with greater needs—that is, those who were older and who were widowed. Although instrumental support declined over the two-year period, in every case it was because the helper's own needs or declining health prevented his or her continuing aid to the sibling. Moreover, a decline in or cessation of help to a sibling was always accompanied by great regret. Gender differences were also found, with sisters both giving and receiving more help than brothers. In regard to social support from siblings, the relationships between brothers were characterized by greater feelings of resentment and less acceptance and approval than observed in the sister-sister or sister-brother dyads.

Bedford (1989b) reports differing findings regarding gender in a study of 71 adults representing a wide age range. In her sample, instances of sustained sibling help in old age were rare, although siblings did help in crisis situations. No gender effects were found, but this may have been due to the fact that the sample was dominated by dyads consisting of sisters reporting about help to brothers.

In a study of sibling relationships of elderly blacks and whites, Suggs (1989) found that siblings in both racial groups exchanged help in the areas of illness, housekeeping, and transportation. Unfortunately, no analysis of gender effects was conducted.

O'Bryant (1988) interviewed recent widows about the extent of help from siblings since their husbands' deaths. As might be expected, sibling help was greater when the sibling lived nearby and there was no adult child in the vicinity. Unmarried sisters (widows and never marrieds) contributed the greatest help, but married sisters also contributed significant amounts of help. The sisters provided female-stereotypic help (e.g., care when sick), while brothers more often provided help with decisions and legal matters. However, sisters' husbands provided more male-stereotypic help of this sort than did brothers. Seemingly, the sisters recruited their husbands for needed male tasks as an extension of their own helping activities. Help to widowers was not investigated in this study.

Cicirelli (1990b), in a study of support by family members identified as primary supporters to 102 hospitalized elderly people, found that the amount of support from siblings was second only to support from spouses in certain areas of tangible support (e.g., bringing needed items to the hospital, helping to plan posthospital care, and agreeing to help with posthospital care).

Because only 11 siblings were named as primary supporters, no gender-specific analyses were conducted; however, most sibling support came from sisters.

Overall, the studies that have explored the support of the elderly by their siblings indicate that some tangible support does occur, although it is relatively infrequent compared with help from spouses and adult children. For the most part, elderly siblings stand ready to assist in times of crisis and special need, or to supplement the efforts of other family caregivers. Existing studies did not focus on the number of hours of care provided by siblings. In terms of task performance, more help was given and received by sisters than by brothers. Not all studies found this gender effect, at least in part because the samples did not contain adequate gender distributions, but no study found the opposite effect—that brothers gave and received more help than did sisters. The kinds of help given tended to follow traditional male and female gender role norms.

Level of Impairment

Middle-Aged Siblings

The effects of the care recipient's level of impairment on sibling helping relationships have received little attention. There seem to be two trends in the way the middle-aged sibship responds to an increasing level of parental impairment. First, adult children tend to provide more help as parents' needs increase (Cicirelli, 1981). Second, as the parent's needs increase, one adult child (usually a daughter) tends to volunteer or to be propelled by circumstances and subtle forces into the role of principal caregiver (Aldous, 1987; Brody, 1990). When an adult child shares a residence with an elderly parent, the major portion of caregiving responsibility falls to that child by virtue of the immediacy of many care needs and the inclusion of other caregiving tasks within the fabric of ongoing household duties. Brody (1990) found that help from the principal caregiver's siblings was greater when the parent lived alone than when the parent lived with the principal caregiver. Studies are needed that investigate sibling helping as a function of level of impairment with parent coresidence controlled in order to determine whether gender differences in helping vary with level of impairment.

In related research, Matthews and Rosner (1988) have indicated that when parents' needs increased, the siblings tended to hire supplementary caregiving services rather than increase their own caregiving involvement. The families studied by Matthews and Rosner were in comfortable financial circumstances. However, this work suggests that gender differences in caregiving are not altered when parents' care needs increase.

Elderly Siblings

The existing literature indicates that elderly siblings do tend to help in crisis situations affecting one of the siblings. Greater help has been found to go to siblings with greater needs. For example, in Gold's (1989a) study, as the older person's level of impairment increased, whether siblings could respond or continue to respond often depended on their own health and needs. In general, instrumental support by elderly siblings declined over time. Although gender differences in sibling help have not been studied in relation to increasing impairment, one would expect that the predominant role of sisters in providing help would not change as level of impairment increases.

Reciprocity and Issues of Fairness

Middle-Aged Siblings

Since the findings regarding task performance and hours of care indicate unequal distributions of parent caregiving among middle-aged siblings, the question arises as to just how equitable and fair these unequal contributions are perceived to be. Matthews and Rosner (1988) indicate that about half of the families they studied experienced conflict over caregiving arrangements, although much of this conflict could be attributed to events in family relationships that had occurred long before caregiving responsibilities became an issue. Nevertheless, current sources of conflict tended to be centered on the issue of whether or not a sibling had met filial responsibilities. This would seem to implicate brothers more than sisters, in view of the finding that brothers' help is more likely to be sporadic or circumscribed. However, Matthews and Rosner do not present specific findings regarding gender differences in conflict over caregiving arrangements. It seems that just how a sibling's dissociation from caregiving responsibilities is interpreted depends upon a complex history of contingencies and loyalties within the family (Matthews & Sprey, 1989).

Brody (1990) has also noted that 30% of principal caregivers, 40% of their sisters, and 6% of their brothers reported strain from sibling interactions regarding parent care. Difficulties arose when the principal caregiver regarded siblings as not doing their fair share, as well as over sibling criticisms of the caregiver's performance. The siblings in Brody's study reported frequent attempts by the principal caregiver to make them feel guilty or to make them assume greater responsibility. It is interesting that such attempts appeared to be directed toward sisters to a greater degree than toward brothers; the brothers' work responsibilities seemed to be regarded as legitimate excuses. Alternatively, the daughters giving care simply may not have expected their brothers to help with traditionally female tasks. As the caregiving load increased, the family strain also increased, as did the caregiver's complaints to her siblings. Overall, the equitable sharing of responsibilities was regarded as a major problem by most of the siblings in this study.

In an ongoing study of 50 adult daughters providing at least 10 hours per week of caregiving help to their mothers, preliminary findings indicated that 63% of the daughters rated the division of responsibilities with their sibling networks to be fair or very fair, while 37% rated it as unfair or very unfair (Cicirelli, 1990a). When classified into groups according to sibling gender, 33% of those with sisters only, 25% of those with brothers only, and 44% of those with both brothers and sisters regarded the division of responsibilities as unfair. Because group sizes were small, differences between groups were not statistically significant. Judgments of fairness or unfairness were not related to the perceived equality or inequality of caregiving contributions. Rather, they seemed to be based on complex considerations of a sibling's proximity, competing responsibilities, interest and willingness to help, gender role norms, and history of family relationships compared with the caregiver's own situation.

If any conclusion can be drawn from the existing studies of gender differences in judgments of fairness regarding siblings' caregiving participation, it is that such judgments are directed toward sisters more than toward brothers. Brothers' lesser contributions appear to be legitimated by their work responsibilities as well as by established social norms.

Elderly Siblings

The question of reciprocity in the exchange of help is more applicable to elderly siblings than is the question of fairness, since it has been held that sibling relationships are characterized by balanced reciprocity (Johnson, 1988). In times of need or crisis situations when reciprocity is not possible, an elderly person may extend help to a sibling based on a shared history of reciprocal aid. But this help is usually temporary unless some reciprocation occurs (Brady & Noberini, 1987; Stoller, 1985).

Mutual helping behavior between elderly siblings has been reported by several researchers (Avioli, 1989; Bedford, 1989b; Gold, 1989a; Suggs, 1989), with more help exchanged between pairs of sisters. One-way help to a sibling in old age may depend on whether help has been received from that sibling in the past. Unreciprocated help seems to be troublesome to both giver and receiver. Elderly sisters' feelings of burden and distress associated with help to brothers may be the result of brothers' lesser participation in reciprocal helping arrangements in the past (Bedford, 1989b). From the perspective of the elderly sibling receiving help that cannot be reciprocated, such aid may be perceived as an admission of weakness and incompetence and thus may be distressing to the recipient (Avioli, 1989; Gold, 1987; Stoller, 1985).

Hence reciprocal helping arrangements among elderly siblings seem to involve pairs of sisters more than they do sister-brother or brother-brother dyads. Nonreciprocal arrangements appear to lead to feelings of burden and distress for both the caregiver and the care receiver.

Stress and Burden of Caregiving

Middle-Aged Siblings

Because care of an elderly parent tends to fall unequally on one daughter, one would expect the burden and stress of caregiving also to fall unequally on that daughter. This may be the case with regard to objective burden measured in terms of tasks or time, but since subjective feelings of burden depend more on how the caregiver perceives the situation than on actual caregiving load (Zarit, Reever, & Bach-Peterson, 1980), the extent of subjective burden experienced by middle-aged siblings may be quite different from what is expected. Unfortunately, there are few findings bearing on this question.

According to a study by Brody (1990), daughters who were the principal caregivers for an elderly parent experienced the most burden and strain; of their local siblings, the brothers experienced the least stress and burden, and the sisters experienced an intermediate amount. Among geographically distant siblings, sisters felt more stressed and burdened than brothers. Above and beyond the burden of trying to provide help to a parent over a distance and in addition to competing responsibilities, the siblings (especially sisters) were subject to complaints from the principal caregiver and feelings of guilt that they should be doing more. These findings have been supported in clinical work (Tonti, 1988).

Brody's (1990) findings are somewhat puzzling when compared with those from Montgomery and Kamo's (1989) study of caregiving sons and daughters. The latter authors found that although caregiving sons engaged in fewer and less intense caregiving tasks than did daughters, the amount of subjective and objective burden reported by the two groups did not differ. By way of explanation, one can speculate that gender norms do not lead sons to anticipate parent caregiving responsibilities (Spitze & Logan, 1990b); when called upon to assume a principal caregiver role, sons may feel particularly burdened because they do not feel that it is a man's role. In a secondary caregiving role, as Brody (1990) observes, brothers feel little strain accompanying their more limited helping role and little guilt that they should be doing more. The work of Coward and Dwyer (1990) is also relevant here. For single-gender sibling networks and only children, caregiving sons and daughters did not differ in perceived stress or burden measured in terms of caregiving problems. However, caregiving daughters from mixed-gender networks had significantly more burden and stress than caregiving sons, paralleling the greater number of hours of care provided.

Overall, sisters experience greater caregiving burden than do brothers. However, when brothers do assume a major caregiving role, their feelings of subjective burden may be disproportionately great in view of their objective burden.

Elderly Siblings

Other than anecdotal reports of the burden experienced by those siblings who assume a heavy caregiving load for an aging brother or sister, only a few authors have dealt with sibling burden. In general, however, sibling caregiving activity is limited, and the withdrawal of elderly siblings from long-term caregiving activities is socially condoned (Johnson & Catalano, 1981); thus burden would be unlikely to occur. However, Bedford (1989b) found that giving help to elderly siblings appeared to be the cause of feelings of burden and distress. Bedford's sample ranged in age from 20 to 89, but feelings of distress associated with helping a sibling increased with age, even though the percentage of subjects giving help to a sibling decreased with age. The dominant group in the older portion of the sample was women helping their brothers. Bedford suggests that if women's needs in later life shift from nurturing to individualistic concerns, this might account for older women's feelings of burden in dealing with brothers' needs for help. Others have advanced the view that giving support to others may be more beneficial to the individual giving the help than to the receiver (Avioli, 1989; Johnson, 1988; Kahana & Midlarsky, 1983). Since the sibling relationship throughout the life course tends to be reciprocal in nature, dependence on a sibling may be more burdensome to the care receiver than to the caregiver. Further research is needed in this area.

Affection and Life Satisfaction

Middle-Aged Siblings

Helping an aging parent is one of the major developmental tasks facing middle-aged siblings (Goetting, 1986). Just how the siblings accomplish this task can have important implications for their affectional relationships with each other and for their general life satisfaction and sense of well-being.

Tonti (1988) has outlined several phases of change that many adult children undergo as they deal with their parents' aging. Most adult children undergo denial of a parent's aging process until some critical event forces them to reappraise the parent's health and functioning. In an initial phase, the siblings tend to move closer to one another emotionally, with increased communication about the parent's situation. In the second phase, the parent's needs increase to the point that the children need to provide some care; the role of a primary caregiver begins to emerge. In the third phase, the parent's needs increase to the point that coresidence with the child who is the principal caregiver becomes necessary. In the final phase, the intensity of the parent's care needs becomes so great that the parent is transferred to a long-term care facility.

How adult siblings handle these changes depends on the history of their relationship. According to Tonti (1988), there is a history of closeness and care in some families, and tasks are divided as equally as possible among the siblings. In other families, siblings tend to distance themselves emotionally from one another under the stress of caregiving. In still others, old patterns of sibling rivalry are reactivated, with active conflict arising among siblings. Parental favoritism, use of excessive or abusive control tactics, or the splitting of responsibility and authority among siblings can cause or exacerbate conflicts. Finally, in some instances, the relationship between the siblings and the parent is so dysfunctional that the siblings are unable to organize to provide care to the parent, leaving it up to formal agencies.

The existing studies of relationships among middle-aged siblings in care-giving situations provide some support for Tonti's clinical observations. Matthews and Rosner (1988) found that conflicts among the siblings they studied stemmed from events in their past that were unrelated to their caregiving responsibilities. Unless conflicts were extreme, however, the siblings managed to maintain caregiving activities. This was true of caregiving brothers as well as sisters (Matthews, Delaney, & Adamek, 1989). Conversely, Brody (1990) reports increased conflicts among siblings as a result of caregiving. In Brody's study such conflicts were more characteristic of relationships between sisters, who assumed the major portion of care responsibilities, than for the other sibling gender combinations.

Preliminary findings from an ongoing study of caregiving daughters (Cicirelli, 1990a) include information on whether the daughters felt that their relationships with siblings had grown closer, stayed the same, or grown less close as a result of their caregiving experiences. Some 65% of the daughters reported that their feelings toward their siblings had stayed the same, 23% said that they had grown closer to their siblings, and 12% felt that their sibling relationships had grown less close. Daughters who felt that there was an unfair distribution of caregiving tasks among the siblings tended to be more likely to report that the relationship had grown less close (16% of those who claimed the distribution was unfair reported that they had grown less close, compared with 7% of those who regarded it as fair). With regard to gender, all of the daughters from sister-only networks reported that their relationships had grown closer or stayed the same, while the groups of daughters with brothers only and daughters with both sisters and brothers were as likely to report that their relationships had grown closer as to say that they had grown less close. Looking at the last two groups from another perspective, all the daughters who felt that their sibling relationships had grown less close as a result of caregiving had at least one brother.

Elderly Siblings

The preponderance of existing research indicates that most older adults report a high degree of closeness with their siblings, with the greatest closeness between pairs of sisters and the least between pairs of brothers (Avioli, 1989; Cicirelli, 1980, 1982; Gold, 1989a, 1989b; Ross & Milgram, 1982; Troll, 1971). Brother-sister dyads report intermediate levels of close-ness. Conversely, rivalry and conflict tend to be greatest between brothers. Most studies have found that rivalry and conflict diminish with age.

However, clinical interviews (Ross & Milgram, 1982) and projective measures (Bedford, 1989a) have suggested the existence of greater sibling rivalry and conflict than indicated elsewhere.

The exchange of instrumental help between elderly siblings tends to be relatively rare, often limited by age and infirmity as well as distance. As a consequence, it has been hypothesized that relationships with siblings who stand ready to assist in time of need, although this resource might never be called on, should lead to increased well-being. Various studies have been carried out to determine the effects of relationships with siblings on older persons' well-being, with mixed results.

An early study found that elders with living siblings had higher morale than those without living siblings (Cumming & Henry, 1961). Cicirelli (1977) concludes that men with sisters have a greater sense of emotional security in old age, while women with sisters are stimulated and challenged. In contrast, Lee and Ihinger-Tallman (1980) did not find a relationship between frequency of contact with siblings and morale of the elderly. A more recent study confirms Lee and Ihinger-Tallman's findings with regard to sibling interaction, but finds that the mere availability of a sister is a significant predictor of life satisfaction in women and approaches statistical significance among men (McGhee, 1985). This knowledge that one has a living sister, termed "existential awareness" by Gold (1989a), may elicit feelings of belonging to a contemporaneous caring family network (even when the sister is seen infrequently) and thus may enhance life satisfaction. Just knowing that the sister is there, on reserve, seems to be sufficient.

Cicirelli (1989a) investigated the hypothesis that a close affectional bond to elderly siblings would be associated with greater well-being and that this would be related to the gender combination of the siblings. The study findings offer partial support for this hypothesis. The perception of a close bond to sisters by either men or women was related to their well-being, as indicated by fewer symptoms of depression. A close bond with brothers was not related to well-being. Further, disruption of the bond to sisters through conflict and indifference was related to increased symptoms of depression. By way of explanation, Cicirelli suggests that sisters' greater effects on well-being might be due to the perception of sisters as more valuable sources of support in old age. This remains to be tested.

Gold (1989a) found that psychological involvement with siblings, acceptance and approval, and feelings of closeness to siblings increased over a two-year period in old age. The existential awareness of a sibling gave greater meaning to later life. There were gender differences, with enhanced relationships (as indicated by closeness, emotional support, and acceptance and approval) when there was at least one sister in the dyad. Avioli (1989) has confirmed the importance of sisters for psychological support, although others have failed to find gender differences (Connidis, 1989; Suggs, 1989).

Overall, the existing studies indicate that having a close bond to sisters is important to the well-being of the elderly, while a bond to brothers is unrelated.

Interaction with the Formal Service Sector

Middle-Aged Siblings

Interaction with the formal service sector regarding parent care occurs in two ways: mediation to secure needed supplementary services when the parent resides at home, and family support of a parent who has entered a long-term care institution. With regard to the mediation of services, Cicirelli (1981) found that the adult child who was the parent's main source of overall help also carried out most mediation activities. Some 34% of these adult children reported that their siblings also provided some help with securing services, with brothers named most frequently. Brothers' mediation activities reflected such areas of traditional male expertise as legal and financial services and dealing with government agencies. Similarly, sisters who were nurses or who had other expertise in the health care field tended to mediate the use of formal health care services.

Elderly Siblings

There is little information, other than anecdotal data, on how an older person's siblings interact with the formal service sector, and no information regarding gender differences. In addition to providing general social support, siblings can serve three important functions in relation to formal services. The first is a pioneering function with regard to the use of formal services. If one sibling makes use of home nursing care, medical clinics, homemaker services, senior housing, and other such services, he or she can make them more familiar and more acceptable to other siblings. The second function is lay advising regarding formal services, with siblings contributing information and advice from their own experience and perhaps mediating the arrangements for such services. Third, siblings can help to monitor the delivery of formal services. They may interpret another sibling's needs and desires to adult children, stimulate adult children to take action to secure formal services for the parent, or act as watchdogs to see that formal services for their sibling are properly provided.

Speculating on the existence of gender differences, one would expect the primacy of sisters that has been found in other settings to be observed also in connection with formal services. An exception might be in certain types of lay advising, where the topic in question involves areas of traditional male expertise.

Conclusions

There is nothing in existing findings to support hypotheses advanced in the introduction that men and women become more androgynous with increasing age, at least in regard to caregiving behaviors. Rather, present generations of adult child siblings and elderly siblings appear to be influenced by sex role stereotypes that override the demands of individual caregiving situations. Although the literature on sibling caregiving is somewhat sparse, the following conclusions are advanced:

- Sisters provide greater caregiving help in both the adult child and the elderly sibling systems.
- In the adult child sibling system, sisters tend to share the caregiving burden more equally than do brothers.
- Sisters and brothers tend to fulfill caregiving tasks depending on how the tasks fit traditional conceptions of male and female roles. This reliance on cultural role expectations appears to be the case in both the adult child and the elderly sibling systems.

Implications for the Future

In speculating about the future, one can predict that sibling participation in caregiving will increase by default. Increased longevity, especially of elderly widows, indicates increased demand for care. Yet economic realities in the foreseeable future point to a limited role for the formal care system. By default, family members (primarily spouses, adult children, and elderly siblings) will have little choice but to care themselves for their elderly family members. However, with smaller sibship sizes, larger numbers of women in the work force, and larger numbers of divorced and never-married adult children, the task will be too great for any one caregiver. The only way families will be able to cope with the caregiving needs of their elderly is through increased cooperation among siblings. Thus, in the future, daughters propelled by gender role expectations into the role of principal caregiver must rely more than they have in the past on sibling assistance, including assistance from brothers. Also, greater longevity suggests that elderly siblings' caregiving activities must assume greater significance in the future. Finally, siblings of both generations must become more flexible in performing a variety of caregiving tasks, in assuming more equitable shares of the caregiving duties, and in shifting from leadership to supporting roles as the situation demands. In fact, women must learn to delegate caregiving assignments, to train and guide men in taking on routine caregiving tasks, and to regard caregiving as a team function (Felder, 1990). In addition, elderly care receivers must be encouraged to accept help from male as well as from female care providers.

PART III

Theory and Research

7

Filial Responsibility

Attitudes, Motivators, and Behaviors

ROSEMARY BLIESZNER
RAEANN R. HAMON

Recent evidence indicates that the attitudes of adult sons and daughters toward providing parent care do not differ, but daughters are more likely than sons to give assistance. In this chapter we review the literature on attitudes of filial obligation, motivations to carry out filial duties, and filial role enactment in the form of parental caregiving, with an emphasis on gender differences in these areas. We conclude with an analysis of theoretical explanations for gender differences in filial attitudes and behaviors and suggestions for future research. Where possible, we compare and contrast filial responsibility in daughters and sons, but readers should note that not all topics have been examined with both groups of offspring.

What Is Filial Responsibility?

Filial responsibility is a sense of personal obligation to assist with the maintenance of aging parents' well-being. It emphasizes duty and a willingness to protect and care for elderly parents (Schorr, 1960, 1980). These attitudes outline appropriate behaviors and responses for the responsible adult offspring, frequently finding expression in shared living arrangements, assistance with household tasks and shopping, maintenance of personal contact, provision of emotional support, and the like (Seelbach, 1984).

Filial responsibility also includes a preventive dimension that promotes self-sufficiency and independence among the aged (Seelbach, 1984). It enables adult children to encourage older parents to perform the tasks that they are capable of doing for themselves. This aspect of filial responsibility can be exhibited in a number of ways. Adult offspring can help parents to seek new and enriching life experiences, acquire new skills, and disregard negative stereotypes about aging. Also, children can respect their parents' autonomy, enabling them to make the decisions that affect their own lives (Cicirelli, 1989b).

Observing that many adult children confront filial obligations, Blenkner (1965) introduced the concept of filial maturity as a unique developmental challenge of mid-life. A filial crisis emerges when persons in their 40s and 50s realize that their parents can no longer fulfill the supportive role they once did during times of emotional and economic hardship. How do adult children react to this realization? Blenkner argues that role reversal, the attempt of children to parent their aging parents, is the result of a dysfunctional perception of the filial role and a pathological condition indicative of abnormal development. She suggests that a healthier resolution of this developmental crisis includes being dependable and seeing parents differently—as persons with their own needs, rights, and histories. Cicirelli (1989b) also asserts that the giving and receiving of care are essential developmental experiences for the mature personality. Being dependable and seeing parents as having needs, giving as well as receiving care, are expressions of filial responsibility that signify progress toward attainment of the stage of filial maturity.

As parent care becomes a normative part of the family experience (Brody, 1985), and as various life-style and societal factors affect adult children's circumstances (see Chapter 2, this volume), more and more of them will have concerns about their filial responsibilities. Filial anxiety, or worry about how much help they might be asked to give and their ability to react appropriately, is a likely response of adult children to the anticipated future stressors of parental decline and need for care. This anxiety is thought to be rooted in the adult child's attachment to, and desire to preserve the life of, the elderly parent (Cicirelli, 1988). L. R. Fischer (1985) and Cicirelli (1988) have observed that adult children can experience filial anxiety whether or not they are currently providing care. As discussed next, both adult children and aging parents hold expectations for the kinds and amounts of assistance offspring should provide their parents; awareness of these norms no doubt contributes to filial anxiety.

Filial Responsibility Expectations

The research on filial responsibility expectations has been diverse in its focus, method, and intent. We review this literature by first looking at research on expectations of single generations and then at studies that examined expectations of more than one generation concurrently.

Adult Children's Expectations

Despite the increasing incidence of intergenerational relationships in later life, only a sparse number of studies exist that address filial norms. In addition, discrepant results contribute to much of the ambiguity in our understanding of intergenerational role expectations.

Using data from a nonrandom sample of 1,006 college and 318 high school students, Dinkel (1944) conducted one of the first studies of filial attitudes. In his examination of the effects of sex, religious affiliation, area of residence, age, and education on attitudes toward support, he discovered that Catholics and rural residents more strongly endorsed filial obligations than did Protestants, Jews, those with no religious affiliation, and urban residents. He found no evidence of significant differences between females and males or between high school-age and college-age students. Dinkel also discovered that the extent of endorsement of filial obligation varied considerably with the degree of hardship present in the situation; students were more reluctant to help when circumstances made it more difficult to do so.

Wake and Sporakowski (1972) replicated and expanded Dinkel's work to include two additional independent variables, birth order and socioeconomic status. They administered an 18-item measure of filial responsibility to a nonrandom, Caucasian sample of 136 high school and 119 college students and their parents. They, too, found no sex differences. Unlike Dinkel's outcome, however, differences in filial attitudes between rural and urban residents were minimal and nonsignificant, and students of varying religious denominations did not differ significantly on filial responsibility beliefs. Although nonsignificant as a single variable, ordinal position was significant when combined with sex: the youngest female children in families had higher filial responsibility scores than did other female siblings.

Other researchers continued this line of inquiry, examining rural-urban, cohort, and racial differences in filial norms (Hanson, Sauer, & Seelbach, 1983; Sauer, Seelbach, & Hanson, 1981). Based on data from a stratified random sample of 1,950 respondents of a housing survey conducted in the southeastern quarter of Wisconsin (17.4% black and 82.6% white), their findings indicated that urbanites were significantly more likely than rural residents (Sauer et al., 1981), and whites were significantly more likely than blacks (Hanson et al., 1983), to endorse filial norms. As with Wake and Sporakowski's (1972) findings, the youngest cohort (under age 30) was more likely than older cohorts to support such norms. The items related to expectations about being available for elderly parents that received the most support were (a) married couples should want a home large enough so that parents are free to move in and (b) married children should live close to their parents (Hanson et al., 1983; Sauer et al., 1981).

Recognizing the potentially stifling effects that situational variables might have on children's sense of filial duty, researchers continued to pursue an understanding of the impact of other restraints imposed by living in contemporary society. Roff and Klemmack (1986), focusing on norms concerning adult children who were members of dual-earner couples, attempted to differentiate between behaviors expected of male and of female children. Taking into account the growing number of women in the labor force, they wondered to what extent traditional norms for female responsibility for aged parents still exist. Members of a probability sample of 315 adults (mean age 36.5 years) responded to a vignette about an elderly woman in need of some assistance. Both sexes thought that sons and daughters in dual-earner couples should share equally the responsibilities of helping and maintaining contact with their parents. Of the 18 norms examined, only 3 evidenced statistically significant gender differences; most adult children thought it more appropriate for sons to assist frail parents with yard work and daughters to aid with housework and meal preparation. Roff and Klemmack conclude that adult children favor behaviors that facilitate independent living for both elderly parents and themselves as well as advocate egalitarian norms for the care of infirm parents.

More recently, Finley, Roberts, and Banahan (1988) conducted telephone interviews with 3.4% of households in the metropolitan area of Huntsville, Alabama, using a random-digit dialing sampling technique. Of the 1,760 participants, 38% (667 respondents) had at least one living parent aged 70 or over. Data from this subsample were analyzed to determine potential motivators (affection) and inhibitors (role conflict and geographical distance) of attitudes of filial obligation. These authors make an important contribution to existing information by analyzing filial obligation for each of four types of parental relationships (mother, father, mother-in-law, father-in-law). All of the respondents interviewed by Finley et al. (1988) endorsed high levels of filial obligation to aging parents. Furthermore, the results indicate that the relationships of the predictor variables to filial obligation vary by the gender of the adult child and by the type of parent. For example, for daughters (but not for sons), affection proved significant in predicting filial obligation in relationships with mothers, fathers, and mothers-in-law (but not fathers-in-law). So too, role conflict, or perceived difficulty in assisting elderly parents in light of competing responsibilities, was inversely related to filial obligation and affected the daughters' (but not the sons') sense of filial duty to their fathers. The more daughters perceived role responsibilities as conflicting, the less obligation they felt in their relationships with their fathers. Role conflict was not a significant predictor for either daughters or sons with respect to the other parent types. Finley et al. conclude by challenging the assumption that affection produces filial obligation in all relationships and vice versa. Instead, they argue that attitudes of filial obligation are a product of individual life circumstances, such as the costs and rewards of the relationship, geographic distance from parents, and competing roles.

Parents' Expectations

Some investigators have specifically considered what elderly parents expect of their adult offspring. Parents consistently pinpoint affection as the most important thing their children can provide them (Schorr, 1980). Streib (1965), for example, questioned a nonrandom sample of 291 male retirees from private industry. Almost two-thirds of these men indicated that maintaining close affectional ties with their adult children was more important than receiving financial help from them. More recently, Blieszner and Mancini (1987) secured qualitative and quantitative data about filial responsibility expectations from a nonrandom sample of 23 white, healthy participants of workshops for older adults, aged 55 to 94 years. Their data replicate Streib's results in a new cohort, revealing that the parents desired affection, thoughtfulness, and open, honest, and frequent communication from their adult offspring; these parents deemed direct caregiving and residential proximity less important (Blieszner & Mancini, 1987).

Seelbach (1977, 1978, 1981) and his associate (Seelbach & Sauer, 1977) examined filial responsibility expectations and realizations, variables associated with different levels of expectations, and predictors of types of assistance provided by adult children. Using participants drawn from the larger Aged Services Project, their sample comprised 595 urban, low-income, predominantly black parents, with a mean age of 70 years. Although statistically significant differences between blacks and whites were non-existent, sex differences did occur; females were more likely than males to think that older parents who do not wish to live alone or who are physically unable to care for themselves should live with one of their children (Seelbach, 1977). Older, widowed, low-income, and frail persons tended to expect more from their offspring; Seelbach (1978) notes that filial expectancies of elderly parents are usually indicative of, and positively related to, their level of need.

In contrast, Marshall, Rosenthal, and Daciuk (1987) did not observe a connection between filial responsibility expectations and apparent need. Starting with a stratified random sample of individuals aged 40 and older from Hamilton, Ontario, the researchers selected a subset of 103 community-dwelling persons aged 70 or older who had at least one child. They found that respondents' demographic and health status variables were unrelated to their filial obligation expectations.

Although the association between parental need and filial duty expecta-tions is not clear, these expectations do appear to be important in relation to parents' psychological well-being. For example, filial responsibility expec-tations are inversely associated with parental morale (Quinn, 1983; Seelbach & Sauer, 1977). The more parents expect from their children in the way of obligations surrounding care during illness, financial help, living nearby, visiting patterns, and general feeling of duty, the lower their life satisfaction. Seelbach and Sauer (1977) propose that parents with extensive expectations may be "out of tune with their offsprings' expectations" (p. 498). Morale seems to be enhanced when parents perceive that their children will fulfill their roles as responsible others in the event of a crisis that requires their help (Blieszner & Mancini, 1987; Schlesinger, Tobin, & Kulys, 1981).

Multigenerational Studies

Relatively few researchers have analyzed the beliefs regarding filial role obligations of more than one generation simultaneously. Even fewer have incorporated analytic techniques that take advantage of paired data. Brody (1981) and her colleagues (Brody, Johnsen, & Fulcomer, 1984; Brody, Johnsen, Fulcomer, & Lang, 1983) are responsible for one such study. Using a nonrepresentative sample of 403 Philadelphia-area women from three generations (225 of whom belonged to 75 family triads), they investigated opinions about appropriate filial responsibility behaviors and personal preferences for providers of various services. Overall, the sense of filial responsibility was strong among the three generations of women; most felt that the old should be able to depend on adult children for help (Brody, 1981; Brody et al., 1983). The majority of these women believed that adult children should adjust their family schedules and help meet the expenses of professional health care for the impaired elderly mother when needed. They did not, however, view adjustment of work schedules and sharing households as appropriate. All three generations rated the adult child first over five other potential provider categories for intimate functions such as confidant and financial manager (Brody et al., 1984). Generational differences emerged, however. The middle-generation women were less likely than grandmothers or granddaughters to prefer adult children as providers of housework, personal care, and financial support (Brody, 1981). The oldest generation was most receptive to formal services for the elderly (Brody et al., 1983). To the best of our knowledge, no researcher has examined grandfather-father-son attitudes in a corresponding manner.

Using paired data from a random sample of 144 parent-child dyads from the Harrisburg area of Pennsylvania, Hamon and Blieszner (1990) analyzed filial responsibility expectations and level of intergenerational consensus on these expectations. Their findings confirm previous research that highlights the significance both generations attach to emotional functions of the filial role; talking over matters of importance and discussing resources available to aged parents were highly endorsed by both parents and their children. Both generations agreed that unnecessary prescriptions for the filial role included living close to parents and writing letters to parents on a weekly basis. Although children's responses reflected willingness in the following areas, parents did not expect to receive financial assistance from children, to live with their children, or to have children adjust their work schedules to help them. These beliefs reflect a sensitivity to familial and social changes that affect intergenerational obligation. Hamon and Blieszner extended previous research by assessing parent-child consensus on 16 filial responsibility items at the dyadic level. Overall, a moderate level of agreement appeared, with the highest consensus apparent when respondents were asked about residential proximity of children to parents, giving parents advice, and appropriate types and frequency of contact. The greatest divergence of agreement occurred when respondents were asked about financial assistance to parents; 86.4% of children agreed that they should provide it, but only 41.1% of parents felt that way. Unfortunately, this report did not include an analysis of gender differences in filial obligation norms.

Motivations for Filial Responsibility

Given that most empirical evidence suggests the endurance of attitudes of filial responsibility, we next consider what prompts and maintains such beliefs. From Hess and Waring's (1978a) discussion concerning parent and child relationships in later life, we might suspect that children who respond to their aged parents' needs fulfill the filial role by choice rather than because of feelings of obligation. Walker, Pratt, Shin, and Jones (1989) found, however, that filial behavior is likely to be the result of a number of both discretionary and obligatory motives.

Several theoretical explanations have been offered for the sense of responsibility for one's aging parents (see Chapters 3 and 5, this volume). First, attitudes of concern for parents may be regarded as a moral imperative. Children may perceive filial norms to be morally and socially expected, the right thing to do. Such beliefs may stem from the Judeo-Christian commandment that instructs children to "honor your father and your mother" (Exodus 20:12). Because this biblical injunction is not gender specific, we would not expect such a moral imperative to vary by gender; however, we did find data concerning the moral aspects of filial responsibility motivation only for females. Among their volunteer sample of 173 daughters in western Oregon providing at least one service to their aged mothers, Walker et al. (1989) discovered that relationship obligation and moral beliefs were, in fact, the most frequently mentioned obligatory reasons for caregiving.

In addition, children may be socialized or socially coerced into adopting filial norms. From the time of birth, humans learn appropriate ways to think and behave. For example, Graham (1983) asserts that women are socialized into a caring role and that caring becomes the defining characteristic of a female's identity and lifework. From this perspective, we would expect daughters to be more motivated than sons to carry out filial obligations.

Although social pressure may be effective in some instances, what children do for their parents rarely is connected with compulsion, given the infrequency with which filial responsibility laws are enforced (Bulcroft, Van Leynseele, Hatch, & Borgatta, 1989). Instead, when parents need comfort or confidants, they most frequently turn to the children with whom they share similar values. Interview information from a nonrandom sample of 117 preretirement couples associated with a midwestern Catholic university indicates that aging mothers most often chose as confidants daughters who lived nearby, were early-born, and had interests similar to their own (Aldous, 1987; Aldous, Klaus, & Klein, 1985). In those instances where sons were confidants to mothers, it was important that the sons were not married. Similarity of interests and attitudes toward treatment of their parents were important characteristics of confidants selected by fathers, although fathers were more likely to choose sons than daughters (Aldous et al., 1985).

Social exchange theory offers another feasible explanation for the filial responsibility motivation. This theory holds that relationships are governed by a norm of reciprocity; people "should reciprocate favors received from others" (Nye, 1979, p. 4) and such rewarding exchanges should equal themselves out over the course of a lifetime. When considering intergenerational exchanges, Nye (1979) asserts that parents undergo a number of costs in bearing and rearing children, such as those associated with food, shelter, socialization, and protection. Consequently, children may be impelled or motivated to endorse filial norms because it is profitable for them to do so.

The pervasive sense of duty experienced by many children may be an outgrowth of feelings of indebtedness (Seelbach, 1984) or irredeemable obligation (Berman, 1987) to parents for all that they have done, and may actually serve to motivate contact and caring (Walker et al., 1989). When adult children perceive an imbalance in exchanges, one could anticipate that they might attempt to reduce their guilt and distress by restoring equity (Nye, 1979). Blenkner (1965) hints that, on occasion, some guilt is functional because it prods children to follow through on filial duties upon which parents have come to depend. Children may endorse filial norms in an effort to avoid the costs that would be inflicted upon them in the way of social disapproval for not being concerned about the well-being of their parents. Because women tend to be socialized as caretakers in the family realm, they would be likely to encounter more costs than men should they not perform well in this area.

Attachment theory has also been posed as a means of understanding adult children's attitudes about and provision of help to older parents (Cicirelli, 1989b). Bowlby (1979) asserts that attachment to parents endures throughout the life span. Attachment in the adult years is defined as "the propensity or tendency for psychological closeness and contact, although this tendency may be only intermittently reinforced with physical closeness and contact" (Cicirelli, 1983, p. 816). Attitudes of filial responsibility may be an outgrowth of positive feelings for one's parent, a result of friendship and mutuality (English, 1979), indicative of filial maturity (Blenkner, 1965). On the other hand, although feelings of attachment or affection may be sufficient to foster attitudes of responsibility, they may not be strong enough sources of motivation to enable children to cope with the strains of actual filial role enactment, such as caregiving (Jarrett, 1985). Moreover, the nature of children's personal relations with their parents also influences their decisions about whether or not to help them (Dinkel, 1944; Walker et al., 1989). For example, Matthews and Rosner (1988) found that both daughters and sons were reluctant to help a parent if they perceived that another sibling had been the parent's favorite child.

Enactment of Filial Responsibility

Having reviewed the influence of gender on filial responsibility attitudes and sources of motivation to carry out filial obligations, we turn now to a consideration of daughters' and sons' performance of parental caregiving tasks. *Filial role enactment* is the term used to describe the behaviors that result from the attitudes and sources of motivation discussed previously. Study after study has shown that the majority of adult children respond to their parents' needs, but that daughters and sons fulfill their filial obligations differently.

Filial Behaviors

Adult children interact with their parents in many and diverse ways (Mancini & Blieszner, 1989; see also Chapter 5, this volume). Here we are concerned specifically with research that provides information about how daughters and sons respond when they perceive that their parents' independence is threatened and their needs for assistance are greater than those associated with routine companionship, emotional support, and the like. Many researchers have reported gender differences in filial behaviors (Horowitz, 1985b; Houser, Berkman, & Bardsley, 1985; Matthews & Rosner, 1988; Stoller, 1990; Stone, Cafferata, & Sangl, 1987). Adult daughters both provide more assistance in general than adult sons and help more with direct hands-on, intensive, instrumental, and emotional support tasks. In contrast, the help given by sons typically involves financial management, advice, heavy chores, and shopping.

This gender-based division of parental caregiving parallels the arrangements found for other family work. Wives do three times more household and family tasks than husbands and take responsibility for tasks that are unrelenting, repetitive, and routine. They cope with multiple demands by reducing their personal leisure time. Husbands tend to perform family work that is infrequent, irregular, and nonroutine. They are less likely than wives to allow family responsibilities to interfere with their leisure activities (Thompson & Walker, 1989).

Influences on Filial Role Enactment

Adult children respond to parental frailty within the context of their past and current family situations. Patterns of caregiving are affected by family structure, the character of family relationships, and competing commitments for time and energy, as well as by level of parental dependency or need and correspondence between filial responsibility expectations and actual behaviors. These influences are elaborated in Chapter 5 of this volume; therefore, we briefly outline here important contextual issues related to filial role enactment:

- The number, sex, marital status, and geographic location of adult children in the family influence who provides what types of support to aged parents (Cicirelli, 1984; Matthews, 1987; Matthews & Rosner, 1988; Moss, Moss, & Moles, 1985).
- The sex of the parent needing care is related to the sex of the child who provides it (Stoller, 1990).
- Long-standing interaction patterns involving favoritism or conflict may determine which adult children perform which assistance tasks (Matthews & Rosner, 1988).
- Family and work roles affect the time and energy adult children have for parental caregiving (Kleban, Brody, Schoonover, & Hoffman, 1989; Lewis, 1990; Stoller, 1983).
- The amount, types, intensity, and duration of assistance required by elderly parents are associated with whether sons or daughters serve as primary caregivers (Cicirelli, 1981; Stoller, 1990).
- Feelings of attachment and attitudes of filial obligation influence the provision of services to parents indirectly through their effects on attachment behaviors such as maintaining geographic proximity and frequency of contact (Cicirelli, 1981).

Effects of Filial Role Enactment

The carrying out of filial duties has an impact on elderly parents, adult children, and the relationship between them. The implicit assumption of most researchers is that the tasks completed by adult children benefit their parents by enabling them to remain in the community instead of moving to institutions. On the other hand, the potential exists for unhelpful interventions by adult children or conflict about filial behaviors as well. Chapter 5 in this volume provides a detailed examination of the effects of filial behaviors on elderly parents and adult children. Below is a review of some key elements in this process:

- Among the problematic aspects of filial helping are the interruption of daily routines and the restriction of activities, physical and emotional strain, and parent-child conflict (Chenoweth & Spencer, 1986; L. R. Fischer, 1985; Horowitz, 1985b; Johnson & Catalano, 1983; Snyder & Keefe, 1985).
- Some possible benefits of caregiving are improved family relationships, more time spent together, feelings of competence, and an appreciation of the care receiver's ability to cope with dependency and the help received from others (Alley, 1988; Walker, Shin, & Bird, 1990).
- A lifetime of kinkeeping by women may pay off when they are old because they are likely to live longer than men and thus develop greater needs for assistance than do their male counterparts (Spitze & Logan, 1989).
- Mothers' satisfaction with the parent-child relationship is based more on their satisfaction with the quality of contact they have with their offspring than on the adult children's filial behaviors (Houser & Berkman, 1984; Walker, Shin, Jones, & Pratt, 1987; Walker & Thompson, 1983).
- The quality of the parent-child relationship deteriorates when filial behavior is not forthcoming as expected (Fisher, Reid, & Melendez, 1989).

Conceptual and Methodological Issues in Filial Responsibility Research

Many questions about gender issues in filial responsibility attitudes and filial role enactment remain to be addressed. In addition to focusing on neglected research topics, conceptual and methodological improvements would expand our knowledge and understanding of filial responsibility issues (see Chapter 9, this volume).

Conceptual Issues

Marshall et al. (1987) have reviewed the literature on filial responsibility; they conclude that discrepant definitions and measures of filial obligation interfere with the interpretation of results across studies. Further, they maintain that researchers have not specified the content of norms carefully enough, have overlooked the fact that global measures of filial behaviors mask specific dimensions of the exchange of assistance, and have given insufficient attention to theorizing about the link between the endorsement of filial norms and filial role enactment in terms of the effects of the situation and context in which assistance actually is (or would be) given.

Hanson et al. (1983) and Lewis (1990) point out that scholars of filial responsibility must give more careful attention to the effects of history and cohort membership on parent-child relations and parental caregiving. Different experiences between the sexes and across the generations in a wide variety of societal and historical dimensions are likely to affect the interaction patterns under consideration here. Moreover, the idea that the filial caregiving situation itself changes over time warrants additional research.

Brubaker (1990a) and Gubrium (1988) advocate for greater emphasis on the entire family history instead of examining filial responsibility norms and behaviors outside the context of ongoing interaction patterns. This recommendation includes studying multiple members and generations of families concurrently (including daughters-in-law; Horowitz, 1985b) and asking questions about characteristics of the parent-child relationship prior to parental dependency and outside of the caregiving situation.

Lopata (1987) has identified a filial duty that has not received research attention: the responsibility of keeping alive the memory of deceased family members and preserving family traditions. This cultural expectation, typically assigned to females, suggests that filial responsibility does not end with parental death. The feelings of offspring about such an indefinite extension of filial obligation and their methods of accomplishing this duty have not been examined.

There is little on record about elderly parents' feelings about receiving care from their children (see Blieszner & Mancini, 1987, for a discussion of anticipated feelings) or about the responsibilities aged parents feel toward their children and whether these differ by the gender of the offspring. Likewise, L. R. Fischer (1985) mentions the need for more information on the emotional reactions of adult children to their parents' dependency and the subjective meanings of different kinds of losses experienced by the different generations in the family. Again, do these responses vary by gender?

If one aspect of filial responsibility is a preventive dimension that encourages self-sufficiency and independence (Seelbach, 1984), then research questions must be raised about the types of parental caregiving that are not helpful, that interfere with self-sufficiency and independence. What causes adult children to be intrusive, beyond helpfulness, and when does this form of interaction slip from relatively benign to abusive? Are there differences in the likelihood that daughters or sons will adopt intrusive filial caregiving styles?

Thompson (1989) summarizes many of the above concerns in her treatise on contextual and relational morality in late-life intergenerational relations. She calls for more research on the everyday circumstances of parents and adult children as a way of understanding when actions and services are helpful and when they are not, the connection between affection and obligation, and the influence of the broader sociohistorical context (e.g., historical change, cultural myths, government policies and services) on parent-child relations. She also notes the need for additional study of the relational processes in mature families, such as attributions, self-disclosure, empathy, and cooperation, and how they affect parental helping. All of these questions could be studied profitably with both daughters and sons.

Methodological Issues

Certain groups have been underrepresented in filial responsibility research, while white middle-class mothers and their daughters have been the focus of many investigations. Although Walker and Thompson (1983) justify their study of mother-daughter dyads on the basis of earlier literature implying that female relationships are more enduring and encompass more activity than male or cross-sex family dyads, the fact that sons do engage in filial behaviors and that fathers are the recipients of such care (e.g., Kaye & Applegate, 1990b; Kleban et al., 1989; Stoller, 1990) suggest the desirability of including the viewpoints of fathers and sons in future research. Moreover, the perspectives of family members from diverse ethnic, racial, and socio-economic groups within the United States and across various cultures internationally are required for a more comprehensive understanding of filial responsibility attitudes, motives, and behaviors.

Lewis (1990) stresses the significance of more research based on representative samples and of employing longitudinal designs and multivariate analytic techniques as several ways of strengthening the literature on filial responsibility. Also, it is imperative that researchers include both female and male family members in the same studies so that gender similarities and differences can be examined and understood more completely. When investigators do have data on both genders, it is crucial that they perform gender-based analyses; many studies cited herein contain responses from both women and men but do not show results for the two groups.

Equally important, the results of qualitative research studies illustrate the advantages of nonstructured interviews for uncovering new dimensions of family caregiving and achieving greater insights into motivations for, and perceived consequences of, filial duty (Blieszner & Mancini, 1987; Fisher et al., 1989; Gubrium, 1988; Matthews & Rosner, 1988; Matthews, Werkner, & Delaney, 1989). The use of in-depth interviewing techniques can reveal both the emotional and the symbolic meanings of filial obligation that are not detected in typical survey approaches.

Adopting a feminist perspective and feminist methodology (Thompson, 1990) would contribute to the advancement of filial responsibility research. Whereas "prevailing approaches [in family studies] emphasize sex differences and neglect similarities, deny diversity within gender, ignore context, offer vague meanings so researchers can fill in any meaning that suits them, and mask power, inequality, conflict, and change" (Thompson, 1990, p. 4), feminist research offers a fresh viewpoint. For example, a feminist analysis would examine gender as a construct evoked through everyday filial interactions (not a predetermined attribute of individuals), connect personal experiences of caregiving to the larger social context in which it takes place, seek previously hidden reasons for adopting the caregiving role, propose models of shared filial responsibility among adult children rather than trying to determine whether daughters or sons should aid parents or are more motivated to do so, and enable research participants to contribute to the identification of the research questions and the interpretation of the results. An extension of this perspective is the notion that research on filial responsibility should be conducted not only for the purpose of pinpointing gender differences, but also to provide data that can be used to enhance the ability of both daughters and sons to choose their filial responsibilities and discharge their filial duties effectively without being oppressed by them.

8

Gender Differences in
Family Caregiving

A Fact in Search of a Theory

GARY R. LEE

The task of this chapter is to consider possible explanations for the preponderance of females as family caregivers to the elderly. In any explanatory task, it is important at the outset to identify precisely what is to be explained. The focus here will be on the greater role played by daughters than sons in the care of aging parents. Many studies have shown that the "first line of defense" for elderly persons requiring care is the spouse, and that it is more common for wives to care for husbands than vice versa (Arling & McAuley, 1984; Cantor, 1983; see also Chapters 2 and 4, this volume). The explanation for this, however, is largely demographic. Because men tend to marry younger women and women have longer life expectancies, wives persist in outliving their husbands. This means that husbands are likely to need care earlier in the marital life cycle than are their wives, and by the time wives need assistance, their husbands are often deceased. While there are undoubtedly other factors involved, the predominant role of demographic reality in this process means that the explanation is relatively straightforward and not particularly controversial.

This is not the case, however, for the division of caregiving responsibility for elderly parents between daughters and sons. Other chapters in this volume have documented the predominance of daughters in the enterprise of family caregiving for the elderly (see Chapters 2, 5, and 7). This is not to say that sons are entirely uninvolved; they do make many contributions. But sons are likely to be primary caregivers for elderly parents mostly when there are no available daughters. If there are daughters, sons are unlikely to provide "routine" care; rather, their roles are more likely to be described as "backup," "circumscribed," or "sporadic" (Matthews & Rosner, 1988). Sons do provide considerable assistance to aging parents in the form of financial aid or advice and transportation, but personal care and household chores are largely accomplished by daughters (Montgomery & Kamo, 1989). These facts are well established empirically, but poorly understood in a theoretical sense. For this reason, the focus of this chapter is restricted to the question of why daughters provide more extensive, varied, and continuing care to elderly parents than do sons, particularly in cases where both sons and daughters are available.

Broader Domains of Family Behavior

The predominance of daughters in the caregiving networks of the frail elderly has been evident to researchers for some time, and is increasingly the focus of theoretical concern. However, having narrowed the object of explanation to this particular phenomenon, it is now appropriate to consider the advisability of broadening it in at least three ways. The provision of care to frail elderly parents is a component or manifestation of the domestic division of labor, nurturance in family role behavior, and kinship relations. Gender differences in family caregiving are intimately related to gender differences in each of these three domains. Each of these domains, in turn, has implications for the understanding of gender differences in the caregiving enterprise.

Scientific theory is more powerful and useful if it is general rather than specific (Stinchcombe, 1987); that is, a theory that explains inclusive classes of phenomena is more useful than a theory that explains only isolated or singular facts, because specific explanations can be deduced from general propositions. Part of the problem with existing theory in the domain of family caregiving is that it often treats family caregiving as a unique domain of behavior, distinct from other aspects of human lives. In fact, family caregiving for the elderly may be a specific manifestation of much more general processes, and explanations of the specific phenomenon at issue here may be derivable from explanations of these more general processes. In the sections that follow, domestic labor, nurturance, and kinship relations are examined in turn for the insights they may provide into the phenomenon of family caregiving.

Domestic Labor

Caring for elderly parents is a task that fits clearly under the conceptual category of domestic labor. This is particularly the case for activities routinely conducted by females—that is, personal care and household chores. Although the tasks performed for elderly parents by their children are not necessarily performed in the children's homes, since most elderly parents do not share residences with their children (Coward, Cutler, & Schmidt, 1989), some degree of residential proximity is required if children are to provide these services to parents on a regular basis (Litwak & Kulis, 1987). Whether the adult child engages in these activities in the child's home or the parent's, the tasks involved are the same.

Domestic labor, in our society and most (if not all) others, is primarily the province of females throughout the life cycle (Rexroat & Shehan, 1987). This is true even when husbands and wives are both employed outside the home (Berardo, Shehan, & Leslie, 1987; Shelton, 1990); it is, in fact, unclear whether or not wives' employment results in any marginal increase in husbands' contributions to domestic labor.

There are some indications that gender-segregated patterns of domestic labor are changing (Menaghan & Parcel, 1990; Pleck, 1985), but these changes appear to be progressing much more rapidly on the attitudinal level than on the behavioral level. Thornton (1989) has shown considerable recent increases in the extent to which both men and women (but particularly women) believe that husbands should share in domestic roles if wives are sharing the provider role. In a similar vein, many studies show that *attitudes* favor a relatively egalitarian division of parent care between sons and daughters, but behavioral differences persist (Finley, 1989; Montgomery & Kamo, 1989; Roff & Klemmack, 1986). This pattern has long been observed for other aspects of domestic labor as well; many couples who hold egalitarian attitudes have very inegalitarian divisions of household labor (Araji, 1977; Hiller & Philliber, 1986). As Condran and Bode (1982) have observed, "Attitudes and sympathies may have changed, but husbands still don't wash the dishes very often" (p. 425). Nor, I may add, do sons provide personal care or household help to their aging parents if daughters (or, in some cases, daughters-in-law) are available to do it.

Others have recognized that the gender-based division of labor in caregiving for the elderly parallels that for domestic labor in general (Dwyer & Seccombe, 1991; Thompson & Walker, 1989; see also Chapter 7, this volume). Few, however, have attempted to capitalize on this fact in the development of explanatory theory. One exception to this is a study by Finley

(1989), who attempts specifically to apply theories of family labor to the caregiving enterprise, without notable success. I will return to her study in subsequent sections.

Nurturance

Caregiving in general has long been recognized as primarily a female domain (Abel, 1986; Chodorow, 1978). This has most frequently been applied strictly to the analysis of child care, however. Parsons and Bales (1955) differentiated instrumental from expressive leadership roles based on small group research, and Zelditch (1955) applied this distinction to the family, arguing that, cross-culturally, wives/mothers specialize in socio-emotional leadership while husbands/fathers take the lead in task accomplishment. The general sentiment among contemporary scholars is that this distinction is too gross and general to apply to contemporary families (see Reiss & Lee, 1988); it also fails to take account of the fact that many domestic and caregiving behaviors are actually instrumental in the sense that they involve task accomplishment and manipulation of the external environment. However, the fact persists that women predominate in the care of young children, particularly infants, in the contemporary United States as well as in earlier times and in other cultures (Crano & Aronoff, 1978; Lee, 1982).

Some of the predominance of women in caring for children may be due directly to the fact that women have babies and men do not; maternity is socially obvious, while paternity is inherently uncertain (Barnard & Good, 1984). Chodorow (1978) argues that mothering behavior reproduces itself, and the unique attachment of the infant to its mother serves to identify caregiving with females. This leads to a nurturant self-definition among women. Walker, in Chapter 3 of this volume, refers to this as the "psychological" explanation for gender differences in caregiving.

Rossi (1977, 1984), as well as many other sociobiologists (see Filsinger, 1988), has drawn on endocrinology to suggest that there are other biological, particularly hormonal, bases for caregiving behavior in females. According to Rossi (1984), females are better equipped hormonally to respond to the needs of infants in appropriate and constructive ways:

> When [biological] gender differences are viewed in connection with caring for a nonverbal, fragile, infant, then women have a head start in easier reading of an infant's facial expressions, smoothness of body motions, greater ease in handling a tiny creature with tactile gentleness and in soothing through a high, soft, rhythmic use of the voice. (p. 13)

These explanations, however, have been applied almost exclusively to the care of infants and young children by their mothers. As noted previously, the predominance of mothers in the care and nurturance of infants may serve to identify nurturance with the female role and make nurturing an integral part of women's self-concepts. When, later in the life cycle, aging parents need nurturing care, its provision by daughters is at least consistent with the gendered division of labor established earlier.

Kinship

The relation between aging parents and their adult children is, first and foremost, a kinship relation, and is often conceptualized as the linchpin or most basic element of the contemporary kinship system (Lee, 1980). In many nonindustrial societies, males are the prime movers in kinship systems, particularly those organized according to unilineal principles of descent; even in matrilineal kin groups, the key relations are between mothers' brothers and sisters' sons (Fox, 1967; Lee, 1982).

However, in contemporary societies with bilateral kinship systems, kin ties revolve primarily around women (B. N. Adams, 1968; Alwin, Converse, & Martin, 1985; L. R. Fischer, 1983; Leigh, 1982; Rossi & Rossi, 1990; Sweetser, 1984). This is probably because kin networks usually have neither substantial economic nor political functions in modern industrial societies (Lee, 1982). Sweetser (1984) contends that, for married couples, ties to the wife's kin are stronger than those to the husband's, unless the latter are crucial to the husband's occupation. Lee (1988) has shown that older persons are more likely to live near and interact with daughters, except farmers, who are more involved with sons; this is clearly consistent with Sweetser's generalization. American culture appears to assign the role of "kinkeeper" to women, to the extent that wives are more likely to keep in touch with their husbands' kin than are the husbands themselves (Bahr, 1976). The primary exception to this is in the area of financial assistance or advice, where ties between males predominate. The connections to gender-differentiated roles in the care of aging parents are, once again, obvious.

If kinship ties revolve around women, it follows that the strongest kinship ties of all are those between mothers and daughters. This is indeed the case (Abel, 1986; L. R. Fischer, 1983; Lee, 1980; Thompson & Walker, 1984; Walker, Pratt, Shin, & Jones, 1989). As mentioned previously, for demographic reasons, most elderly persons in need of care from children are women. Stoller (1990) has also shown that there is a positive correlation between the genders of care receivers and their caregivers. This may be partly because kin ties are stronger among women, mothers are closer to their daughters than to their sons, and caregiving for elderly parents involves the activation of a kinship relation.

The differential roles of sons and daughters in caregiving for elderly parents, then, are specific manifestations of gender differences in domestic labor, nurturance, and kinship relations. Yet none of this helps directly in explaining the specific difference at issue here. It does help us, however, to form the question at a more general level, and therefore to search for more general, and thus more powerful, explanations. The next section examines some explanations for family caregiving in general, and gender differences in caregiving in particular, that have been proposed in the existing literature.

The Status of Proposed Explanations

Cicirelli (1989b) has advanced three explanations for why adult children provide assistance to their aging parents. While none of these is specifically intended as an explanation of gender differences, each may be applicable to this issue. The explanations fall under the headings of equity, obligation, and attachment.

The *equity* argument is based on both equity and exchange theories. It suggests that the parties to an exchange relationship attempt to maintain balance in costs and rewards, are distressed by imbalance, and attempt to redress imbalance when it appears. Parent-child relations are characterized by lifelong imbalance because of the costs sustained by parents in the raising of their children. Caregiving for elderly parents provides children with an opportunity to redress this imbalance and return the relationship to a more equitable level. Brody (1985) describes a sense of "indebtedness" on the part of adult children, which engenders feelings of guilt even among those who are devoting a great deal of energy and resources to parental care. Brody found that three-fifths of the women in her sample who were primary caregivers for their aging mothers "said that . . . they felt guilty about not doing enough for their mothers" (p. 26).

The equity explanation is largely indistinguishable in most respects from Cicirelli's (1989b) *obligation* explanation, in which a sense of duty to help parents is based on gratitude for earlier help from parents as well as cultural norms. Walker et al. (1989), in a study of mothers and daughters, found that daughters were very likely to report motives for caregiving based on obligation, while mothers were more likely to perceive that their daughters were motivated by discretionary feelings such as affection than by obligation.

Clearly, feelings of obligation play a major role as motives for caregiving, although Cicirelli (1983) found that the effects of perceived obligation on commitment to provide care were indirect via attachment behaviors. These feelings of obligation are closely related to norms of filial responsibility, as discussed by Blieszner and Hamon in Chapter 7 of this volume.

The roles of equity and obligation in explaining gender differences in family caregiving are dependent upon the observation of greater feelings of indebtedness and duty among adult daughters than among sons. Previous research, however, has not demonstrated the existence of such differences (Finley, 1989; Montgomery & Kamo, 1989). Sons report feeling just as obligated as do daughters to provide care to aging parents. They are not, however, equally likely to act on these feelings, at least not to the extent that daughters do. In light of these facts, equity and obligation theories do not appear to be particularly useful in the explanation of gender differences in family caregiving for the elderly.

Cicirelli's (1989b) third theory of family caregiving is labeled *attachment*. This explanation revolves around the affectional bond between parent and child, which is established early in the child's life and, presumably, continues throughout the life span. The caregiver is motivated to maintain or preserve the object of attachment (i.e., the aging parent), and so provides care when this object is perceived as vulnerable. Cicirelli (1983) has shown that feelings of attachment have modest positive effects, direct as well as indirect, on the commitment to provide care for elderly parents.

Here there is good evidence of a sex difference. Ties between mothers and daughters are the strongest of any intergenerational relations throughout the life course, in attitudinal and affectional as well as behavioral terms (Lee, 1980; Rossi & Rossi, 1990). As noted earlier in this chapter, even though the American kinship system is formally bilateral, ties through females are stronger and more viable than those through males. If adults are motivated to care for aging parents (particularly mothers) by feelings of attachment and affection, it is reasonable to expect that these feelings are stronger among daughters than among sons because mother-daughter bonds are stronger than mother-son, father-daughter, or father-son bonds. This is consistent with Cicirelli's (1989b) attachment theory.

The problem here is the link between affection or attachment and caregiving. Cicirelli (1983) found positive correlations between attachment and caregiving behavior, but others have found either very low or nonexistent correlations between affectional closeness and the exchange of assistance (Dressel & Clark, 1990; Rossi & Rossi, 1990). Finley, Roberts, and Banahan (1988) found correlations between affection and caregiving for daughters, but not for sons. It is clear from these and other studies that affection is not necessary for caregiving, and that care is frequently provided by children to parents even when the relationship is characterized by considerable conflict.

Cicirelli's (1989b) attachment theory, as applied to gender differences in family caregiving, is consistent with known differences in kinship relations and behaviors between men and women. However, it does not take account of, or offer an explanation for, women's greater roles in domestic labor in general or nurturance in particular. It does not, therefore, offer the generality we are seeking in an explanation of gender differences, because it is focused entirely on the caregiving relationship to the exclusion of clearly related role behaviors. We need to examine more closely existing efforts to explain family caregiving as a manifestation of gender differences in other familial role behaviors.

As mentioned previously, Finley (1989) has attempted to apply four different theories of gender differences in domestic labor to the explanation of why daughters provide more care for aging parents than do sons. Although Finley's (1989) study has been discussed elsewhere in this volume (see, for example, Chapter 5), a brief recapitulation here is necessary to set the context for further discussion.

Finley (1989) tested four distinct hypotheses. First, she hypothesized that women have more available time to care for parents than do males; controlling for a measure of role conflict, however, did not reduce the gender difference in caregiving. Second, she suggested that women may feel more obligation to care for parents than do men because of gender role socialization. Gender, however, was found to be uncorrelated with filial obligation, although obligation was correlated with caregiving. Third, the "external resources" argument implied to Finley that women have less power in determining their behavior because they have lesser access to external resources, such as those provided by employment and education; women are forced to perform more menial tasks because of this lesser power. However, controls for employment status and education also failed to reduce the effect of gender on caregiving. Fourth, Finley hypothesized that there is role specialization in caregiving, whereby females provide more personal care and males are more involved in care management and supervision. However, she found that daughters are more involved in the provision of all types of care than are sons, and that sons and daughters are equally responsible for arranging for the provision of care by other sources.

In short, none of the theories of domestic labor that Finley tested proved to be of use in explaining why daughters provide more care than do sons. This casts some doubt on the utility of the contention that caregiving is part of domestic labor. However, it must also be noted that these same theories have been relatively ineffective in explaining why women do more domestic labor than men in terms of housework and child care (Berardo et al., 1987; Rexroat & Shehan, 1987; Shelton, 1990; Thompson & Walker, 1989). Women's greater role in family caregiving may still be a component of women's greater role in domestic labor; this difference itself, however, remains unexplained.

One other important characteristic of Finley's study needs to be considered here. This is the fact that, in all cases in her sample, the recipient of care was the respondent's mother. We know that kinship ties are stronger among women, and that there is a tendency for caregivers to be of the same gender as the receivers of care (Stoller, 1990). It is entirely possible that the outcomes of Finley's tests would have been different if aging fathers and their children had also been included in her analysis.

Each theory offered by Cicirelli (1989b) and Finley (1989) to account for gender differences in family caregiving for the elderly has some appeal, but each encounters problems in terms of logical consistency, empirical support, or both. The same is true for the three "perspectives" (psychological, socio-logical, and feminist) developed earlier in this volume by Walker (Chapter 3), which I will not recapitulate here. Based on my critiques of these explanatory attempts, however, it may be possible to synthesize a set of propositions that advance the cause of explanation at least marginally beyond its current state. This is the intent of the concluding section of this chapter.

An Attempt at Theoretical Synthesis

The following propositions are offered not as a path-breaking set of new ideas, but rather as a summary of what is already known in a form designed to facilitate the explanation of gender differences in caregiving for the impaired elderly. These propositions vary somewhat in terms of their confir-mation status—that is, some are more debatable than others. Each, however, has a substantial body of supportive evidence behind it, much of which has been reviewed in this chapter.

- *Women are more involved in kinship networks and relations than are men.* This is important because, after all, the parent-child relation is a kinship relation. Except for financial exchange and direct involvement in economic enterprises, ties between related women generally are activated before and in preference to either ties between related men or cross-sex ties.

- *The majority of elderly persons needing family care are women.* This is attributable to the demographics of longevity; women tend to outlive men in general, and wives tend to outlive their husbands in particular. This is of central relevance here because of the fact presented as the next proposition.

- *There is a tendency for caregivers to be of the same gender as care receivers.* It does not follow, from this fact alone, that if husbands outlived their wives we would find more caregiving behavior among sons than among daughters. However, in combination with the other propositions advanced here, it suggests that mothers are more likely to turn to daughters than to sons for most types of assistance if both sons and daughters are available.

- *Women are more strongly identified with nurturing roles than are men.* As suggested above, this may stem partly from biological influences, partly from the fact that women bear and nurture infants and young children, and partly from social causes. It is consistent with Walker's psychological perspective (Chapter 3, this volume), which argues that nurturing is a more integral component of women's self-concepts than of men's. It is also consistent with the fact presented as the next proposition.

- *Women are more heavily involved in domestic labor of all types than are men.* While the explanation for this difference is the subject of continuing debate and research, the fact itself is beyond dispute. Even when women and men are equally involved in economic activities outside the home, the domestic division of labor is rarely equal. In spite of the failure of Finley's (1989) four theories of domestic labor to account for the gender difference in caregiving, caregiving is still a dimension of domestic labor. If we understood more about the antecedents of domestic labor, we would understand more about the antecedents of family caregiving for the elderly.

None of these propositions is self-explanatory, nor do they, as a set, neatly suggest some singular theory by means of which they may all be explained. They do, however, help to place family caregiving for the elderly in a broader context involving general and persistent gender differences in domestic labor, nurturance, and kinship behavior. It is the persistence of these behavioral differences between men and women that needs to be explained, because family caregiving for the elderly is a special case of these overarching differences.

No ultimate explanation of male/female role specialization in these domains is forthcoming here; these questions have been the subject of research and theory for more than a century without approaching a final resolution. It is reasonable, however, to suggest directions in which we might look for explanatory strategies. There are two such directions that seem to me potentially fruitful because of their generality; they are highly interrelated.

One is a variant of what Walker (Chapter 3, this volume) calls the psychological perspective. (I would, incidentally, choose a different label; *psychological* implies reductionism and micro-level reasoning, which is not precisely what is going on here.) This is most closely connected with the nurturance argument elicited previously. The cornerstone of this logic is that women, and not men, bear children and, throughout human history until the twentieth century, have been the only ones capable of feeding infants. This creates both a strong mother-child bond, from which follows the asymmetry of our bilateral kinship system, and continuing identification of nurturance and caregiving with women throughout the life cycle. Chodorow's (1978) theory of the "reproduction of mothering," which is a large part of the basis of this argument, has been seriously challenged on grounds of internal consistency (R. M. Jackson, 1989), but nonetheless indicates how other nurturing behaviors, and nurturant self-concepts, are more likely to develop among women than among men.

The second possible direction involves the theoretical tradition known as "gender stratification" (see, for example, Friedl, 1975; Huber, 1990). It is, in many ways, complementary to the nurturance argument. The two basic premises of gender stratification theory are that "producers in the family economy have more power and prestige than consumers," and "the most power and prestige accrue to those who control the distribution of valued goods beyond the family" (Huber, 1990, p. 4). This theoretical tradition shows how, over the course of human history, women have been systematically excluded from valued producer roles in the family and the economy by their necessary roles in childbearing and child rearing. This has relegated women to domestic roles under most technological and ecological conditions. Although the ultimate causes of these gender-based role differences have been altered drastically under modern technological and economic conditions, processes of cultural change are slow. This is similar, but not identical, to the feminist perspective elucidated by Walker in Chapter 3 of this volume.

The major modification I would suggest to gender stratification theory, in this particular application, is that gender differences in caregiving behavior are not necessarily best interpreted in terms of power and prestige. If education and employment status are reflective of power and/or prestige,

Finley's (1989) analysis and others that show minimal effects of women's employment on caregiving would be inconsistent with this theory. It is possible, however, to deduce hypotheses regarding gender-based role *specialization* from gender stratification theory without contending that this specialization is necessarily an outcome of power imbalances, at least in an immediate sense.

If these explanations have merit, it is reasonable to expect some change in gender differences in family caregiving in the foreseeable future. Women's roles are changing in the sense that women are progressively more involved in the productive economy and less restricted to the domestic sphere by the demands of bearing and rearing children. Women are adding the "provider role" to their role repertoires. Attitudes are rapidly becoming more supportive of this, and of corresponding changes in men's roles in the direction of increasing involvement in domestic labor such as housework, child care, and related activities (Thornton, 1989). Behavioral changes in the latter dimensions, however, are following much more slowly; Ogburn's (1923) enduring concept of "cultural lag" seems highly relevant here.

However, women still do bear children, and the hormonal differences between men and women detailed by Rossi (1977, 1984) do not seem in imminent danger of drastic change. It is, of course, entirely unreasonable to argue that women take the lead in providing family care to the elderly because their hormones direct them to do so. But, to the extent that gender differences in nurturance of infants are antecedents of gender differences in other forms of nurturant behavior, it would be equally unreasonable to discount these factors.

The explanatory directions suggested here imply clearly that gender differences in the provision of care to elderly parents are part and parcel of gender differences in other domains of family behavior. It follows from this that we are not likely to see changes in caregiving behavior in isolation from changes in these other domains. The psychological explanation advanced by Walker in Chapter 3, together with our knowledge of the endocrinology of nurturance, implies that there may be limits to the mutability of human behavior in caregiving and related roles. However, gender stratification is not immutable, although it is very stubborn. As the roles of women and men become more similar in the economic and familial spheres, we may see reductions in gender differences in caregiving roles as well. The prospects for the complete elimination of such differences remain unknown.

9

Methodological Issues in the Study of Gender Within Family Caregiving Relationships

AMY HOROWITZ

As evidenced in the earlier chapters of this collection, the proliferation of research in family caregiving over the last two decades has been phenomenal. This body of research has clearly established that family care to the frail and disabled elderly is not idiosyncratic behavior, but rather a societal phenomenon with clearly identifiable characteristics. In an earlier review of the caregiving literature (Horowitz, 1985a), the importance of gender, as one of the most significant factors determining patterns of family care, was highlighted. Research conducted since this review continues to confirm that attention to gender issues is critical if we are to appreciate fully the complexity and variability of the caregiving experience. Although the vast majority of studies continue to be descriptive, we have also witnessed an increasing sophistication in both the conceptual and methodological approaches applied to the study of family care. This trend has been observed in the general caregiving research as well as in research specific to the study of gender influences within the context of family care (Gwyther & George, 1986; Zarit, 1989). In fact, these more recent research efforts, utilizing multivariate conceptual and analytic models and relatively larger, more representative samples of caregivers, have more clearly called attention to the methodolog-

AUTHOR'S NOTE: I would like to acknowledge Joann P. Reinhardt, Ph.D., of the Lighthouse Department of Research for her very helpful comments on earlier drafts of this chapter.

ical limitations that have characterized much of the previous research in family caregiving. It is this latter body of methodologically problematic studies, however, upon which we have based our current understanding of gender differences in the care of the elderly.

The purpose of this chapter is to review the range of methodological issues that arise in the study of gender differences in family caregiving and to explore the extent to which these problems may cloud our understanding of gender influences and/or limit our ability to examine key questions relative to gender differences in the care of the elderly. The methodological concerns that will be discussed include issues relevant to sample recruitment, small sample sizes, the traditional focus on primary caregivers to the exclusion of the larger family caregiving network, reporting and measurement biases, and the predominance of both cross-sectional and quantitative research designs. Relevant to each of these areas is the sophistication (or lack thereof) of the analytic techniques used. As will be more fully developed later in the chapter, it is argued that many of these general issues are interdependent, with the most serious problems and analytic constraints stemming from the variety of sample deficiencies.

It is not the intent of this chapter to provide a substantive review of the literature on gender differences in family care. That task has been successfully addressed by authors of the other chapters within this volume. Specific trends in research findings will be referred to, however, when relevant to the methodological issue being addressed. Nor is it the intent of this discussion to provide a prescription for "problem-free" research, for there are no easy solutions to the multitude of methodological problems that confront researchers concerned with gender differences in family care. Rather, the goals of this review are to identify clearly some of the methodological problems that do exist in the study of gender-specific caregiving, to discuss their implications for the substantive interpretation of research findings, and to suggest directions for future research that may help us better understand the phenomena of family caregiving as it is influenced by the gender of the actors.

Biases in Sample Recruitment
Leading to Male Underrepresentation

One of the most consistent findings in the literature is the predominance of women as the primary caregivers to older people (see Horowitz, 1985a, for a review; see also Brody, 1985; Brody, Dempsey, & Pruchno, 1990;

George & Gwyther, 1986; Horowitz, 1985b; Montgomery & Datwyler, 1990; Stone, Cafferata, & Sangl, 1987). Most study samples of primary caregivers report gender distributions of approximately 75% female to 25% male or, if limited to spouse caregivers, two-thirds female to one-third male. There are several reasons, however, to hypothesize that men are underrepresented in samples of primary caregivers relative to their actual assumption of this role and thus to question, if not the general direction, at least the accuracy of these typical gender distributions.

First, the vast majority of studies reported in the literature select samples either from publicly supported programs serving the disabled elderly or from organizations providing support services to family caregivers. Male caregivers, however, are far less likely than their female counterparts either to participate in caregiver support groups or to utilize formal services at any stage during their caregiving careers (Noelker & Wallace, 1985; Snyder & Keefe, 1985; Toseland & Rossiter, 1989). Furthermore, the utilization of formal services to complement informal care tends to be more common in the later stages of the caregiving career, as the disability of the older relative increases beyond the ability of the caregiver to manage without such assistance (Horowitz, 1985a). It has been suggested, however, that nonspouse male caregivers may abdicate the role of primary caregiver as the demands of the role increase (Montgomery & Kamo, 1989). As a result, men would be less likely to be found caring for the most severely impaired elders, who are the primary recipients of community-based formal services. Thus when either support groups for caregivers or formal home care or day-care programs for older adults are used as sampling frames for primary caregivers, we can be assured that male primary caregivers will be underrepresented to some extent.

Second, even if we can initially find them, men are generally less likely than women to participate voluntarily as study subjects, regardless of the research topic (Rosenthal & Rosnow, 1975). Lower participation rates of men have been attributed to their relative unwillingness, compared with women, to discuss personal feelings and experiences as well as to their perception of having less time available for research participation. In any case, the response rates of males and females typically differ in caregiving research, resulting in further underrepresentation of males. For example, Horowitz (1985b) reports that only 58% of the sons, compared with 78% of the daughters, who were identified as the primary caregiver to an older parent participated as study respondents.

Third, access to male caregivers, especially nonspouses, is often blocked by the older care recipient long before the researcher ever has the opportunity to seek the direct cooperation of the caregiver. It is not uncommon, especially in studies of the physically rather than severely cognitively impaired elderly, for investigators first to select a sample of older disabled adults, who then identify and give permission to contact their primary and/or network of caregivers. This technique has been used not only in small local studies of caregiving (e.g., Horowitz, Silverstone, & Reinhardt, 1991) but also in the National Long-Term Care Survey (U.S. Department of Health and Human Services, 1984), which has served as the data base for a multitude of recent research studies (e.g., Coward & Dwyer, 1990; Dwyer & Coward, 1991; Dwyer & Seccombe, 1991; B. Miller, 1989; Stone et al., 1987; Stone & Short, 1990). My own experience, however, has been that older persons are significantly less likely to give permission for a researcher to contact a son than to contact a daughter. It is hard to estimate the extent of this bias, since such data are seldom reported in the literature. However, it appears that gender biases and expectations play an important role in this process. The comments of older parents suggest that they believe that sons are "too busy" to be interviewed, while daughters are not. Furthermore, it may be hypothesized that, as a function of the closer emotional bond with female offspring, older parents perceive this "imposition" to pose a much smaller risk to their relationships with daughters than to their relationships with sons.

While it is not suggested here that a "bias-free" sample, even if such a sample were possible in an ideal world, would result in an equal distribution of male and female caregivers, these inherent biases in caregiving samples have important implications. First, it must be recognized that men who participate in caregiving research are likely to be somehow different from their nonparticipating counterparts. In all probability, they represent the most committed and involved of male caregivers (in fact, it may be for this reason that samples of male caregivers are primarily dominated by spouses). While this bias clearly holds true for female caregivers as well, it can be argued that there is a qualitative difference in the case of men, precisely because research participation represents a behavior more atypical for males than for females.

Second, and most critically, we must not only acknowledge that male caregivers are underrepresented in caregiving research relative to their incidence of being identified as either primary or secondary caregivers, but consider the implications of these sampling biases in the interpretation of study findings. One example of how these biases may manifest themselves is in the interpretation of research results regarding the magnitude of mental health effects. George and Gwyther (1986) have argued that the measurement of caregiving effects must include standardized measures of physical, social, and mental health status, in addition to specific caregiving "burden" and "stress" measures, so that it is possible to compare caregivers to noncaregiving populations and thus better understand the unique consequences of caregiving relative to other life stresses. Several investigators have followed this recommendation and have found that caregivers do tend to score more negatively than noncaregiving populations on a variety of standard mental health measures (see, e.g., Anthony-Bergstone, Zarit, & Gatz, 1988; George & Gwyther, 1986; Pruchno & Potashnik, 1989). However, Schulz, Visintainer, and Williamson (1990), in an extensive review of the literature on the psychiatric and physical morbidity effects of caregiving, have noted that studies in which sample selection strategies depend on service utilization tend to find higher rates of symptomatology than studies in which caregivers are recruited from the general population. They conclude that the latter sampling approach is likely to give a better indication of the real prevalence of psychiatric morbidity in a caregiving population, while the former is likely to yield somewhat inflated rates of morbidity. While elevated depression scores among service-utilizing populations is probably a function of the stress that led to the utilization of support services, the fact that men are underrepresented in such samples, interacting with their tendency to report less stress than women (Horowitz, 1985a), must be seen as a contributory factor to this discrepancy in findings. Thus sample biases in recruitment contribute to biases in study findings and lead us to question some of our most basic "truths" about the caregiving experience.

There are no easy solutions to these sample selection dilemmas. However, as a first step to understanding the extent of the bias better, it is strongly recommended that investigators begin systematically to report response rates, at all levels of contact, in published reports. Second, the field would benefit greatly from studies that specifically focus on sample biases. Only one example was found in the recent literature (Dura & Kiecolt-Glaser, 1990), and this study was limited by its small sample size (a topic that will be covered in depth in the following section). Thus future studies of sample biases must be as sensitive to issues of sample size as general studies of caregiving experiences.

Limitations Due to Small Sample Sizes

Unfortunately, most caregiving research continues to be conducted on relatively small and/or unspecified samples. Moreover, the constraints imposed by small sample sizes lie at the heart of a wide range of methodological and, especially, analytic limitations in the study of gender-specific caregiving.

Even under the best sampling plans, there is no doubt that men represent a low-incidence subgroup within general samples of primary caregivers. Unless there is an oversampling of males (which is rare) or the study is limited to spouse caregivers (in which case the gender distribution is less likely to be as extreme), investigators often find themselves with too few cases of males for extensive and/or comprehensive gender analyses. This problem pervades the caregiving literature, as exemplified by the following quotes. Although these are offered out of context of the specific study purpose, they are presented here to underscore the extent and seriousness of the problem:

(1) "Because of small sample size, no formal analyses were conducted for the younger men" (Anthony-Bergstone et al., 1988, p. 246).

(2) "The small male sample size prohibited testing the usefulness of the three time period model separately for male and female caregivers" (Pruchno, Kleban, Michaels, & Dempsey, 1990, p. 196).

(3) "Results must be interpreted cautiously because the number of men included in the study was relatively small" (Pruchno et al., 1990, p. 198).

(4) "The small size of the sample of sons necessitated a reduction in the number of independent variables for the regression analyses" (Montgomery & Kamo, 1989, p. 218; see also Brody et al., 1990, p. 216, for a similar statement).

(5) "Only spouses, nonspouses and daughters were analyzed, as other types of relationships were too small in number for full regression analyses" (Morycz, 1985, p. 348)

(6) "Predictive power of particular variables was constrained by the size of the sample" (Morycz, 1985, p. 354).

(7) "Stray cases (sons, nieces/nephews, siblings) were deleted from this analysis (comparisons of wives, husbands, and daughters) due to the numbers being too small for the preferred statistical analyses" (Young & Kahana, 1989, p. 665).

(8) "It was not possible to obtain adequate numbers of participants in certain cells of interest (e.g. husbands, sons, and other male caregivers). . . . Also, given the fact that the sample was broken down still further in terms of presence or absence of cognitive impairment of the care-receiver, some cells had zero participants (e.g., sons caring for a demented parent)" (Gallagher, Rose, Rivera, Lovett, & Thompson, 1989, p. 455).

These limitations and caveats on study findings due to small sample size are even more disconcerting when one considers the range of factors, in addition to gender, that influence the caregiving experience and that must be incorporated in multivariate analyses, either as control variables or to define subgroups, in order to understand the independent influence of gender more accurately. The importance of the kin relationship, for example, in predicting both caregiving behavior and experiences has been consistently identified in the literature (Dwyer & Seccombe, 1991; Horowitz, 1985a; Young & Kahana, 1989). The reactions, motivations, and stresses of caregiving wives are quantitatively and qualitatively different from those of daughters, just as the experiences of husbands differ from those of sons. As a field of inquiry, we have progressed far beyond the point where it is acceptable simply to contrast data on males and females to arrive at conclusions about gender differences in caregiving without taking into account the interactive effects of the kin relationship.

While the importance of the kin relationship is well established and is generally incorporated in study designs, a multitude of other factors also need to be considered. In recent years researchers, some utilizing large data sets and multivariate analytic strategies, have begun to challenge many generalizations about gender differences in caregiving and to provide greater in-depth understanding of the conditions under which gender does or does not make a difference. Coward and Dwyer (1990), for example, have examined the composition of the sibling networks of adult child caregivers. Caregivers were separated according to whether they were only children, in single-gender networks, or in mixed-gender networks. Gender differences were identified only for those in the last group. In contrast, sons and daughters in only-child and single-gender networks reported similar numbers of hours per day spent in parent care and experienced comparable levels of stress and burden. Matthews (1987) has also reported that the size and gender distribution of the sibling network affected the division of labor in parent care, in that larger sibling networks (i.e., four or more) and those that included a brother were more likely to have at least one sibling who did not engage in the care of the parent. Furthermore, findings from other studies indicate that the age of the spouse caregiver moderates the relationship between gender and burden (Fitting, Rabins, Lucas, & Eastham, 1986); that employment status differentially influences the care provided by sons and daughters (Stoller, 1983; Stone & Short, 1990); that the closer proximity of the adult child reduces observed gender differences in parent-child interactions (Mercier, Paulson, & Morris, 1989); and that when marital status is controlled, older unmarried women and men do not differ in their living arrangements (Spitze & Logan, 1989).

Research findings such as those noted in the previous paragraph provide some evidence of the complex relationship between gender and patterns of caregiving, and suggest that gender may not be the "all-powerful" predictor of differences under certain conditions. This research also highlights the limitations inherent in gross comparisons of males and females without further specification of the larger context within which caregiving is embedded. Other key control variables, such as cohort, social class, and ethnicity, to cite just a few examples, have yet to be explored extensively. Does age/cohort moderate the relationship between gender and caregiving experiences for adult children as well as for spouses? That is, do gender differences become less pronounced among adult children in their 30s and 40s who matured during a period of social change that included the women's movement? Are males and females who are comparable in social class and financial resources also comparable in their tendency to purchase rather than provide care services? Are expectations for gender-appropriate caregiving behavior different in various ethnic communities? These are only a few examples of the types of questions that depend upon the availability of large and/or well-specified samples of caregivers in order to ensure that the cells of interest have sufficient numbers for multivariate analyses.

In addition to constraining analytic options, small and unspecified samples have also precluded researchers from even attempting to address various critical research questions relevant to gender issues. For example, because evaluations of intervention effectiveness typically rely on small, local samples, and because women predominate among support service users, we know absolutely nothing about the men who do use such services and what benefits may accrue to them. This knowledge might, in turn, provide evidence on how to adapt existing services to attract male caregivers (Toseland & Rossiter, 1989; Zarit & Toseland, 1989), since it has been suggested that differences in the sources of stress for men and women are likely to call for different types of interventions (Gwyther & George, 1986; Noelker & Wallace, 1985). This is an area that has been relatively ignored for a variety of reasons, not the least of which are the difficulties in recruiting appropriate and sufficiently large samples of male respondents.

Another critical issue that has been ignored concerns the relative importance of the caregiver-care receiver gender interaction, especially in parent-child dyads, in influencing patterns of family care. Typical samples of family caregivers are characterized by "normative" caregiving patterns: older wives caring for disabled husbands and daughters caring for older widowed mothers. Such patterns predominate as a function of gender differences in morbidity and mortality as well as of gender influences in the selection of the primary caregiver to older parents. Yet, although less typical, some daughters do provide care to older fathers, and sons can be found in the role of primary caregiver to older mothers as well as fathers.

Although very little is known about how the gender of the care receiver interacts with the gender of the caregiver to influence the course and experience of caregiving, there is some preliminary evidence to suggest that this is a factor of significance. For example, spouse caregivers have been found to turn to children of the same sex to provide support (Barusch & Spaid, 1989) and husband caregivers have been reported to receive more assistance from their sons than from their daughters (Kaye & Applegate, 1990a). Finley, Roberts, and Banahan (1988) report that, although filial obligations were similarly high among sons and daughters in their study, the predictors of obligation differed not only by the gender of the child but by the gender of the parent referenced. Furthermore, Stoller (1990) found that when non-spouse caregivers were identified by older persons, they tended to be of the same sex, with older fathers more likely to name sons than daughters. This latter finding offers a tentative alternative hypothesis for the predominance of daughter caregivers. That is, most parent-care situations involve older widowed mothers and thus same-sex caregivers. Older fathers, for whom sons might be the more likely caregivers, are less often in situations where they require assistance from adult children because they are more likely to have spouses available to assume primary responsibility. Unfortunately, widowed fathers in need of caregiving assistance represent such rare events that their unique caregiving circumstances remain largely unexplored. Thus large and/or carefully selected samples are critical if we are to pick up atypical dyads of caregivers and care receivers and explore differences that result as a function of gender interactions.

In sum, the field of family caregiving research has matured beyond the point where research on small, local, unspecified samples of caregivers can further contribute to our knowledge base on gender differences in family caregiving. Such samples simply do not provide the analytic power required to address the current questions of interest. In lieu of a major influx of research monies to support a new generation of large sample studies, we must look for alternatives to overcome the constraints imposed by small samples.

One, less satisfactory, alternative has been simply to eliminate gender as a confounding factor. That is, many investigators have chosen to focus solely on the caregiving experiences of women (e.g., Brody, 1981; Crossman, London, & Barry, 1981; Fengler & Goodrich, 1979; Matthews, 1987). The rationale has been that since women predominate as primary caregivers, their experiences represent the norm of caregiving. Such studies have clearly contributed to our understanding of caregiving by wives and daughters and, to a lesser extent, by sisters, granddaughters, nieces, and daughters-in-law. At the same time, it is obvious that such research does nothing to advance our understanding of gender differences in the experience of caregiving.

In reaction to the predominance of research on women, as well as to the limitations posed by small numbers of males in general caregiving studies, other investigators have focused solely on the experiences of male caregivers (e.g., Kaye & Applegate, 1990a). Research of this type has brought attention to this often ignored group of caregivers, and thus serves an important polemic function. In addition, male-only samples allow for more in-depth exploration of issues unique to the male caregiving experience and therefore represent an important preliminary strategy that can serve to suggest substantive topics for future research.

There are, however, obvious disadvantages to single-sex samples. Although findings from male-only samples can be contrasted with the general literature on caregiving experiences, because of extensive variation in both sampling criteria and measures across studies, such research contributes less to our understanding of gender variations than do studies that include both males and females and that permit comparative analyses within the same study boundaries. Furthermore, whether by design or outcome, studies of male caregivers have largely translated into studies of husbands. Kaye and Applegate (1990a) have found male caregiving to be predominantly a spousal experience; it is less frequently played out within the context of a mother-son relationship.

A more promising alternative is the increased utilization of available data sets that include representative samples of elders and/or their caregivers. As noted earlier, investigators who have conducted secondary analyses on data available from, for example, the Supplement on Aging to the 1984 National Health Interview Survey, the U.S. Census, the National Long-Term Care Survey, and the National Survey of Informal Caregivers (Coward, Cutler, & Schmidt, 1989; Coward & Dwyer, 1990; Dwyer & Coward, 1991; Dwyer & Seccombe, 1991; B. Miller, 1989; Spitze & Logan, 1989; Stone et al., 1987; Stone & Short, 1990), have made major contributions to our knowledge base on gender influences in caregiving. Fiscal realities, coupled with the imperative to go beyond gross descriptive research, compel us to increase our creativity in formulating research questions that can be examined fruitfully within the data bases now available for secondary analyses.

Another alternative is to target and define samples of caregivers more specifically so that they are consistent with the research questions of interest. "First come, first recruited" caregiving samples will continue to produce findings that describe "normative" caregiving patterns. As we become more interested in variations from the norm, these samples will simply not meet our needs. Sample designs must be a function of the questions being posed, and as our questions become more sophisticated and specific, so must our sampling strategies and criteria. To give just one example, if the interest is in exploring whether gender differences among spouses and offspring are of similar magnitude when caring for physically versus cognitively impaired elders, samples must be stratified to ensure adequate variation in gender, impairment type, and kin relationship to conduct the appropriate analyses. Researchers must continue to struggle with the appropriate balance between large, heterogeneous samples and those that are carefully defined to meet specific research needs.

Sole, Primary, Secondary, and Potential Caregivers

Our understanding of the caregiving contributions and experiences of men has also been severely constrained by the predominant focus on the "primary" caregiver; that is, the one family member who takes primary responsibility for managing care and/or who provides the vast majority of services to the frail elderly relative. This concentration of research on the primary caregiver is not surprising given that, with the exception of Matthews and her colleagues (Matthews, 1987; Matthews & Rosner, 1988; Matthews & Sprey, 1989), most research has continued to confirm the central role played by a primary caregiver in the care of the disabled elderly (e.g., Brody, Hoffman, Kleban, & Schoonover, 1989; Horowitz, 1985a; Tennstedt, McKinlay, & Sullivan, 1989). At the same time, however, there has been increasing awareness of the importance of distinguishing among different *types* of caregivers in order to add depth to our understanding of the role of gender in influencing the caregiving experience.

Dwyer and Coward (1991), for example, argue that samples limited to only those adult children who have already assumed the caregiving role, rather than including the entire sibling network, may obscure any gender bias that may exist in caregiver selection and involvement. That is, they argue that all *potential* caregivers must be taken into account if we are to understand better the role of gender in determining who provides care, as well as what types of care, to impaired parents. Dwyer and Coward's findings, using all living children of a national sample of impaired elders, support previous research regarding the greater involvement of daughters, compared with sons, in both ADL and IADL assistance to elderly impaired parents, and thus provide an even stronger empirical base for estimating the effects of gender on both actual and potential caregiving behavior. Further support is provided by Horowitz (1985b) who examined the sibling networks of adult son primary caregivers and found that the role of primary caregiver was often taken on by default by male offspring; that is, the vast majority of sons were only children, members of male-only sibling networks, or the only geographically available children. Such research further highlights the fact that studies that are confined to *identified* caregivers may give only a partial picture of the importance of gender in influencing caregiver behavior.

Another distinction that is seldom made, but that has important implications for understanding gender-specific caregiving involvement, is that between primary and sole caregivers. Although the word *primary* implies that there is a network of secondary caregivers available, this is not always the case in actual experience. Stone et al. (1987) report that only slightly more than half of all primary caregivers receive assistance from other informal and/or formal providers, with the remainder more accurately described as *sole* caregivers. Furthermore, while spouses constitute the majority of sole caregivers, daughters were twice as likely as sons to assume the primary responsibility with no assistance. Again, this distinction provides additional depth to our understanding of gender differences in caregiving, and future researchers would be well served to incorporate variables specifying caregiver types in their analytic models.

In contrast to the relatively limited focus on distinguishing either potential from actual caregivers or sole from primary caregivers, recent research has been giving increasing attention to the contributions and experiences of secondary caregivers (e.g., Brody et al., 1989; Kleban, Brody, Schoonover, & Hoffman, 1989; Matthews & Sprey, 1989; Tennstedt et al., 1989). As a result, we have gained a better understanding of the involvement of men as the husbands, brothers, and sons of the women who serve as primary caregivers to their older parents and husbands. In these roles males provide significant services for the elders and support for primary caregivers, and experience levels of caregiving stress that we have only begun to explore. Overall, we are coming to appreciate that unless our research designs include these secondary caregivers, we will continue to have only a partial picture of both the family caregiving experience as a whole and the role of males within this experience.

While the movement toward the study of the family caregiving *system*, rather than the caregiving dyad, represents a significant development in caregiving research, many studies of secondary caregivers remain methodologically limited because they collect data about, rather than from, secondary caregivers (e.g., Matthews & Rosner, 1988; Tennstedt et al., 1989). Thus our understanding of the role of secondary caregivers in general, and especially of men who occupy this role, derives largely from the perceptions of primary caregivers. There is evidence, however, that we may be wise to question the validity of such reports. Where multiple respondents have been interviewed, discrepancies in responses have been more the rule than the exception. For example, husbands of adult daughter caregivers have been found to perceive their wives' burden as more severe than do the wives themselves and to be less likely than their wives to report that caregiving has negatively affected the marital relationship (Kleban et al., 1989). Sisters caring for an older mother were found to differ substantially in their perceptions of how responsibility was divided with respect to specific tasks, how close the families were, and how adequately their parents' needs were being met (Matthews, 1987). Townsend and Poulshock (1986) have also reported that older people tended to underreport the total number of helpers when compared with their adult child caregivers. This last finding raises questions about *who* is the most appropriate source for identifying the network of secondary caregivers.

Thus our current body of knowledge about the contributions of secondary caregivers, male or female, remains only suggestive. It is critical that future research not only address questions relevant to the larger family caregiving system, but include multiple respondents within study samples. This is not, in any way, to underestimate the very difficult methodological challenges posed by multiple respondent designs, both in terms of sample recruitment and data analysis. These problems do exist, but they are not insurmountable. Furthermore, such research will also require a philosophical shift on the part of some investigators, who, by training and often by temperament, seek to bring some order and logic to the complexity of human behavior. Multiple-respondent studies will most likely reveal multiple "truths" about any one caregiving situation that may not be capable of resolution, but that, by its very existence, will add to our understanding of an extremely complex family experience.

Reporting Biases in Mental Health Effects

While there are exceptions, the majority of studies find that men tend to report lower levels of burden, stress, depression, and other mental health effects of caregiving than do women (see Horowitz, 1985a, for a review; see also Barusch & Spaid, 1989; Brody, 1985; Fitting et al., 1986; Gallagher et al., 1989; Horowitz, 1985b; B. Miller, 1989; Noelker & Wallace, 1985; Pruchno & Potashnik, 1989; Young & Kahana, 1989). Such gender differences appear to apply to proximate secondary caregivers (Brody et al., 1989), geographically distant caregivers (Schoonover, Brody, Hoffman, & Kleban, 1988), and caregivers to the institutionalized elderly (Brody et al., 1990), as well as to primary caregivers to the disabled elderly living in the community.

Many reasons have been offered in the literature to explain this gender difference. It has been hypothesized that male caregivers tend to receive more emotional as well as concrete support from informal networks, and that this support serves to reduce caregiving burden (Johnson, 1983; Noelker & Wallace, 1985). Others have suggested that older husbands become more invested in the marital role as they age and become more nurturing, while wives, in contrast, seek to continue and expand their lifelong involvement with larger social networks (Noelker & Poulshock, 1982). Therefore, it is hypothesized that the demands of caregiving are likely to be accepted more by husbands and resented more by wives. Daughters have been found to have stronger emotional ties to their mothers than do sons and therefore are hypothesized to be more emotionally affected by the decline of the parent and the responsibility for care (Robinson & Thurnher, 1979). Brody (1981, 1985, 1990) has also called attention to the stresses imposed on the "women in the middle," as well as to the fact that women have been socialized as nurturers. In the latter role, they are likely to see themselves as responsible for the total care and well-being of their parents and, yet, can never meet their own expectations. The resulting disparity intensifies the strain of caregiving.

While all of the above explanations for gender differences in the mental health effects of caregiving have merit, we cannot forget an alternative hypothesis that may call into question our current understanding of these reported differences. That is, it has been hypothesized that men simply do not express stress in the same way or to the same degree as do women (Davis, Priddy, & Tinklenberg, 1986; Kleban et al., 1989). As a result of gender-specific socialization patterns, men tend to place a higher value on the *appearance* of competence. Admissions of coping failure are not easily made. Men may, therefore, underreport both the burden and the depressive symptomatology they experience as a consequence of caregiving. While several investigators have noted this caveat in their research findings (e.g., Barusch & Spaid, 1989; Pruchno & Resch, 1989; Schoonover et al., 1988; Zarit, Todd, & Zarit, 1986), few have further explored its implications.

This is an issue that has plagued mental health epidemiologists for decades and one for which there is no easy solution. It is, however, a methodological issue that we must continue to recognize and attempt to address. The trend toward using standardized measures of mental health status is a positive one, in that male caregivers can be compared with their noncaregiver counterparts. Whatever reporting biases exist would affect both groups equally. While this helps us understand the relative stress created by caregiving for males, it still does not address the degree to which we can have faith in the gender differences that have been reported. To address this issue, we must continue to examine the multiple dimensions and sources of caregiving stress (e.g., financial strain, task burden, emotional stress, social activity limitations) and look at gender differences within the various dimensions, in order to achieve a better understanding of exactly how, and in what areas, men and women differ in their reported experience of the caregiving role.

Cross-Sectional Versus Longitudinal Designs

In an earlier review, it was noted that cross-sectional designs predominate in the study of family caregiving (Horowitz, 1985a). As a result, we have only a limited understanding of the dynamic nature of the caregiving experience, and how the behaviors and reactions of caregivers may vary over time as a function of changes in the needs of the older relative as well as changes in the internal and external resources available to the family caregivers. Unfortunately, with few exceptions, the reliance on cross-sectional research has continued.

In addition to a variety of other constraints that are beyond the scope of this discussion, cross-sectional study designs may also be a factor in underestimating the extent to which males participate in caregiving over time. Montgomery and Kamo (1989) have noted that as the needs of an older parent increase beyond those for transportation and financial assistance, daughters are more likely than sons to retain the caregiving role. In contrast, a pattern of brief, less intense caregiving characterizes the behavior of sons, and they are less likely to continue to help throughout the length of the parent's disability period. As a result, Montgomery and Kamo (1989) have suggested that if sons do abdicate the caregiving role at earlier stages than do daughters, cross-sectional studies will inevitably underestimate the extent to which sons actually participate in caregiving. Findings from research conducted by Stoller and Pugliesi (1989) support this hypothesis in that, contrary to other studies, sons and daughters were equally identified as caregivers for moderately impaired parents. Brody et al. (1990) also found that although sons continued to provide support to institutionalized parents, the parents of daughters in nursing homes were more impaired than those of sons, suggesting that daughters may be keeping their parents in the community for longer periods of time and at higher levels of disability.

In addition to the limitations imposed by cross-sectional designs, this issue again highlights the importance of initial sampling decisions. That is, if we are interested only in patterns of caregiving to the most severely impaired elderly, then it is appropriate to select our samples accordingly, but, at the same time, we must be aware that we will continue to document the predominance of women as caregivers. However, if our interest is in the continuum of the "caregiving career," as well as in understanding the extent to which men engage in caregiving throughout its various stages, then only longitudinal study designs, with baseline measures taken at early stages of an elder's impairment, will provide us with the framework to explore these questions. Here, again, secondary analyses of available longitudinal data sets, such as the Supplement on Aging to the National Health Interview Survey and the Long-Term Care Survey, can help achieve this goal.

Qualitative Versus Quantitative Designs

Just as the literature has been dominated by cross-sectional rather than longitudinal research designs, it has also been characterized by quantitative rather than qualitative research (Abel, 1990b). In many respects, the current generation of quantitative studies has been built upon the foundation established by the early qualitative research in family caregiving. This does not mean, however, that qualitative research should be abandoned. On the contrary, we still have much to learn from in-depth qualitative studies about the meaning attached to caregiving as well as the social and emotional context of caregiving, especially as it is differentially experienced by males and females (Mancini, 1989b; Mancini & Blieszner, 1989). For example, in one of the few recent qualitative studies reported in the literature, B. Miller (1987) found that husband and wife caregivers differed in their perceptions of control over the caregiving situation and the degree to which they were comfortable in assuming authority. Issues of control were more problematic for wives because they were accustomed to deferring to their husbands' authority. Wives were also more concerned with maintaining the dignity of their demented spouses. Men, on the other hand, were more comfortable being in charge of another person, as this was seen as a logical extension of their role as authority figure at home and at work. Findings from qualitative research can thus contribute to a better understanding of the *causes* of the stresses experienced by caregivers and how such causes may differ for men and women.

Qualitative research can, therefore, help address a methodological problem that has recently been identified in quantitative research. That is, as both the questions being asked and the analytic strategies have become more sophisticated, there has been a move away from simply considering gender as one of many predictor variables and toward simultaneous gender-specific multivariate analyses in order to identify whether predictors remain similar in type and/or strength for men and women (Brody et al., 1990; Montgomery & Kamo, 1989; Morycz, 1985; Pruchno & Resch, 1989; Pruchno et al., 1990). The problem has been, however, that although a variety of significant predictors of mental health effects are identified for women, most of these studies report that these same variables fail to have sufficient explanatory power in the case of men. Pruchno and Resch (1989) have suggested that since we have not yet been able to identify those variables that are most useful in predicting the mental health of men, future research needs to address more complex constructs, such as the meaning attached to the caregiving role, in order to increase our understanding of the caregiving experience and effects for male caregivers. Qualitative research can make an important contribution in this area.

Conclusion

By focusing in this chapter on the methodological problems that have characterized this field of study, it is not my intent to present a bleak portrait of the current state of the art. On the contrary, there has been a great deal of progress over the last several years in both the conceptual models and the analytic strategies applied to the study of gender issues in family care. Overall, we have become more precise in identifying the conditions under which gender does or does not influence the course and consequences of the caregiving experience. It is precisely because of these advances, which have added a deeper layer to our understanding of the role played by gender, that we have become more cognizant of the problems that have plagued previous research efforts. Future research must now build upon this knowledge and, as our questions about the caregiving experience become more sophisticated, so must our research strategies.

The purpose of this review has been to highlight some of the methodological problems that confront researchers in the study of gender issues in family care to the disabled elderly, as well as to suggest some directions for future research that may address and/or mitigate these problems. The major issues discussed are summarized below:

- Men have been underrepresented in caregiving samples because of the predominance of research on service-utilizing populations, the tendency for men to have lower response rates than women, and the greater likelihood of care receivers to refuse permission to contact male offspring.
- Research has suffered from the limitations imposed by small sample sizes, especially the constraints on multivariate analytic options.
- A predominance of research has been on primary caregivers, a practice that has contributed to the underestimation of the total contribution of men; there has also been a tendency to collect information about, rather than from, secondary caregivers.
- Reporting biases in mental health effects, specifically the tendency for men to underreport negative effects, have been insufficiently explored.
- The predominance of cross-sectional designs, and the implications of these designs for underestimation of the contributions of men to caregiving, especially for the less severely disabled elderly, has limited understanding of the nature of the caregiving experience.
- Quantitative research has failed to identify the variables that are most salient in predicting mental health effects for male caregivers.
- There has been a relative absence of qualitative research in the field, and as a result we have limited understanding of the meanings attached to caregiving and the contexts within which the caregiving experience is embedded.

The following recommendations are offered in an effort to address these concerns:

- Greater attention should be given to the implications of sample biases in the interpretation of findings.
- There should be systematic reporting of response rates for males and females at all levels of contact with the study sample, including contacts with the elders who provide access to their network of caregivers.
- More research should be undertaken that is specifically focused on understanding the extent and sources of sample biases.
- More research should be undertaken utilizing available large data sets for secondary analyses.
- There should be greater targeting and specificity in sampling plans so that they are consistent with the specific research questions of interest.
- More research should be focused on the total family caregiving network, utilizing designs that include multiple respondents.

- There should be increased emphasis on longitudinal studies, beginning at the early stages of the caregiving career, in order to capture fully the contributions and experiences of male caregivers.
- There should be increased emphasis on qualitative research, which will enrich our understanding of the context of caregiving, including the different sources of stress for male and female caregivers.

10

Gender and
Family Care of the Elderly

Research Gaps and Opportunities

JEFFREY W. DWYER
RAYMOND T. COWARD

The volume of research on family caregiving that has been published, and the frequency with which gender is included as a significant differentiating characteristic in the caregiving context, has grown tremendously over the last decade. Yet, this area of research is still evolving. As a result, there are a number of gaps in our present knowledge base and opportunities for future research that, if addressed, will enhance our ability to facilitate the creation of gender-sensitive family and aging policies that can be implemented successfully in the practice environment.

This chapter is organized around six areas of family caregiving research that we believe have particularly significant implications for understanding the role of gender in the social context of caregiving. These areas are divided into two sections: one that addresses *how* we should build a knowledge base for the study of gender and family care of the elderly, and a second that focuses on *what* aspects of family caregiving hold the greatest potential for furthering our knowledge.

In our judgment, a gender-sensitive family caregiving research agenda for the 1990s should emphasize the application of theory to research, the replication of research findings, and the use of longitudinal studies. In addition, our understanding of the role that gender plays in the caregiving context will be significantly improved if future research concerns itself with making cultural comparisons, with disentangling the effects of gender from other covariates, and with understanding whole families rather than only caregiving dyads.

Before we begin our discussion of these issues, however, four caveats are in order. First, we have not limited the issues addressed in this chapter to those that apply *exclusively* to the impact of gender on family caregiving. That is, many of the topics discussed in this chapter are also applicable to the broader family caregiving literature (e.g., the application of theory to research and the use of longitudinal studies and cultural comparisons). Second, we do not contend that our list of priorities is all-inclusive, only that these are among the most important issues in the gender/family/aging literature. Third, with one exception, we do not focus on methodological issues, because these have been addressed in Chapter 9 of this volume. Finally, we use selective examples to make our points, rather than citing multiple studies; where appropriate, we also make direct reference to other chapters in this volume.

Building a Knowledge Base

The Application of Theory to Research

Studies that have focused on gender and family care of the elderly have typically not been driven by theory; rather, they have examined specific "problems" in the caregiving environment (e.g., perceived inequities or the negative consequences of caring for an older person) (Lee, 1985b). Hagestad (1987) has argued, for example, that "much of the current knowledge on the later phase of parent-child ties has come about because social scientists have responded to pressing social and political issues, rather than having as their primary goal the building of systematic knowledge" (p. 405).

Theory, however, should assume a more prominent role in the process of research. Merton (1968) has identified five functions of theory in the research context: (a) to orient and direct research, (b) to summarize facts (i.e., empirical generalizations), (c) to organize facts into a system (theoretical propositions), (d) to provide a mechanism for predicting facts (causality), and (e) to point out gaps in knowledge. Unfortunately, to date, the use of theory in the study of gender and family care of the elderly has been limited primarily to the first two of these "functions": orienting research and summarizing facts. We believe that future efforts in this line of inquiry should expand the use of theory to Merton's last three functions as well. Specifically, we would argue that investigators should focus on the development of theoretical propositions and systems of causal statements that will enhance our understanding of the gendered nature of family caregiving and point out gaps in our present knowledge base. Thus, in addition to developing and refining our theories of gender differences (a recommendation offered in Chapter 8 in this volume), we also need to expand the number of empirically based investigations that attempt to apply theoretical propositions to the explanation of specific caregiving behaviors.

Replication

All scientific study should be oriented toward identifying and verifying empirical realities. Verification occurs in two ways: (a) predicting outcomes with a level of confidence that exceeds chance, and (b) building consensus through replication (Lastrucci, 1967). It is this latter method of verification, replication, that is frequently missing in the literature described throughout this volume. Too much of what we "know" (or think we know) about specific aspects of the relationship between gender and family care of the elderly has a relatively "thin" empirical base. To correct that deficiency, we believe that researchers in this area should focus on two types of replication studies, and that, in addition, two discipline-based issues need to be addressed in order to facilitate such research.

Types of replication studies. The most common type of replication occurs when researchers ask similar questions and test comparable hypotheses with different data sources. By achieving like results over repeated trials, it is possible to build consensus regarding the empirical reality under study. We can confidently state that daughters are more likely to provide caregiving assistance to parents than are sons, for example, because this finding has been reported in dozens of studies using a wide range of samples of elders and their helpers.

In contrast, there are many other important aspects of the relationship between gender and family care of the elderly that have not been confirmed through repeated studies. For example, several of the authors in this volume have alluded to an observed tendency for caregivers to be of the same gender as care receivers, yet these observations are based on evidence from only one or two studies. In our opinion, before this and similar propositions become "conventional wisdom" in the family caregiving literature, much more replication is needed. We need to ask, for example, whether the tendency for sons to care for fathers and daughters to care for mothers is observed when the genders of all siblings are compared—both those who are currently providing help and those who are not. In addition, does this pattern hold true for elders of all racial and ethnic groups? Is the pattern observed among elders who are severely impaired? As a discipline, we should be cautious about accepting propositions and suppositions that are based on findings that have not yet been replicated.

Replication studies should also focus on developing reliable instruments with common components that can be used by others involved in similar research. Measurement focuses on the relationship between an observable, empirically grounded indicator and some underlying unobservable concept (Carmines & Zeller, 1979), and is a critical part of the research process. Among the important qualities of a good measuring procedure or instrument is that it yields the same results over repeated trials—in other words, that it is reliable. Therefore, because reliability is based on replication, we believe that future caregiving studies that focus on gender would be enhanced by greater emphasis on developing and using standardized measurement tools.

At present, many of the most frequently addressed concepts in caregiving research use very different empirical indicators. For example, even among commonly used measures such as ADL and IADL indices, there is a great deal of variability in the specific items included (Wiener, Hanley, Clark, & Van Nostrand, 1990). Similarly, the measurement of caregiver stress and burden, common dependent variables in gender-oriented research, has been accomplished in a variety of different ways and with an assortment of different instruments. As a consequence, our ability to compare findings across studies is severely limited, and replication is often not possible.

Facilitating replication. In order for an enhanced emphasis on replication to be successful, however, two additional, more general, issues need to be addressed. First, some professional journals and editors seem to be reluctant to publish replication studies, appearing instead to prefer research that reports genuinely "new" findings. In our opinion, these gatekeepers need to be convinced that, at least in this area of research, replication is necessary in order for the discipline to build consensus, to gain confidence in our understanding of the gendered nature of family care, and to resolve existing controversies. Although this suggestion may seem to be simultaneously idealistic and unrealistic, given the realities of academic publishing, we would argue that the mechanism for accomplishing this goal is already available. Specifically, in reference to the review process, M. K. Miller (1991) has stated that "it is first and foremost your peers that must be persuaded of the merit of any manuscript" (p. 7). Hence it may be that those of us who are involved in the review of manuscripts in this area should be more tolerant, accepting, and supportive of replication studies.

Second, replication is not possible unless concepts, measurement instruments, and analytic techniques are clearly defined and described by researchers in the literature. Lastrucci (1967), for example, argues that verification is problematic if

> the problem has been loosely formulated, if it has not been made clear which data are pertinent, if all relevant variables have not been accounted for, if the methodology has been inadequate or inept, if the techniques were inappropriate to the data, or if the conditions of analysis were such that empirical demonstrability is impossible. (p. 235)

Too frequently, researchers adopt shorthand methods for describing the methodological or analytic aspects of a study, and thus make it impossible for others to replicate the findings. We believe that those who study the gender/family/aging nexus should be encouraged to conduct their research, and to report their findings, in a manner and style that makes possible the replication of their work by others.

Longitudinal Studies

Although Horowitz has addressed the importance of longitudinal research elsewhere in this volume (see Chapter 9), we feel compelled to repeat it here. Longitudinal research is certainly not new to aging studies. For example, both the Baltimore Longitudinal Study, which "provides 30-year data on several generalized social support measures" (Antonucci, 1990, p. 209), and the Duke Longitudinal Studies, which focus on medical, psychiatric, psychological, and sociological perspectives with data from several decades (Palmore, 1974), have contributed a great deal to our understanding of changes in the aged population over time. Unfortunately, in the caregiving research literature, longitudinal studies are notably absent.

There are a number of topics within gender and family caregiving research that lend themselves to longitudinal analysis. For example, there is evidence in the literature that some caregivers, particularly wives, can provide care over long periods of time (see Chapter 4, this volume). Yet we know very little about the evolution of the caregiving "career" or the ways in which roles and responsibilities ebb and flow over time. In a similar manner, our understanding of the consequences of providing care would be enhanced by data on families and individual family members *before* they began to provide care. At present, because we rarely have measures of the dynamics within a family before the onset of caregiving, it is difficult to separate the *consequences of caregiving* from other dynamics (both positive and negative) that existed prior to an elder's impairment and subsequent need for care. Because the negative consequences of caregiving are more frequently associated with female than with male caregivers, such longitudinal analyses would provide us with better insight into the gendered nature of family care throughout the caregiving experience. There are, of course, many other examples of topics that could benefit from longitudinal analyses; the challenge lies in creating the means to conduct such research.

Existing longitudinal data sets. Primary data collection using a longitudinal research design can be prohibitively expensive and time-consuming. Fortunately, however, there are now several data sources available that can be used by investigators to explore caregiving phenomena from a longitudinal perspective. Although components of these data sets have been used in several studies cited in this volume, we would argue that these resources can be "mined" more completely than has been the case up to now.

The following are brief descriptions of three such data sets, emphasizing their longitudinal features. More complete descriptions are available from the distributors of the data.[1]

- *The 1982-1984 National Long-Term Care Survey* (NLTCS) (U.S. Department of Health and Human Services, 1989): This survey was designed to gather data on a national sample of noninstitutionalized elders who experienced at least one ADL or IADL impairment for a period of at least three months. In 1982, 6,393 elders were interviewed regarding their health status, use of services, and sources of assistance (see Macken, 1986, for a discussion of these data). In addition, data were collected from the elders describing all household members, people who were providing help, and children (both resident and nonresident). In 1984, 4,530 of the elders in the 1982 sample who were still living in the community were reinterviewed. Matching Medicare records for the period 1978-1986 are available for all of these elders. In addition, the longitudinal file includes death and institutionalization records for those elders who were in the original 1982 sample but were not living in the community in 1984. The instrument used in 1984 was nearly identical to that used in 1982, although information is available about important events that occurred during the intervening two-year period. For example, if the elder was institutionalized between 1982 and 1984, the data indicate when and for how long. The 1984 wave of the NLTCS was replicated in 1988, but those data are not yet available as this volume goes to press.

- *The 1982 National Survey of Informal Caregivers* (NSIC) (U.S. Department of Health and Human Services, 1984): The NSIC is linked to the 1982 National Long-Term Care Survey described above. A sample of elders from the 1982 NLTCS who reported receiving assistance with ADL tasks from at least one unpaid caregiver were asked to identify all helpers who provided ADL assistance. The NSIC data set consists of interviews with 1,924 unpaid caregivers of elders from the 1982 NLTCS (see Stone, Cafferata, & Sangl, 1987, for a more detailed description of these data). The data available for these caregivers are extensive and cover information ranging from tasks performed, stress, and burden to employment consequences and basic demographic data. Moreover, the caregiver information can be linked to the elder information from the NLTCS to provide a particularly rich data source when the entire caregiving network is the focus of study. In both of these data sets (i.e., the NLTCS and NSIC) the genders of nearly all participants in the potential caregiving networks of impaired elders are known. The NSIC data, now available only for 1982 (although these data can be used in longitudinal research by linking them to the longitudinal file of the NLTCS), will soon have a 1988 follow-up component available along with the 1988 NLTCS.

- *The National Health Interview Survey: Longitudinal Study on Aging* (NHIS: LSOA) (National Center for Health Statistics, 1990): Data are now available from 1984, 1986, and 1988 for a large sample of community-dwelling elders. Although the characteristics of the respondents vary somewhat from year to year, the Version 3 file contains data on 7,527 people who were age 70 or older at the time of the initial interview (1984). The NHIS:LSOA was originally designed to measure changes in functional ability and living arrangements, but, because the genders of the elders and other household members are known, it has the potential to be useful in gender-oriented family caregiving research. Therefore, although this data set does not contain information on all older people (i.e., it does not include those 65-69), it does provide data on all elders across the full range of functional abilities. Hence it differs from the NLTCS in that it is representative of the general aged population age 70 and over, rather than only those who are impaired. Matching insurance, death, and Medicare records are available in addition to information about movements in and out of institutions.

These are but three examples of existing data sets on which longitudinal analyses can be performed. Our point in describing them is to remind readers that questions about the gendered nature of family care of the elderly that require a time dimension to answer *might* be accomplished without the expense and difficulty of longitudinal primary data collection. We sincerely hope that in the future these and other existing data sets will be used more extensively by family caregiving researchers.

An Agenda for Future Research on the Gendered Nature of Family Caregiving

A general approach to research on gender and family care of the elderly that focuses on the application of theory, the replication of findings, and the use of longitudinal studies will provide important insights into the gendered nature of caregiving relationships. In addition, however, there are three specific areas of research that are likely to be fruitful. The following sections briefly describe these areas and, collectively, represent an agenda for future research that addresses substantial gaps in our present knowledge.

Cultural Comparisons

Social gerontologists have long recognized the influence of culture on the lives of older people. Keith (1990) has argued, for example, that "research investigating social and cultural influences on aging has two important goals: first, the *location* of the aging experience in specific social, cultural, and subjective contexts; and, second, interpretations of the *mechanisms* through which these contexts influence the experiences of aging" (p. 91). From a gender perspective, cultural comparisons are important because culture influences both who gives and who receives care (Targ, 1989).

Inasmuch as culture influences both customs and beliefs, family care of the elderly is affected by the socialization of individuals regarding both gender roles and the status of older people in a society (Woehrer, 1982). Montgomery and Kamo (1989) argue, for example, that culturally based prescriptions and proscriptions influence patterns of family care for the elderly by defining appropriate behaviors for each gender. Therefore, to the extent that we can understand, from a cultural perspective, both the roles and responsibilities that are assigned to people of different genders and the responsibility for older persons that is allocated to the family, we will be better able to adopt appropriate policies and devise useful interventions that will benefit specific groups of people who share similar cultural backgrounds.

In a decade review (1980s) article titled "Families in Later Life," Brubaker (1990b) notes that he is compelled to repeat a call for more research on ethnic and minority comparisons in later-life families that had been sounded in a similar review of the 1970s (Streib & Beck, 1980). Although Brubaker's comment is directed toward the broader gerontological literature, it is the case that most of what we know about gender and family care of the elderly pertains to white, middle-class caregivers and elders in the United States. Therefore, we believe that more research needs to be directed at identifying both direct and indirect effects of specific cultural variations—for example, among social classes, among persons from different racial and ethnic groups, and in families that reside in different regions and in communities of different sizes (i.e., rural-urban comparisons). In addition, we recommend that comparative research be conducted to explore further any cross-national variations in these phenomena.

Disentangling the Effects of Gender from Other Covariates

Our review of the existing literature has led us to conclude that the effects of gender on family caregiving have not been fully disentangled from the effects of other factors with which gender covaries. That is, to date, research has identified a large number of factors in addition to gender that influence who provides care, what kind of care is provided, and how much care is given. These other factors include characteristics of the caregiver, characteristics of the care recipient, and the circumstances surrounding the provision of care. Many of these other influences, however, also covary with gender. Yet few studies have been designed in a way that would permit the investigators to isolate that part of the variance in caregiving outcomes that is due solely to gender (Dwyer & Coward, 1991). In this context, we briefly describe three factors that future research needs to disentangle from gender in order to understand better the specific effects of each.

Gender and age. The association between gender and age affects both care recipients and caregivers. First, as age increases, the proportion of older people who are female increases. Indeed, more than 70% of persons over age 85 are women (Soldo & Agree, 1988) and their health status and service needs constitute a substantial public policy concern (Manton & Soldo, 1985; Soldo & Manton, 1985). Second, because the old-old are less likely than younger elders to have marital partners, they are more likely to rely on adult children for assistance. Although daughters are the primary source of help from adult children, whatever the age of the parents, the prominence of daughters becomes even more apparent as the parents get older (see Table 2.2 in Chapter 2). Nevertheless, some caregiving research continues to treat people over age 65 as a homogeneous population, and very few studies have attempted to differentiate the effects of age from those of gender. As a consequence, the precise relationships among gender, age, and caregiving have been obscured.

Cohort comparisons. A second disentangling that needs to occur is between gender and the cohort in which a caregiver or care receiver is a member. The gender-related norms and expectations of succeeding cohorts of older people are changing dramatically. More important, perhaps, is that those people most influenced by the gender revolution of the last quarter century will become old themselves during the early part of the twenty-first century (Goldscheider, 1990). Their norms and expectations about giving and receiving care are likely to be very different from those of the present cohort of elders. Therefore, as Stoller has argued (see Chapter 4, this volume), we must avoid letting the experience of current cohorts of caregivers and care receivers constrain our predictions about the social context of caregiving in the future.

Gender and health/disability. Finally, the nature of the care recipient's disability is another gender-related issue that requires further attention. Verbrugge (1989) has shown that differences in the health of the elderly population vary a great deal by gender. Although men and women die from essentially the same causes, the rates at which they experience specific conditions vary (see also Figure 2.1 in Chapter 2). For example, women experience higher prevalence rates of most nonfatal chronic conditions, but the prevalence of fatal conditions is greater among older men (Verbrugge, 1989). Yet men are more likely than women to rate their health as excellent as age increases. Data such as these indicate that there is still a great deal to be learned about the experience and reporting of health and disability and, because these measures vary by gender, there is a need for research that disentangles the effects of health and disability from gender.

We could provide more examples of factors that covary with both gender and patterns of family caregiving, but our point here is simply to suggest that future research on gender and family caregiving would be enhanced by using research designs and methods that permit us to identify more accurately the degree of variation that can be directly attributed to gender. Without such an effort, our understanding of the association between gender and other important characteristics of the caregiving context will continue to be obfuscated.

Identifying additional factors. Finally, there is also a need to continue to pursue research that identifies other characteristics of caregivers and elders that may influence the observation of gender differences in family care. For example, although negative caregiving outcomes are typically found to be greater among caregiving daughters than among sons (i.e., stress, burden, hours of care), Coward and Dwyer (1990) found that these differences were present only among adult children from mixed-gender sibling networks, and not among those from single-gender and only-child networks. It is precisely this kind of partialing of different influences that needs to continue. Future investigators may want to examine the impact of length of marriage and multiple marriages on the experience of stress and burden among spouses, especially wives (see Chapter 4, this volume). If, as Gwyther suggests (Chapter 13, this volume), the provision of care to a frail spouse is viewed as part of a lifelong commitment to that individual, do the shorter time frames characteristic of second or third marriages influence this relationship? Similarly, given the current prevalence of divorce and remarriage, it is clear that many millions of families in the twenty-first century will face the challenge of parent care within the context of "blended" families, yet little is now known about the role of stepchildren and stepsiblings in the caregiving context (see Chapter 6, this volume). Although these are only three examples, they should serve to illustrate that there are a number of aspects of the caregiving situation that remain unexplored from a gender perspective.

Study Families Rather Than Caregiving Dyads

Studying the entire family system (both those providing care and those who are not) will also improve our understanding of the complex dynamics that lead specific family members to become caregivers. Such information cannot be derived from caregiving samples that focus exclusively on individuals who are already providing care. The choices that are made by family members when a frail older member requires care and the full range of assistance provided by family members can be appreciated only if the entire family becomes the focus of research. Mancini and Blieszner (1989) have argued that dyadic studies typical of caregiving research "can be misleading in that they typically do not account for the influence of other family members" (pp. 285-286). This failure to examine the entire family network has a particular impact on the study of gender, because, in addition to being the predominant primary caregivers, women are also more likely to be secondary caregivers and, unless the entire family network is studied, the contributions of men may not be measured at all.

Focusing on the entire family system should increase our knowledge of aspects of caregiving that are not now commonly addressed in the literature. As we learn more about the multiple dimensions of family caregiving, specific types of relationships that have not been the focus of research in the past will begin to receive attention. Specifically, this approach is likely to increase our awareness of the contributions of men, which are not addressed at present because our methods for retrieving information are biased against assessing them properly (see Chapter 9, this volume). An enhanced understanding of the contributions of men will make it easier to inform policy and develop effective interventions that account for their involvement.

Conclusions

Our purpose in this chapter has been to establish an agenda for future research, both how it should be done and what topics should be addressed. As these opportunities are pursued, there are two additional aspects of research in this area that we believe should be given consideration. First, many of the research issues described throughout this volume would benefit from the contributions of an interdisciplinary research team. Statisticians, economists, social workers, psychologists, sociologists, and others, working together, can make great strides in dealing with some of the most pressing, and perplexing, research problems in this area. Second, during the decade of the 1980s, several sophisticated analytic techniques have been used with increasing frequency in the family and aging literatures. LISREL, simultaneous equations, logit analysis, event history analysis, and other techniques provide the means to address many of the most important research questions in the gender/family/aging literature in ways that were not possible previously. As a result, research questions that focus on gender and family care of the elderly can be analyzed as systems of equations or while controlling for other covariates. Together, the use of interdisciplinary research teams and the availability of advanced analytic techniques offer important opportunities to advance the literature in this area during the coming decade.

Note

1. The data and documentation for the NLTCS and the NSIC are available through the Inter-university Consortium for Political and Social Research, P.O. Box 1248, Ann Arbor, MI 48106. The data and documentation for the NHIS:LSOA are available from the National Technical Information Services, 5285 Port Royal Road, Springfield, VA 22161.

PART IV

Implications for Policy and Practice

11

Employment, the Family, and Employer-Based Policies

KAREN SECCOMBE

During the 1990s we are likely to witness the continuing clash of two demographic trends: acceleration in the numbers of frail elderly who require some assistance in carrying out the various activities of daily living, and increases in the percentage of women who are employed outside the home. Because women have historically been viewed in American society as a reserve labor force, ready, willing, and able to care for those in need, our social policies toward long-term care have not kept pace with women's changing roles. This chapter discusses the reciprocal relationship between caregiving and employment—both the impact of caregiving on women's employment and the ways in which women's employment is changing, and will continue to change, the nature of the caregiving relationship. Employer-based options and policies are being added to the agenda of caregiving discussions throughout the country. These options will be explored in this chapter, and both the opportunities for and constraints on women's employment and the family economy will be discussed.

The Traditions of Working and Caring

Since colonial times, two generalizations can be noted regarding American women's roles: their economic dependence within the family, and their orientation toward caring for others (Cott, 1977; Degler, 1980; Ehrenreich

& English, 1979; Hayden, 1981). During the preindustrial economy of colonial America, work was allocated largely on the basis of sex. Women's contributions—unlike those of their European counterparts, who were routinely employed in agricultural work—were largely confined to the domestic sphere. Nevertheless, women's work within the home was essential to the survival of the family and the household economy. In addition to the more obvious chores of cooking, cleaning, and taking care of children, women in early America wove cloth, made clothes, cobbled shoes, and were actively engaged in the cultivation and preservation of food. Women's work was highly valued; the colonies relied on the production of these "cottage industries."

During this period, a few women could be found working in businesses and trades (Dexter, 1924; Leonard, Drinker, & Holden, 1962), but often these were widows carrying on their husbands' enterprises. Women's contributions to the family economy, historians note, were most often found within the confines of the home. Their job was to care dutifully for other family members. That dominant ideology accentuated differential sex roles. Norton's (1980) research on 450 eighteenth-century families found that sex roles were clearly and rigidly defined; the populace held very clear ideas about which tasks were "feminine" and which were "masculine."

The separate spheres of men's and women's lives became accentuated during the Industrial Revolution. Goods and services were gradually produced outside the confines of the family, and therefore women played a less active role in economic life. It was men who became the breadwinners, involved in the market economy. Women were designated to play a supporting role. A woman was to maintain an orderly household, to be warm and cheerful, and to provide the support necessary to keep her husband employed. Motherhood became a woman's highest calling.

Caring for the physical and emotional needs of men and children developed into a moralistic ideology. The home, as made by women, was an oasis from a hostile world. It was a refuge from the turbulence caused by industrialization, a place where men and children were nurtured so that they could cope with their daily existence. Biological, religious, medical, and social arguments were invoked to justify this division of labor. Women were viewed as too weak and delicate to participate in the crude work world of men. Women lacked the strength, stamina, and worldly intelligence needed for participation in the paid labor market. In addition, a woman's presumed strengths—sensitivity, morality, fragility, and nurturing—were considered liabilities outside the confines of the home.

This woman of leisure was a middle-class ideal. It did not fit the reality of all women, especially single women, poor women, ethnic minority women, and those in the working or lower classes. For example, although only 5% of married women were employed outside the home in 1890, these women were largely blacks or immigrants who worked in the textile manufacturing plants prominent in New England. Other married women sought employment because of personal misfortune (Smuts, 1959).

Thus the ideal woman resided in the home, away from the market economy, away from politics, and away from the corruption and greed of the new industrial capitalists. She was to be the heart and soul of the hearth in an increasingly hostile world. She was the family caregiver.

Until recently, however, most families did not have to address the issue of caring for frail elderly relatives because few people survived to old age. Conversely, today, adults have more parents than they have children (Preston, 1984). Additionally, women can expect to spend more years caring for an aging parent than for a dependent child. The average woman will spend 17 years caring for a child and 18 years caring for or helping an elderly parent (U.S. House of Representatives, Select Committee on Aging, 1987). At the same time, she is likely to spend an increasing proportion of her life span working outside the home.

The Increase in Women's Labor Force Participation

Industrialization took the production of many goods and services out of the home and into the marketplace, where large numbers of men, and a small but increasing number of women, were gainfully employed. As shown in Table 11.1, by 1890, 84% of males were participating in the paid labor force, a figure higher than the 77% found today. Some 18% of women were involved in paid labor during 1890, and they made up only 17% of the work force. However, unlike males, their labor force participation rates continued to rise steadily, with a particularly large increase found during World War II. Between 1940 and 1945 more than 5.1 million women joined the ranks of paid laborers. This jump in employment during World War II occurred primarily among young women under the age of 25.

The characteristics of women workers have changed dramatically since that time. While the typical female in the labor force of the past was young, single, without children, and poor, today she is often older, married, a mother, and residing above the poverty line (Blank, 1988; Fox & Hesse-Biber, 1984). The entrance of married women with children into the paid labor force may

Table 11.1 Labor Force Participation Rates, Selected Years, 1890-1987 (Total Labor Force)

Year[a]	Percentage of Males in Labor Force	Percentage of Females in Labor Force	Females as a Percentage of All Workers
1890	84.3	18.2	17.0
1900	85.7	20.0	18.1
1920	84.6	22.7	20.4
1930	82.1	23.6	21.9
1940	82.5	27.9	25.2
1945	87.6	35.8	29.2
1947	86.8	31.8	27.4
1950	86.7	33.9	29.0
1955	85.9	35.7	30.7
1960	83.9	37.8	32.5
1965	81.3	39.3	34.3
1970	80.3	43.4	37.2
1975	78.4	46.4	39.3
1980	77.8	51.6	42.0
1985	76.7	54.5	43.7
1987	76.6	56.1	44.3

SOURCE: Blau and Winkler (1989). Reprinted by permission.
a. Figures for 1947 and after include persons 16 years old and over; for the years prior to 1947 the statistics include those aged 14 and over. Figures for 1950 and subsequent years include employed and underemployed civilians plus members of the Armed Forces stationed within the United States only.

represent the single largest change in family structure in this century, with pervasive and significant implications for many aspects of family life.

It was not until after World War II that older married women entered (or reentered) the labor market in increasing numbers. Less than 30% of women who were between the ages of 45 and 54 were employed in 1940, as opposed to almost 50% in 1960, and two-thirds today (U.S. Department of Labor, 1985, 1988). It is these middle-aged women who are also likely to constitute the generation of women who care for older family members. They have been referred to as "the women in the middle," because they are likely to have family responsibilities of their own to juggle with increased employment and caregiving demands (Brody, 1981, 1990).

Modern employment trends among women include both increased entry into the labor market and decreased exit from it. In addition to middle-aged women, the 1970s and 1980s witnessed a tremendous growth in paid employment among younger married women with children. For example, in the

1960s, 36% of all women between the ages of 25 and 34 years were employed; by the late 1980s that figure had doubled to 72% (U.S. Department of Labor, 1988). Moreover, this phenomenon is not restricted solely to the unmarried. In 1987, 57% of married women with husbands present and children under the age of 6 were in the labor force, as were 71% of married women with children ages 6 to 17 (U.S. Department of Labor, 1987). It is expected that these women are likely to stay employed. In other words, these women will, by and large, be employed relatively continuously until they retire. Thus we will have a new generation of female workers who anticipate continuous employment, yet, in all likelihood, will one day be called upon to meet the demands of caring for aging frail relatives. Although these women will face new difficulties logistically in providing long-term care assistance given their expanded role in the market economy, caregiver roles and expectations continue to persist.

The Relationship Between Employment and Caregiving

How does women's increasing participation in the paid labor force affect the care provided to frail elderly relatives? And how does caregiving affect women's patterns of employment? These are certainly pertinent questions given the heavy reliance upon informal sources of caregiving found in this country.

American culture is one of many that attaches great value to intergenerational ties. Americans of all generations generally believe that adult children should take responsibility in caring for aging parents (Brody, Johnsen, Fulcomer, & Lang, 1983; Finley, Roberts, & Banahan, 1988; Walker, Pratt, Shin, & Jones, 1989; see also Chapters 5 and 7 in this volume). Moreover, families do indeed provide care for their frail elderly relatives. Despite the myth of family abandonment (Shanas, 1979b), we find that families, and women in particular, tend to provide the bulk of caregiving assistance (see earlier chapters in this volume).

The term *family care*, however, is misleading. It is generally a woman who provides care—as a wife to her husband, as a daughter or daughter-in-law to an aged parent, or as a friend or other kin (Abel, 1986, 1989; Kivett, 1985; Matthews & Rosner, 1988; Stoller, Pugliesi, & Gilbert, 1988). Males tend to provide intermittent assistance with caregiving tasks, usually those that have been traditionally defined as masculine or that minimize their involvement in personal care (Dwyer & Seccombe, 1991; Montgomery & Kamo, 1989; Stoller, 1990). Additionally, since a male caregiver is more likely to be the spouse of a frail elder rather than the child (Stone et al., 1987), he may be retired and therefore may face little or no interference between work and caregiving demands. Thus the demands of caregiving have less impact on men's lives, generally speaking, than they do on women's.

The number of women who combine employment and caregiving to frail elderly persons has grown dramatically in recent years. Of the approximately 2.2 million individuals who provide unpaid informal assistance for older adults, 31% are employed full- or part-time outside the home (Stone et al., 1987). An employee survey by the Travelers Companies (1985) found that 20% were providing some care to an elderly person for an average of 10 hours per week. Women provided more hours of care than did men, however, averaging 16 hours per week. In fact, 8% of the Travelers employees were spending the equivalent of another full-time job providing care, averaging 35 hours a week. Other studies report similar conclusions. A study completed by the management of *Personnel Journal* found that 12.5% of employees were directly responsible for providing some type of assistance with elder care on a daily basis, and another 12.5% shared the responsibility by providing occasional backup help (Magnus, 1988). A study conducted by Retirement Advisors, Inc. (1986), using a sample of 144 persons aged 50-68, found that 28% were currently caregivers and an additional 9% were anticipating this role within the next five years. The University of Bridgeport Corporate Eldercare Project (Creedon, 1987) surveyed workers over the age of 40 in three companies and found that more than 23% of respondents reported caregiving responsibilities.

While these studies do not contain representative samples of workers within the United States, and their generalizability is limited as a result, they nonetheless illustrate the magnitude of the elder-care issue. Data from the U.S. Department of Labor (1986) suggest that the prevalence of employed caregivers will continue to increase, given longer life expectancies, the rising median age of the labor force, and further increases in female labor force participation. Thus the number of persons who experience the multiple role demands of employment, caring for frail elderly persons, and fulfilling other family and personal obligations and responsibilities is likely to increase in the future (Stoller & Pugliesi, 1989).

The Effects of Employment Upon Caregiving

Most of the research focusing on those who provide care has not found women's employment status to be a major factor affecting the amount of time or the type of help provided to aging parents (Brody & Schoonover, 1986; Horowitz & Dobrof, 1982; Matthews, Werkner, & Delaney, 1989). Men's contributions to caregiving, in contrast, are decreased by employment. Stoller (1983), for example, through face-to-face interviews with a regional probability sample of 753 noninstitutionalized elderly, found that being employed decreased the average level of sons' assistance by more than 20 hours per month. In contrast, employment had no significant effect on the amount of time daughters spent caring for aged parents.

In related research, Noelker and Townsend (1987) found that gender and employment status were two of the most important sociodemographic variables associated with providing caregiving services; virtually all daughters, whether employed or not, served as caregivers when needed, compared with only 35% of employed sons and 54% of unemployed sons. In addition, Brody and Schoonover (1986), using a nonrandom sample of 150 Philadelphia-area families, compared the amount and types of care provided to aging mothers by two groups of daughters, those who were employed and those who were not, and found that the two groups of mothers received the same amount of care overall. Employed and nonemployed daughters provided equal amounts of help with shopping, transportation, household tasks, managing money, service arrangements, and emotional support. Employed daughters did offer less personal care and cooking than nonemployed daughters, but the differences were offset by purchased help.

Finally, Matthews, Werkner, and Delaney (1989), utilizing a sample of 50 pairs of sisters who were recruited primarily through classified advertisements in newspapers, compared the contributions to the care of frail parents by sisters when one was employed and the other was not. They found that, generally, employment status was not a significant predictor of the amount or type of care provided. There was evidence, however, that when a parent's functional health status declined, it was the nonemployed sister who was more likely to contribute more tangible services. Similarly, Horowitz and Dobrof (1982) found that long-term caregiving was negatively correlated with part-time employment rather than full-time employment, as predicted. Moreover, they found that, among females, marital status was the most important predictor of caregiving; those who were married, with or without children at home, were most likely to limit the amount of care they provided to aging relatives.

The Effects of Caregiving Upon Employment

A second pertinent question involves the way in which caregiving responsibilities affect caregivers' employment. It seems that employed caregivers, females in particular, deal with their multiple responsibilities by sacrificing their own free time, modifying their work demands, and maintaining rigid schedules (Cantor, 1983; Gibeau & Anastas, 1989; Stone et al., 1987).

Data from the 1982 National Survey of Informal Caregivers (Stone et al., 1987), based upon a nationally representative sample of frail elders, reveals that 9% of nonemployed respondents reported that they left their jobs in order to provide care to frail aging relatives. The figure was higher for women than for men, regardless of whether or not the caregiver was a spouse or an adult child: 14% of wives and 12% of daughters reported they had quit work to become caregivers, while only 11% of husbands and 5% of sons had done so. Regional studies, using nonrepresentative samples, have reported that perhaps as many as one-fourth of female caregivers have left work to care for older family members (Brocklehurst, Morris, Andrews, Richards, & Laycock, 1981; Brody, Kleban, Johnsen, Hoffman, & Schoonover, 1987). Yet dropping out of the paid labor force to care for an aging relative increases the chance of impoverishment for women.

Other caregivers manage to remain on their jobs. These employees, who moonlight as caregivers, are no longer a rare breed. Recent studies reveal that approximately one-quarter of workers are actively involved in caregiving (Creedon, 1987; Scharlach & Boyd, 1989; Travelers Companies, 1985). Stone et al. (1987), for example, found that 29% of the employees they studied changed their work schedules, 21% reduced the number of hours worked, and 19% took time off without pay. Again, generally women, especially daughters, were more likely to do this than were male caregivers. It should be noted that Stone et al. did find, however, that husbands were more likely than wives to report taking a reduction in the number of hours worked and taking time off from work without pay. Brody, Johnsen, and Fulcomer (1984) found that 28% of nonworking daughters interviewed in one study had quit their jobs to take care of their frail mothers.

Scharlach and Boyd (1989), in a survey of one large employer in Southern California ($N = 1,898$), found that caregivers reported that working made the emotional, physical, and overall situation of caregiving more difficult. The only manner in which working eased the burden for a few respondents was financially. Additionally, Scharlach and Boyd (1989) found that caregivers, when compared with other employees, were more likely to report interference between their jobs and family responsibilities. As a consequence, they were more likely to miss work. Moreover, almost one-fourth of caregivers indicated that it was "somewhat" or "extremely" likely that they would be forced to quit their jobs to provide care, and 9% had considered quitting due to caregiving during the previous two months. Likewise, Gibeau and Anastas (1987) report that 44% of the caregivers identified in a national sample reported conflicts between their work and family responsibilities. In addition, 8% had considered quitting work, but had not done so because they felt they could not afford to. Other conflicts included missed meetings (20%), losses in overtime pay (13%), missed conferences (13%), forgone promotions (5%), and reduced job offers (3%).

In other contexts, multiple roles have been found to be beneficial to self-esteem, psychological well-being, and physical health (Linville, 1987; Thoits, 1983; Verbrugge, 1983). Yet the caregiving literature unequivocally points to the stress, strain, and burden caregivers experience, especially those who are employed. Caregivers report that they feel isolated, lonely, and depressed, yet at the same time they often report feeling guilty, as though they somehow are not doing quite enough (Cantor, 1983; Horowitz, 1985b; Montgomery, Gonyea, & Hooyman, 1985; Pilisuk & Parks, 1988).

New options are needed if families are to continue to be a part of the caregiving process. Modifications in the personnel policies of the workplace are an important start. These changes must be made if an optimal balance between family responsibilities, including caregiving, and paid employment is to be achieved.

Employer-Based Policies

In recent years employers have become interested in ways to increase productivity and worker morale by eliminating some of the conflicts between work and family life (Bureau of National Affairs, 1986; Galinsky, 1986; Raabe & Gessner, 1988). Although systematic data are limited, awareness of the connection between corporate policies and employee productivity seems to be on the rise, resulting in recent corporate innovations aimed at promoting better integration between work and family responsibilities. Some examples of these innovations include flexible alternatives in work scheduling, maternity benefits, information and referral services, and corporate child-care services. Options such as these are far from universally embraced, however. It is estimated, for example, that only 2,500 of the nation's 44,000 largest employers offer any kind of child-care services to their employees (Bureau of National Affairs, 1986).

While the situation has likely improved in the decade since Louis Harris and Associates (1981) conducted their national survey and found that only 16% of personnel managers thought that employees' family demands influenced their decisions about work schedules, employer policies in the United States still lag behind those in many Western European nations in the extent to which they foster the integration of work and family for both women and men (Bohen, 1983; Kamerman & Kahn, 1981). For years, Western Europeans have had the benefits of extensive paid maternal and paternal leaves, child-care services, flexible work scheduling, and other policies that facilitate family life. In the United States, most of these issues are left to the discretion of the individual employer rather than codified into law. Furthermore, formal policy may be deliberately avoided by corporations, so that needs may be handled informally, on a case-by-case basis (Denton & Love, 1988). While case-by-case approaches are often touted by business as maximizing flexibility, they also open the door for accusations of inconsistency and unequal treatment.

The programs in the United States that have been developed to help create and maintain the needed balance between work and family life are generally oriented toward helping workers cope with their responsibilities as *parents*; therefore, issues such as day care and maternity leave are major points of discussion (Denton & Love, 1988; McNeely & Fogarty, 1988; Raabe & Gessner, 1988; Zimmerman & Owens, 1989). But family responsibilities are not limited to child care. Family versus workplace conflicts are compounded by the fact that caregiving may also revolve around a frail elderly relative. Yet *elder-care policies* in the workplace are so new and innovative that one author refers to them as "still at the threshold" (Magnus, 1988, p. 19).

Several studies suggest that employers are aware that elder care is an issue touching the lives of many employees, but very few corporations throughout the United States have designed programs aimed at helping employees who are caring for elderly relatives (Denton & Love, 1988; Magnus, 1988; Travelers Companies, 1985; Warshaw, Barr, Rayman, Schachter, & Lucas, 1986). A survey of personnel executives from 101 companies, employing over 1 million persons, found that more than two-thirds of the respondents reported that elder care is an issue to be concerned with, yet only 10% of them had studied the extent and nature of the problem within their firms. Moreover, even fewer had done anything about implementing policies toward alleviating the problem (Magnus, 1988). Similarly, in a study of corporate responses to the needs of employed caregivers in the New York area, Warshaw et al. (1986) found that one-half of the studied corporations knew that their employees had caregiver needs that were infringing upon their productivity, but only 15% had initiated programs or policies to help caregivers. Those programs that did exist were largely informal rather than codified into policy. Creedon (1987) suggests that program development may be constrained by several factors, including executive resistance to new benefits of any type.

Flexible Work Scheduling

There are a variety of workplace options available to ease the strain experienced by employees caring for frail elders. One of the most popular includes *flexible work schedules*. This could include flexible job hours (flextime), increased opportunities for part-time work, and leaves of absence with or without pay. Each of these policies offers obvious advantages for workers. Flextime allows for varying work schedules, sometimes on a short-term emergency basis and at other times as a more permanent feature of the workplace. For example, instead of working the traditional hours of 9 a.m. to 5 p.m., a person may choose to begin work earlier or later in order to coordinate caregiving responsibilities with others.

Flextime is an important resource; it was rated as the most helpful program by caregivers of the elderly in a large firm located in Southern California (Scharlach & Boyd, 1989). Yet few employers offer this program to their employees on any systematic basis. Denton and Love (1988) reviewed the elder-care policies of 20 corporate employers in the Chicago area, including 3 public utility companies, a government agency, 3 financial or insurance institutions, 3 health service corporations, 2 social service agencies, a professional membership organization, a social science research group, 4 manufacturing firms, a mining company, and an engineering firm; 5 of the corporations were local, 2 were regional, 10 were national, and 3 were multinational. Of these corporations, Denton and Love (1988) found that 7 companies provided flextime formally; 4 other companies furnished flextime informally under certain circumstances, generally awarded at the discretion of the management. The remainder did not offer it at all.

Part-time work allows an individual to remain in the work force, but with reduced hours. This option was evaluated favorably by slightly more than half of the caregivers in the study by Scharlach and Boyd (1989). Unfortunately, part-time positions often do not include important fringe benefits, such as health insurance. Because many persons rely upon these benefits for financial security, part-time employment, as it is currently compensated, may not be a viable option for everyone (Seccombe & Beeghley, n.d.). One relatively new option for part-time work is referred to as "job sharing," in which two people split one position, preferably with fringe benefits included. The state of New York, for example, has a part-time shared job project and registry (Wagner, Creedon, Sasala, & Neal, 1989).

Family Leave

In recent years the leave of absence, sometimes referred to as "family leave," has come forward on the public agenda (Wisensale & Allison, 1988, 1989). Unfortunately, caring for elders is often excluded from family leave policies. A recent review of the 28 states that introduced family leave legislation in 1987 indicated that only 4 states passed their bills, and only 1 of those states, Connecticut, included caring for elderly relatives in its provisions (Wisensale & Allison, 1988). Furthermore, of the 24 states that introduced but did not enact family leave legislation, only 5 had proposed that elder care be included in the policy. In 1988, only 13 states introduced family leave legislation; of these, only 3 states passed it (Wisensale, 1990).

Clearly, not everyone agrees that elder care is an issue large enough or important enough to create legislation that would assist family caregivers by providing leave time from employment or other workplace flexibilities. Wisensale and Allison (1988) found lobbyists positioned predictably along different sides of the debate. Representatives of business, for example, generally argue that family leave will increase costs, hurt small businesses, and encourage discrimination toward people with families, and will ultimately be detrimental to women employees. They argue that family leave should be voluntary rather than mandated by state legislation. Labor unions, in contrast, claim that family leave policies will improve employee morale, help retain a work force, and assist all workers, including those who do not have a collective bargaining unit. Women's groups take the position that family leave policies will help single parents, dual-worker couples, and women who choose to have both families and careers. Interestingly, lobbying activists on behalf of the elderly have been absent from the debate.

Denton and Love (1988) found the managers they interviewed from 20 Chicago-area corporations to be adamant in their belief that family leave policies should be up to the discretion of the employer. The managers were convinced that legislation would disrupt the programs already existing within their organizations, and balked at the universal coverage that would be required.

Federal family leave legislation, which would include responsibilities to frail elderly relatives as well as to young children, has been introduced in the U.S. Congress as well as on a state-by-state basis. Federal legislation has been somewhat more successful than most state initiatives, and legislation recently passed both the House of Representatives and the Senate. In 1990, however, President Bush vetoed the legislation, arguing that family leave policy should not be mandated by federal law but should instead be left to the discretion of the employer.

Unions historically have been active in increasing the level of job perquisites provided to workers, and several of them have recently adopted platforms that directly pertain to caregiving. Both the Service Employees International Union (SEIU) and the American Telephone and Telegraph Company (AT&T), for example, have negotiated contracts with parental leave provisions that allow employees leave time to provide care for parents or parents-in-law (Wagner et al., 1989).

Additional Policies and Employer Options

Other options that could assist employed caregivers include *senior day-care centers* and *information and employee assistance programs.* Senior day-care centers, modeled somewhat after traditional day-care programs designed for children, can ease the stress of caregivers by providing supervision for elders during the working portion of the day. Companies can either provide on-site day care within their own facilities or use a voucher system in which they reimburse employees for the costs of private day care in the community. Of the 20 Chicago-area corporations in their study, Denton and Love (1988) found that none offered such a service, although several offered day-care assistance for children. Managers at 2 of the 20 corporations thought that day care for elderly persons could be feasible; the remainder did not. Yet there is a need for elder-care services as well. Scharlach and Boyd (1989) found, for example, in their sample of caregivers in one Southern California firm, that more than three-fourths reported that proposed senior day-care centers would indeed be helpful to them in balancing work and family demands.

Information and employee assistance programs cover a wide range of services, including printed material, referral services, lunchtime seminars, and trained counselors who provide individual or family therapy to assist employees with a host of personal problems. Originally employee assistance programs were designed to help employees affected by drug and alcohol abuse, but counselors are expanding their practices to include other personal, family, and employment issues as well (Denton & Love, 1988). Denton and Love (1988) found information and employee assistance programs to be widespread. Of the 20 corporations in their study, 11 held seminars, often with outside experts; 8 published company newsletters in which articles on caregiving were professed to be welcome; and 16 offered employee assistance plans, with another in the planning stage. Scharlach and Boyd (1989) report that 59% of the caregivers in their sample found their existing employee assistance programs helpful, and 68% found their lunchtime seminars to be helpful. Of those services still at the proposal stage, information on senior services was the most popular option among caregivers; fully 85% felt that this information would be helpful.

In sum, it appears that a large and growing number of workers have family demands that go beyond simply caring for oneself, a spouse, and children. Elder care is a common phenomenon and will continue to be so in the future. Second, because women, who have largely been the principal caregivers, play an increasing role in the labor market as well, they are particularly vulnerable to the stresses inherent in juggling the demands of family and work responsibilities. Third, it appears that many employers recognize this fact and are cognizant of the ways in which family responsibilities, such as elder care, affect employee stress, productivity, and morale. Fourth, despite the large numbers of primarily female workers affected and acknowledgment of the problem by management, the corporate and business world has been slow to provide solutions to eliminate or reduce the strain associated with these multiple roles.

A look at history shows us that many changes have indeed occurred within the family, with the expanding number of elders who require some assistance in carrying out their activities of daily living and the increase in the percentage of women who are joining the paid labor force being two of the most important. Unfortunately, these changes have not been accompanied by changes in the structural components of society. The United States, more so than many Western European countries (Kamerman & Kahn, 1981), continues to ignore the clash of these two demographic trends and instead continues to rely upon women to serve as caregivers while ignoring fundamental policy imperatives.

Gender Justice

From the above discussion it is clear that corporate policy and gender are interrelated; that is, women are affected to a greater degree than are men by corporate policies on elder care. Nevertheless, this relationship is customarily ignored (Kirp, Yudof, & Franks, 1986; Osterbusch, Keigher, Miller, & Linsk, 1987). A cogent argument could be made that the current configuration of programs, or the lack thereof, represents antifemale sentiment. Businesses, backed by federal and state government, operate on two traditional assumptions: (a) that they are the body best equipped to judge the needs of an employee, that such needs should be taken into account on a case-by-case basis, and that mandating legislation such as a family leave policy or day care undermines private capitalistic enterprise; and (b) that women are able, willing, and ready to render caregiving services when needed while men continue the tradition of working outside the home.

Osterbusch et al. (1987) discuss several of the implications of these assumptions. First, they suggest that such assumptions reduce the chance to legitimate families as the targets of services. Relying upon unpaid caregivers becomes a primary way to control costs, yet it is done under the guise of protecting women's presumed caregiving nature. Second, these assumptions encourage government to intervene only when no family is available for caregiving. When family members provide any form of care, their chances of eligibility for public services are reduced. Third, women increase their likelihood of poverty by reducing their work hours, eliminating overtime, or quitting their jobs to continue the uncompensated tasks involved in caring for relatives. Osterbusch et al. suggest that social policy must contribute to, rather than undermine, gender justice:

> The conception of community care policy options must extend to include the general structure of family caregiving and the effects of these policies on women who are the spouses, daughters, and other relatives of ill and disabled elderly persons. The social dynamics underlying present community care policies are rooted in traditional concepts about the family, women, and the responsibility of the State. These concepts have generally supported a laissez-faire approach to family caregiving, including an appropriate concern for preserving the liberty of the family to make its own decisions about allocating career tasks. However, the privacy of these decisions is largely illusory. The capacity of women to freely choose caring is severely limited by the paucity of caregiving alternatives and the constriction of their choices elsewhere. (p. 218)

It seems plausible that caregivers will benefit most from a combination of support services and social policies designed to meet a wide variety of elder needs and elder and caregiver preferences, such as respite care, day care, payment to caregiver families, and homemaker chore services, to name but a few. The work site is an important place in which to begin to delineate alternative strategies of relieving the stress caused by the multiple role demands of employment, responsibilities to a spouse and children, and caregiving to a frail elderly relative. According to Stone et al. (1987), almost one-half of all caregiving daughters are employed outside the home, and this figure is expected to continue to rise. Thus it is in the best interests of all of society to develop fair and just policies and programs to enable all persons, men and women, to pursue their employment of choice without having to jeopardize the personal and family commitments they make.

12

Social Policy and
Gender Inequities in Caregiving

NANCY R. HOOYMAN

Family care of the elderly is a critical social and health care policy issue that affects women at their core, constricting their economic autonomy and personal rights, roles, and responsibilities. As a result of a declining fertility rate and longer life expectancy, couples for the first time in history have more parents than children for whom they face the potential for caregiving responsibilities. Yet the male half of the marital partnership rarely occupies the role of primary caregiver to an impaired parent, making the term *family care* a misnomer (Brody, 1984; Lang & Brody, 1983). As other authors have noted in earlier chapters, care responsibilities in our society remain primarily ascribed on the basis of gender, with women caregivers predominating both as clients and as unpaid and underpaid providers of maintenance services to dependent elders (Balbo, 1982; Land & Rose, 1985; Pateman, 1988). Specifically, 80% of family caregivers to the elderly are women, who spend an average of 17 years caring for children and 18 years caring for older relatives (Older Women's League, 1989; Stone, Cafferata, & Sangl, 1987). As a result, the average woman spends nearly half of her life fulfilling the role of family caregiver to dependents. Despite gains in women's economic status in the last two decades, most policies and services still assume that women have both a monopoly on care skills and an obligation to be the primary providers

AUTHOR'S NOTE: I wish to acknowledge the assistance of Betty Kramer, M.S.W., Ph.D., in the production of this chapter.

of dependent care, thereby placing women in a "compassion trap" (Adams, 1975).

This chapter focuses on structural gender inequities in elder care, how these inequities interact with and are perpetuated by inadequate community care policies, and how the outcome thereby perpetuates dependence on the unpaid labor of female family members for elder care. This analysis begins with an examination of some of the assumptions and values underlying current policies that serve to perpetuate gender inequities in elder care. After a discussion of how the values of privatization and the ideology of separate spheres result in structural economic inequality for women, the negative impacts of current health and social service policies upon female caregivers' economic status, especially in old age, are examined. A feminist perspective is then used to critique selected policy and program initiatives as well as to suggest future directions for policy development for family caregivers.

For purposes of this chapter, *caregiving work* is defined as custodial or maintenance help or services, rendered for the well-being of older individuals who, because of chronic physical or mental illness, cannot perform such activities for themselves (Waerness, 1985). Throughout this analysis, caregiving values per se are not under attack. The importance and necessity of caregiving work are taken as givens. For many women—and some men—family caregiving is their preferred and chosen life's work. It is the gender inequities created by current social structures that must be changed, not the activity itself or the humanizing imperative to care. Drawing upon a political economy perspective (Estes, Newcomer, & Associates, 1983; Osterbusch, Keigher, Miller, & Linsk, 1987), this critique is directed at the socially constructed assumption (e.g., the compassion trap) that caregiving is women's natural role.

Health and Social Policies

A basic limitation of current policies is that public expenditures are skewed toward long-term nursing home care and short-term acute hospital care (Estes, 1989; U.S. Senate, Special Committee on Aging, 1990). Because of the absence of affordable mechanisms for private payment and of adequate universal public support for long-term care, most older people must pay out of pocket for nursing home care and other long-term care services. When they have exhausted their resources to the point of impoverishment, they generally rely on Medicaid. Yet, even when the elderly are eligible for Medicaid, maintenance services and assistance with daily life tasks are not covered. This gap occurs because the primary insurance mechanisms—Medicaid and Medicare—fund largely institutional care, not in-home services. As a result, many older people are forced into the difficult choice between moving into an institution and getting little or no care. In order to understand why policymakers have failed to make long-term care a societal responsibility, it is useful first to examine the social values regarding family responsibility that underlie current policies and, in turn, affect the gender-based distribution of care responsibilities.

Private Responsibility and the "Public Burden" Model of Welfare

Social and health care services in the United States have historically been organized on the premise of private responsibility; in other words, families have the primary and natural responsibility for dependent care. Accordingly, most policies are based on individualistic values of self-care, personal initiative, and independence, which are counter to the norms of reciprocity, exchange, and interdependence that must underlie the provision of elder care by family members. As a result, most policies are residual in nature; that is, publicly funded services for the elderly or their caregivers are typically provided only after family resources are exhausted or the family has proven itself incapable of meeting care standards (Faulkner & Micchelli, 1988). In effect, families are expected to assume caregiving burden as a "private good" until they break down to the point of "eligibility" for government support (Osterbusch et al., 1987).

Basic to this public burden model of welfare is the premise that the individual elder, not the family, is the unit for service. Eligibility for means-tested social assistance benefits is determined according to the older recipient's financial need, not that of his or her informal helping system (Briggs & Oliver, 1985; Titmuss, 1968; Walker, 1985). Such definitions of eligibility serve both to exclude as many persons as possible and to limit benefits to the minimum required for survival outside a nursing home, thereby "saving" public costs. Hence the equity concerns of social welfare are subordinate to the efficiency criteria of the marketplace (Osterbusch et al., 1987).

Cost-Effectiveness and Privatization

Reflecting this assumption of private responsibility, policy debates are frequently framed in terms of the need to reduce or control expenditures and to achieve a balance between incentives and disincentives to care (Oster-busch et al., 1987). Underlying such debates are policymakers' misconceptions that publicly funded services will substitute for the family. Despite evidence to the contrary, fears persist that the provision of formal services will result in families' abdication of their responsibilities (Olsen, 1986; Wenger, 1984). This fear of substitution plays itself out through cost-containment initiatives, which aim to ensure that formal interventions do not reduce the family's amount or type of care and thereby artificially frame formal services as antithetical to informal family supports.

The myth of substitution also underlies instances of withholding service and income benefits when the family retains caregiving functions. In fact, some policies appear to penalize families who provide custodial care. For example, in the controversial 1989 catastrophic care legislation (which was later repealed), older people with family caregivers would have qualified for fewer hours of respite or homemaker services than those without such family supports. When cost containment is the priority, community-based services are often limited to crisis or casualty interventions, thereby penalizing long-term maintenance while implicitly rewarding the breakdown of a caring relationship (Moroney, 1980; Walker, 1985).

Closely related to the presumption that formal services will substitute for the family is the notion of a "woodwork effect"; that is, that if more benefits were available, more elderly and their family caregivers would come "out of the woodwork" and utilize services (Montgomery & Borgatta, 1989; Oster-busch et al., 1987). Accordingly, restricting publicly funded services is defined as a way to limit potential demand. For example, under the Medicaid 2176 Home and Community-Based Care Waiver programs, states may apply for waivers to provide nonmedical home and community-based long-term care services—such as homemaker, chore, and adult day-care services—but only as a lower-cost substitute for institutional care. Therefore, services must be targeted to persons who would otherwise require Medicaid-financed nursing home care. To prevent states from making home care an entitlement program, a ceiling was imposed so that the average per capita costs with the waiver do not exceed costs without the waiver. Because these restrictions limit payment for home support to those who are so ill or disabled as to be eligible for nursing home care, waiver programs may reach people too late to divert them from institutionalization.

In contrast to the woodwork effect, service providers frequently encounter difficulties in recruiting family caregivers for respite, support, and education programs. The more appropriate metaphor might be "beating the bushes" (Abel, 1987; Montgomery & Borgatta, 1989). Those who fear the woodwork effect also fail to recognize the benefits of early intervention with families. For example, caregivers who experience higher levels of stress tend to use more services, suggesting that preventive approaches could lower service utilization (Bass & Noelker, 1987).

In sum, policies that rely on caregivers' sacrifice can be considered "cost-effective" and "efficient" only if the emotional, physical, and financial costs incurred by caregivers are omitted from the calculations. As noted throughout this book, most caregivers will persevere to the breaking point. Under such conditions, cost-containment approaches make the public purse the beneficiary of policies while victimizing caregivers, primarily women, as unpaid servants.

The Ideology of Community Care

Closely related to such emphases on efficiency and cost-effectiveness is the ideology of community care. This perspective views uncompensated family care as kinder, more sensitive, more attuned to individual needs, and more compatible with traditional values than that provided by paid caregivers (Briar & Ryan, 1986). However, economic considerations, not quality-of-life issues, tend to underlie this perspective as espoused by policymakers.

During the budget cutbacks of the 1980s, public officials often referred to families or voluntary resources as "filling the gaps" in services (Carriko & Eisenberg, 1983). An underlying assumption of this chapter is that such appeals to the informal sector of families, neighbors, and volunteers perpetuate gender inequities in care. In practice, community care is based on women's unpaid domestic labor. Care *in* the community—with the dependent person supported by informal caring networks and community and institutional services as needed—must be differentiated from care *by* the community, where the emphasis is on informal family care provided by women (Lewis & Meredith, 1988). Current community-based and cost-containment efforts tend to support the latter.

In sum, the typical policy approach toward family caregivers is a "public burden" model of welfare, where public expenditures for social and health services are defined as a drain on the economy (Titmuss, 1968; Walker, 1985). Under this model, the economic objectives of profit maximization, growth, and cost-efficiency are defined as legitimate, while achievement of the social objectives of community care and well-being is believed to rest ultimately on sound economic policy. Therefore, the equity concerns of long-term care policy become subordinate to the efficiency criteria that dominate economic policy.

The Ideology of Separate Spheres
and Policy Inequities

Policies affecting family caregiving have also been shaped by the ideology of separate spheres, which segregates caregiving to women's sphere within the home and profit making to men's sphere within the marketplace. In the most basic sense, the ideology of separate spheres took two conflicting philosophies—the old one of community, responsibility, and duty, and the new one of individualism—and resolved the conflict along gender lines: Women would nurture as carers, men would achieve as breadwinners. The domestic sphere of women thereby became culturally linked to the compassion trap of expressivity, nurturing, and emotion, while the public sphere of men became characterized as instrumental, competitive, and rational (Chodorow, 1978). Although this ideology elevated caregiving to new importance as a function of family life, caregiving nevertheless remained a private activity to be performed in isolation, behind closed doors (Ehrenreich, 1983).

Although caregiving work underpins the economy, it is peripheral to the marketplace norms of competition and financial gain as defined by men. Nonmonetized and nontechnological, caregiving has been unrecognized and devalued in a society that defines work in terms of measurable output and wages rather than nurturance and maintenance (Bernard, 1983). What this means for women's roles and status is that women are expected to perform unpaid work in the home that is regarded as nonwork. As a result, assumptions underlying current public policies arise from a social system in which women as a class are at an economic disadvantage.

Current Policies, Economic Costs of
Care, and Gender Inequities

Debates about policies to support or encourage family caregiving have largely ignored the issue of gender, presuming that the processes and outcomes of such policies are gender neutral (Osterbusch et al., 1987). However, to assume that women and men are similarly affected by such policies acts to the disadvantage of women, who, as other authors have documented in this book, carry an unequal share of caregiving tasks across the life span. Accordingly, women, especially in old age, experience more economic costs from caregiving than do men. A public burden model of welfare that regards the marketplace as an efficient and sufficient mechanism for distributing services to families thereby accepts and perpetuates the constriction of social, economic, and health choices for women throughout their lives.

After devoting their lives to attending to others' needs, many women in old age face years of living alone on low incomes with inadequate medical care and with their welfare resting on the presence and willingness of younger female relatives or underpaid care attendants (Minkler & Stone, 1985; Older Women's League, 1986). For most women, years spent out of the full-time paid labor force to perform caregiving services that are essential to the economy and the family are not compensated by private pensions or Social Security in old age. Thus women face a catch-22 dilemma between performing their care obligations across the life span at the cost of their financial security or deviating from societal expectations to pursue employ-ment-related stability as their primary goal, but often without public or familial support for the latter choice. Those who do pursue employment not only encounter low salaries and few retirement benefits, but also find that their domestic responsibilities do not diminish. Instead, double duty becomes the norm, with their leisure or free time shrinking, but not their other obligations (Bernard, 1983). As a result of such double duty, many women end up physically or emotionally exhausted. The sexual division of labor and the occupational segregation of the work force make clear that the social construction of gender—not the individual's biological legacy—is the major determinant of inequities in employment and family roles across the life span.

Current Policies and Gender Inequities

This section examines how inadequate public policies interact with women's lower socioeconomic status throughout their lives to restrict their options for providing care, especially in old age. Women's decisions about caregiving are not solely private choices, but must be viewed within the framework created by long-term care policies.

Medicare

With an emphasis on acute care, Medicare funds primarily skilled nursing home care and medically oriented home health care, covering less than 2% of overall long-term care expenses (Lave, 1985). Medicare's home health benefit is extremely restrictive: Recipients must be under a physician's care, homebound, and in need of skilled nursing care. In 1989 only 3% of Medicare benefit payments covered home care (U.S. Senate, Special Committee on

Aging, 1990). Since medical social services must be oriented to the treatment of a patient's physical condition, beneficiaries do not receive services, such as homemaker and nutritional services, that they need to live independently in the community.

Efforts to control Medicare costs, especially the 1983 implementation of a prospective payment system in hospitals (diagnostic related groups, or DRGs), have often placed increasing pressure on family caregivers. For example, older patients are more likely to be discharged prematurely and thus to return home sicker and to require more intensive in-home services (Coulton, 1988; Estes, Wood, & Lee, 1988). With home health agencies unable to accommodate the growing demand for in-home services, family members, typically women, are increasingly forced to serve as mediators, supervisors, planners, and providers for both in-hospital and posthospital care (Estes & Arendell, 1986; Fischer & Eustis, 1988; Sankar, Newcomer, & Wood, 1986). In fact, hospital discharge planners often assume that wives, daughters, and daughters-in-law are able and willing to provide care and, therefore, contact them first regarding discharge plans (Polansky, 1985).

Recent legislative changes have made it increasingly difficult for Medicare patients to find agencies to serve them. Although home health agencies grew in the early 1980s to capture the Medicare market, inadequate Medicare reimbursement policies in the second half of the decade encouraged agencies to reduce the size of their Medicare clientele (Estes et al., 1988). For example, the Health Care Financing Administration (HCFA) attempted in 1985 to restrict funding for home health benefits by reducing both the ceilings on allowable costs per visit and the number and frequency of visits by home health aides. After HCFA instructed fiscal intermediaries to define *medical necessity* more strictly, the rate of Medicare home health denials rose, with more than 200 home health agencies dropping their Medicare certification in 1986-1987. Because the number of visiting nurses associations and public sector agencies did not grow proportionately in the 1980s, they could not accommodate the publicly funded clients who were abandoned by private agencies (Kane, 1989; U.S. Senate, Special Committee on Aging, 1990).

Medicaid

Because Medicare is primarily oriented to short-term hospital stays and acute care, older people who require long-term custodial care for chronic diseases generally depend upon Medicaid. Medicaid is the primary source of public financing for long-term care, funding approximately half of the nursing home expenditures for intermediate and skilled care in the nation

(Mechanic, 1987; U.S. Senate, Special Committee on Aging, 1990). Medicaid's eligibility policies and benefit structure have created financial incentives to use nursing homes rather than community services, because home care benefits are limited and the income eligibility is higher for nursing home residents than for the elderly poor living in the community (U.S. House of Representatives, Committee on Energy and Commerce, 1986).

Limitations inherent to Medicaid have negative impacts upon women as both care recipients and care providers. One example is the discretion of states to determine eligibility, service access and utilization, and reimbursement of providers. This discretion results in wide variations in long-term care expenditures among states. With reductions in the amount of federal funds allocated to states since the passage of the Omnibus Budget Reconciliation Act in 1981, states have reduced Medicaid benefits, eligibility, and utilization, and have increased copayments (Harrington, Estes, Lee, & Newcomer, 1986). Since women are more likely than men to have low incomes, they have been hurt disproportionately by states' discretionary Medicaid reductions.

In general, older women experience disproportionately the negative effects of medical expenses. Medical expenses take an especially heavy toll on older people living alone. For example, when medical expenses are taken into account, the proportion of older people living alone on incomes below the poverty level increases from 19% to 27% (Commonwealth Fund Commission, 1987). With women predominating among the low-income elderly living alone, they tend to have fewer community-based service options and fewer resources to purchase medical equipment and supplies and to undertake physical adaptations to their homes. Yet these low-income women living alone may not be poor enough to qualify for Medicaid support, since the Medicaid income eligibility standards are more generous to older couples than they are to those who live alone.

The fact that Medicaid funds primarily institutional care also has negative impacts on women caregivers. Since only one-fourth of noninstitutional care is publicly subsidized, most elders and their families must pay privately for home care or go without these services (Doty, 1986). As the number of for-profit home health services has grown, 66% of the elderly who use community-based care pay at least part of the cost, and almost 50% pay the entire cost (Soldo & Manton, 1985). Not surprisingly, higher-income elderly are more likely to be able to purchase privately funded services, and private-paying clients receive more hours of home health care than do those who rely on public funds (Kane, 1989; Liu, Manton, & Liu, 1985). The affluent are also more likely to rely disproportionately for personal care services on aides, companions, and attendants who are not affiliated with established organizations and whom they recruit independently (Brody & Schoonover, 1986).

A more subtle gender inequity may also result from these class differences in service utilization. Agencies tend to treat families who can pay privately for services differently from those whose relatives depend on public funds. Since agencies serving private-pay clients increase their business by relieving families of care responsibilities, they tend to encourage relatives to abdicate burdensome tasks. In contrast, publicly funded programs operate under strict spending caps. The more relatives of clients dependent on Medicaid relinquish their care responsibilities, the more agencies risk exceeding their funding limits. Hence publicly funded agencies are unlikely to urge families to reduce their level of care. Instead, they are likely to be concerned with locating relatives who have not been providing care. Low-income women are therefore likely to encounter health and human service providers who automatically expect that they will provide care.

Even though Medicaid does fund nursing home care for low-income elderly, residents must exhaust their own resources before qualifying for Medicaid benefits. Even those who enter as private-pay patients usually "spend down" to Medicaid eligibility within a year (Doty, Liu, & Wiener, 1985; Rivlin & Wiener, 1988). At the same time, with the growth of proprietary nursing homes, profit-making considerations tend to govern admission criteria. Since the Medicaid rate of reimbursement is substantially below the private-pay rate, proprietary nursing homes usually limit the number of Medicaid beds, thereby discriminating against publicly funded patients, who may be relegated to institutions with the poorest quality of care (Rivlin & Wiener, 1988). Publicly funded patients who are very disabled and thus require heavy care may face the most difficulty in locating nursing home care, creating the paradox that Medicaid recipients with the greatest need for skilled nursing home care are the least likely to receive it (Lave, 1985; Lewin & Associates, 1987).

In the past, couples had to spend down all their resources to qualify for Medicaid payment for nursing home care, a procedure that left many older wives destitute. Fortunately, this gender bias of Medicaid has recently been recognized in the courts and by changes in state policies regarding spend-down requirements. However, states still limit the assets that can be used for home and family maintenance and for emergencies, ranging, in Washington state, for example, from $3,000 to $15,000 for married individuals. Nevertheless, an older wife who is faced with locating a Medicaid-funded nursing home bed, perhaps in a poorer-quality institution than that available to private-paying patients, may feel increasing pressure to continue to care for her husband at home.

As noted earlier, one positive change in Medicaid funding is that states can apply for waivers to provide nonmedical home- and community-based long-term care services. The states must demonstrate that the costs of these services do not exceed the cost to Medicaid from care in institutions. Some states have preestablished upper cost limits on such care, as in New York's Nursing Home Without Walls program. Because of such restrictions, the Medicaid waiver program has not significantly increased the level of support available to low-income women. Waivers have been granted sparingly and have been targeted to a small number of people in a restricted geographic area rather than statewide (Doty et al., 1985). As a result, the Medicaid waiver program reaches only 3% of the population at risk of institutionalization (U.S. Senate, Special Committee on Aging, 1990). An additional limitation is that some states provide services only at the point of discharge, or when an older person has already applied to a nursing home, thereby reaching people too late to divert them from institutional care (Lave, 1985).

A fundamental reason the Medicaid waiver program has not substantially expanded support to female caregivers is that the program's overall goal is cost containment, not the promotion of caregiver welfare. Benefits are usually based on the gap between the informal care already provided and the care necessary to keep the older person from being institutionalized. Since the Medicaid waiver program assumes that home care is less expensive than nursing home placement, the target for benefits must meet the "but for" criterion; that is, the person would be in a Medicaid-financed nursing home but for the services provided by the community-care program. The "but for" approach discounts the unpaid caregiving of friends and relatives (e.g., women) from the total amount of benefits to be paid. Accordingly, an older person without friends and family to provide care will receive a higher benefit than an equally disabled person who is receiving care from family. When family caregiving is taken into account for determining eligibility, low-income women and their families are indirectly penalized for their caregiving (Estes et al., 1983; Osterbusch et al., 1987). Although some states now allow relatives who meet program restrictions (often children or grandchildren, but not spouses) to be paid providers of in-home care, caregivers in most states are not adequately compensated for their services. In sum, for most elderly and their families, the Medicaid waiver program offers a fragmented, inadequate supply of community alternatives to nursing home care (Justice, 1988).

Programs Funding Social Services

The two major programs that fund social services for community-based elderly are the Social Services Block Grant (formerly Title XX) and Title III of the Older Americans Act (OAA). Both are shared federal-state programs, with states responsible for the implementation of federal legislation and regulations.

The Social Services Block Grant program, which funds primarily home-maker and chore services, is designed to assist families and older relatives to maintain self-sufficiency and independence. However, the program is limited to community-based services defined by each state and does not cover medical care except when it is "integral but subordinate" to the provision of a social service. Therefore, its ability to support the long-term care population significantly is relatively limited (U.S. House of Representatives, Committee on Energy and Commerce, 1986).

The Older Americans Act is intended to foster the development of broadly defined, comprehensive, and coordinated aging services—information and referral, meals, transportation, homemaker services, adult day care, and home care, including personal care services and respite. An advantage is that OAA services may be provided without the restrictions of Medicare and without the income tests of Medicaid. Therefore, Title III funds of the OAA may, in some cases, be used to serve persons whose Medicare and Medicaid benefits have been exhausted or who are ineligible for Medicaid.

Both programs are limited in their impact, however, by the relatively small allocation of resources (U.S. House of Representatives, Committee on Energy and Commerce, 1986). Moreover, the Omnibus Budget Reconciliation Act reduced federal funds and removed state matching funds and state reporting requirements for these programs (Bertghold, 1987). Community agencies that had relied heavily on Title XX funds tried to recover their losses by restructuring their programs toward the medical services reimbursed by Medicare (Wood, Fox, Estes, Lee, & Mahoney, 1986). The programs most likely to be eliminated or reduced were homemaker, chore, and personal care services—the very programs that could best minimize demands on family caregivers. These changes in the Social Services Block Grant and the Older Americans Act, along with those in Medicare and Medicaid, have sharply reduced low-income individuals' access to noninstitutional care, thereby increasing demands upon women as caregivers.

Responding to the gaps and fragmentation of federally funded services, states have also developed other initiatives to substitute community-based care for institutional care, such as screening and comprehensive medical and social assessment procedures to determine the most effective and least costly care options, reorganizing access to community services through case management or "gatekeeping" procedures for clients, and operating nursing home preadmission screening programs through local public health departments.

The number of private sector initiatives for the financing and delivery of long-term care is also growing—these include long-term care insurance; life-care or continuing-care retirement communities that combine residential living with medical, nursing, and social services in specialized facilities; and home equity conversions that convert assets in home equity into a lifetime stream of income that can be used for long-term care. However, only those elderly with financial means can take advantage of these private initiatives.

Proposed Policies and Programs

In the last decade, a number of policies and programs have been proposed—and, in some instances, funded—to attempt to address family caregivers' needs. These policies and programs typically focus on financial compensation, education, training, respite, and support groups. This section provides a critique, from a feminist perspective, of these initiatives.

Financial Compensation for Family Caregivers

Financial incentives for family care of the elderly have been debated in Congress since 1965. Many of these debates imply that families need to be induced to perform what they have already been doing for years, or that financial remuneration is detrimental to quality care. There are, however, some encouraging signs of legislative recognition of the financial burdens of care, with 34 states providing some type of economic support for family caregivers. These initiatives include tax supports in 14 states, direct-payment programs in 10 states, and tax and direct-payment programs in 10 states (Biegel, Schulz, Shore, & Morycz, 1989). It is unclear, however, whether the purpose of these programs is to offset expenses incurred, to enable families to purchase outside help, or to compensate caregivers for their services.

Federal tax supports for caregivers have several limitations. They cover expenses primarily for families with dependent children and younger disabled adults, not for families caring for impaired elders (Diamond, 1985). Since the tax credit is not refundable, it is of no benefit to family caregivers, such as low-income women, who owe no taxes or who do not itemize deductions. It is deductible only when all taxpayers in the house are employed, thereby penalizing women who have quit their jobs to provide care or who have never been employed. An additional limitation is that the tax credit is only for the actual expenditures for care up to $2,400 a year, not for direct care provided by a relative, and thus takes into account only a small part of the family's actual effort. As a result of these restrictions, only a fraction of caregivers are eligible for the tax credit (U. S. House of Representatives, Select Committee on Aging, 1987).

Proposed changes in the dependent tax credit would broaden the eligibility criteria, increase the level of credit to compensate family care costs, and expand the types of expenses that could be claimed. However, these changes still fail to address gender inequities, as proposed benefits neither lower the threshold of access to alternative forms of families nor compensate caregivers for the opportunities they forgo by assuming care responsibilities (Abel, 1987).

Initiatives that directly compensate caregivers for their services are also limited. Under the Community-Based Care Waiver program, Medicaid regulations deny payment for personal care to children over the age of 18, spouses who are defined as financially responsible for the recipient, and families who live apart from the care receivers. The denial of eligibility to spouses tends to affect wives more than it does husbands. Fortunately, some states have utilized other definitions of *family members* to circumvent these restrictions (Osterbusch et al., 1987). Some states also provide supplemental payments for personal care, home health, and other home care services (U.S. House of Representatives, Committee on Energy and Commerce, 1986). In most cases, however, these payments are not sufficient to benefit caregivers. Other restrictions limit the eligibility of family caregivers, such as providing payment only if no other home help is available, licensing caregivers, paying family members only if they had to give up employment, and requiring that the caregiver be employed by a provider agency (Osterbusch et al., 1987). State policies and programs need to be expanded and formalized to allow family members to be paid Medicare providers as well.

A fundamental limitation of the financial incentives approach is that it does not address nonrational, nonmonetary motives for providing care. In most instances, financial supports are not the primary factor in families' decisions to become caregivers (Biegel et al., 1989; Lave, 1985). Rather, caregivers tend to place higher priority on the need for flexible, highly individualized support services (Lewis & Meredith, 1988; Sommers & Shields, 1987).

**Education, Support Groups, and
Respite for Caregivers**

Education and support programs are a recent development oriented toward reducing caregiver burden; however, their cost-effectiveness is often evaluated according to whether or not they prolong the caregiving relationship, rather than according to caregivers' well-being. In such instances, education and training can reinforce traditional gender-based inequities in care responsibilities. Individual and group interventions that aim to enhance caregivers' self-efficacy and self-esteem (Gallagher, Lovett, & Zeiss, 1988), for example, may inadvertently imply that personal inadequacy is the source of caregiver burnout. Although such interventions may ease stress on a short-term basis, they still assume that caregiving is primarily the responsibility of individual family members, and offer no long-range, collective solutions that address underlying structural factors.

Such educational approaches also attempt to impose criteria of efficiency and cost-effectiveness on processes governed by standards of quality. For example, time-management training has been used to enhance caregivers' coping ability under the presumption that increased efficiency at task performance is an antidote to the stresses of multiple demands (Clark & Rakowski, 1983). Efficiency is a misplaced standard for caregiving, and questions related to cost-effectiveness are the wrong ones to ask. Instead of asking what is the cheapest way to keep older persons alive, we should be determining the best ways to care for them (Sommers & Shields, 1987).

In addition, perfecting efficient techniques based on standardized knowledge does not necessarily promote good caring, especially since caregivers' patterns of thought and affective relationships may differ sharply from the most rational way to do things. As a dominant societal value, efficiency implies that female caregivers are the cause of their own stress, and that women can reduce their feelings of burden by better managing their time and multiple demands. Under such conditions, education and training interventions may actually increase caregivers' stress.

Support groups for family caregivers are also limited in their potential to alter the structural imbalance of care responsibilities. When support groups function as a safety valve to let the caregiver blow off emotional steam and then return to the same situation, they do not offer long-run solutions to caregiver stress. In fact, support groups that focus only on individual competence can promote personal adjustment rather than the social reform necessary for the funding of in-home services. Another limitation is that support groups tend to reach caregivers who have the time to attend and are already connected to service systems, not those who are the most isolated and, therefore, may be experiencing the greatest stress. Support groups can ease the burden on family members, improve the quality of relationships, and promote the older person's dignity, but they cannot provide affordable community-based alternatives to nursing home care—the underlying source of most caregivers' stress (Abel, 1987).

Respite is one of the needs most frequently identified by caregivers (Crossman, London, & Barry, 1981; Horowitz & Dobrof, 1982; Montgomery & Borgatta, 1989; Montgomery & Prothero, 1986). When respite care provides tangible relief from the daily burdens of care, such services are invaluable. Unless caregivers can afford to purchase in-home or adult day care on a regular basis, however, their access to publicly funded respite services is limited. Assuming that a caregiver can find trustworthy care providers, it may take her months or even years to experience relaxation and relief from their presence. As a result, the shift of responsibility for care provided by respite programs is temporary and generally minimal. Evaluations of respite programs have focused primarily on patient care issues and cost-effectiveness, with little attention paid to the program's impact on caregiver functioning (Gallagher et al., 1988). Such evaluations overlook the fact that some respite services may still imply that caregivers, presumably refreshed by their short breaks, will continue to be primarily responsible.

Future Directions

To develop policies that address gender inequities in caregiving, it is important to recognize the interrelationships among the suppression of women, affiliative and caring values in our society, and the ways in which caring relationships underlie economic security. A just and equal society—a caring society that can meet the needs of all individuals who require maintenance—is not possible as long as inequality between men and women persists. To address gender inequities in elder care and, thus, to rebalance the roles of women and men, fundamental social institutions—the family and the workplace—must be reorganized. This may well entail abolishing the role of full-time individual caregiver in favor of a variety of forms of collective care performed by both men and women.

Most feminists would agree that an overriding imperative for creating a more caring society is to redefine the boundaries of the private and public spheres, the personal and the political, family and work. Strategies are needed not simply to integrate women into the public sphere (e.g., to move women into the labor force), but rather to extend the imperative of caring to men as well as to women. In such a society, women and men would act according to their abilities, potentials, and needs, rather than in response to traditional gender-based modes of thought and behavior.

As a first step in moving toward such a society, it is essential to break out of the mind-set that caregiving is a private duty. The assumption that family caregivers' welfare—and thus women's welfare—should be a central goal of social and health policy, not a means to low-cost care, is fundamental to this discussion of future changes. Policies and programs are needed that are gender responsive as well as cohort responsive, and that foster the inter-dependence of generations (Osterbusch et al., 1987).

Gender-Responsive Policies

Gender-responsive policies would take into account the special situation of women as caregivers, broadening their options for freedom and autonomy, but would not be gender specific; for example, leaves of absence would be available to both men and women as caregivers (P. Adams, 1990). By recognizing informal family caregiving as a social good, employers and policymakers would take the first step in developing programs and services that better support women both as caregivers and as employees. One strategy is to attach market value (e.g., direct payments of adequate wages and retirement benefits) to the socially necessary work of caring for dependents (whether performed by women and men in the home or by employees of public social services, voluntary organizations, or for-profit agencies). If caring *in* the community is the goal, rather than caring *by* the community, then all caring, particularly for the elderly, would be paid for—both outside the family, in residential homes and day centers, for example, and inside the family, through home help or home care nurses (Holter, 1985). Public care would be organized in a manner that neither implies a compassion trap for women nor involves a low level of welfare for society's members who are most in need of care.

Attaching an economic value to caregiving would also entail abandoning the term *caregiver* itself, which defines a compassion trap; by implying "caring" and "giving" for free, caregiving always leaves the receiver in debt. From this perspective, the concept of caregiving itself is a trap, because it is an attempt both to empower caregivers, by praise through implying self-sacrifice, and to disempower care recipients, who are indebted for the caring and the giving (MacDonald, 1988). In developing new policies, it is useful to distinguish between caring *about* and caring *for* someone: Caring *about* implies ties of affection, while caring *for* can be seen as an obligation that can be performed by nonfamily members as attendants as well as divided between the private and public spheres (Aronson, 1986; Jarrett, 1985).

Carried a step further, caregiving work would be accorded economic value by directly paying the caregiver, perhaps through an attendant allowance, as a recognized right for performing a service to society. This suggests that both family and nonfamily care providers be called attendants, since both attend to those aspects of living that cannot be accomplished by another because of a disability or a chronic condition. Under the concept of attendant care, one party to the exchange gets a service while preserving autonomy in meeting his or her needs, and the other receives an income through a homemaker wage or attendant allowance. By receiving funds that can be used to pay an attendant, an older person preserves his or her autonomy. Likewise, attendants would be adequately compensated with both wages and benefits, including vacations and health care, that recognize the importance of their caregiving work.

In sum, attending work, recognized as a legitimate economic category, would have its own criteria of value and rewards for both men and women, and therefore would be more likely to be perceived as a choice. This, in turn, would likely result in an increased capacity to cope and enhanced life satisfaction among families (Osterbusch et al., 1987). However, this strategy of monetary compensation is fraught with the paradox of financially rewarding nonmonetary, nonrational motives, and thereby making intimate relationships instrumental. Rather than starting with questions about wages and jobs, we might ask: How shall we care for and support both dependents and their caregivers?

Gender-responsive policies that address the needs of both caregiver and care receiver must include tangible services to provide relief, to redistribute caregiving tasks more fairly, and to advocate for humane and dignified care alternatives that adequately address the needs of frail elders. Such services should be delivered to a *caring unit* rather than a *marital unit*, and should be provided early on in the caregiving process rather than after a caregiving situation has reached crisis proportions. Child care, after-school programs, adult day care, respite, home help, and congregate meals are examples of publicly provided services that can provide both relief and practical help.

Thus a long-range strategy is needed to combine economic policies designed to improve women's position in the labor market with social policies to ensure that society, not individual women, assumes the responsibility for dependent care. One way to do so is through gender-responsive policies to further the integration of men's and women's public and private lives and to eliminate the gender-based division between the spheres of employment and home/family (Ehrenreich & English, 1979). A first step toward such an integration is through pay equity strategies—equal pay for men and women, elimination of sex discrimination in the labor market, and improvement in the minimum wage.

A second step, as discussed in Chapter 11 of this volume, is to make workplace modifications that will enable men and women to share caregiving tasks more equitably and thus to integrate their public and private lives. These include benefit packages with the options of day-care and in-home services for employees' older relatives, counseling and referral, and restructuring the work setting to accommodate both men's and women's family responsibilities through flextime, part-time jobs with full benefits, job sharing, and shorter workdays.

Cohort-Responsive Policies

Cohort-responsive policies would take account of the circumstances of current cohorts of younger and middle-aged women and the context in which they will grow old and face increasing responsibilities to care for older relatives. Social Security and pension systems need to be changed so that they are no longer based on traditional male employment patterns that penalize women for taking time off to provide care. Marriage should be treated as an economic partnership under Social Security, so that women would not be penalized by zero earnings for the time spent staying at home to care for children or for frail or disabled relatives. Mandatory and portable pensions are needed. Family and medical leave policies that protect caregivers' retirement benefits and that provide paid coverage for caregiving spouses and adult children of the elderly are needed to take account of the multiple caregiving and employment demands faced by women across the life span. Comprehensive and dependent care policies that encompass child care, family allowances, housing assistance, and health care exist in Scandinavian countries and can provide models to emulate (P. Adams, 1990; Hokenstad & Johansson, 1990).

Although part-time schedules and leaves are important first steps, they may still perpetuate gender-based inequities, since women generally use such options more than do men (Hartman, 1988). As a long-run strategy toward reclaiming time for families to maintain themselves, shortening the workweek is preferable to encouraging flextime and part-time work. Recalling that the 40-hour workweek was based on the wife's economic dependence on the husband, a more fundamental long-run strategy would be to make the 30-hour workweek the norm, through amendments to the Fair Labor Standards Act. This would require overtime premiums after a 30-hour week or a 6-hour day to assure that both men and women have time for family concerns. A further step would be the development of an insurance system for paid dependent care, perhaps as part of an expanded unemployment insurance scheme through new federal legislation (Hartman, 1988). Such insurance could also cover the needs of new entrants and reentrants who have been out of the labor market for a period of family care.

Intergenerational Policies

Finally, policies are needed to foster the interdependence of generations, to recognize that today's younger caregivers are tomorrow's older caregivers and care recipients. To the extent that the older population is protected through adequate insurance against the expenses associated with long-term care, their children and grandchildren will be indirect beneficiaries. As part of a social infrastructure that builds communities and supports family life across the life span, a publicly supported national health care system is critical. Housing and neighborhoods could be designed to meet the needs of all family members, through communal facilities that provide meals, meeting places, day care for children and adults, and readily accessible transportation. In other words, in order for the community to provide increasing amounts of care, we need policies to care for the community as a whole (Hartman, 1988).

Conclusion

Skeptics will contend that such major policy changes are not feasible. Yet social intervention on a grand scale occurred in the face of economic crises in the 1930s. Today's crises facing women and families are also severe. The burdens on women who are attempting to bridge the separate spheres without adequate social support are growing, and social policies that once seemed daring are no longer adequate. Social justice demands that women and men have choices about how to care for dependent family members as well as choices in the marketplace. For those who do choose to assume the primary role of providing compassion and care, public resources must be available to support them (Briggs & Oliver, 1985).

Callahan (1988) has argued that even with adequate social supports, we are still faced with moral claims that confront caregivers with imperative duties that include impossible demands. If we must ask caregivers to meet these demands, and if they agree, then it becomes essential that we reward and sustain them through new social forms more fitting to current demographic trends and economic conditions. The challenge for our society is to redefine its responsibility to the growing numbers of both caregivers and care receivers, so that caregiving work is equitably shared by gender. Such a redistribution is essential if we are to move toward a society where individuals are able to receive and to give to others the care that they want and need, and where both women and men experience equity in their employment and dependent care responsibilities.

13

Research on Gender
and Family Caregiving

Implications for Clinical Practice

LISA P. GWYTHER

Male and Female Caregivers Speak
for Themselves

It is an act of complete love—the most unselfish thing I have ever done. (a husband, quoted in Kaye & Applegate, 1989, p. 418)

I am helping [mother] meet death just as she helped me meet birth. (a son, quoted in Kaye & Applegate, 1989, p. 418)

Where can I find a load of patience when all my love for him is not enough to make me sweet? (a wife, quoted in Hampton Roads Alzheimer's Association, 1990, p. 5)

She [a daughter] spends twenty hours a week on top of her job to take care of her mother. You tell her to do less and she says, "How?" Yet, the more she does the more her mother wants. You offer to do more . . . and she says she's the only one who knows how to do it. The more she does, the less satisfied she is. She blames [me]. . . . "If you have to ask what to do, don't bother," she says. (a daughter's husband, quoted in Stafford, 1988, p. 179)

AUTHOR'S NOTE: I would like to acknowledge gratefully the support of AARP Andrus Foundation research grants from 1981 to 1990.

Relating Research to Practice

These quotes illustrate the range of coping responses, reactions to, and uses of informal support based on the gender and the relationship of the caregiving dyad. The preceding chapters of this book provide a rich data base on gender differences in family care and their impact on behavior, attitudes, and caregiving outcomes. Although scholarly research demands conservative analysis and cautious interpretation, clinical practice demands immediate response to and interpretation for families facing conflicts or problems associated with elder care. The complexity of the preceding research findings and their potential interpretations and implications for practice defy simplistic cookbook approaches based on a single variable such as gender.

The demands of elder care are not predicted solely on the basis of gender, duration of care, diagnosis, or severity of illness of the care receiver (George & Gwyther, 1986; Horowitz, 1985b). The cohort, cultural or ethnic context, relationship, family history, coping styles, and subjective appraisal may be equally as important as needs or gender in predicting caregiving outcomes and social support.

Three Encouraging Trends for Practice

If we look specifically at the research on gender differences, three encouraging trends emerge for practice. First, this research focuses on the family as a unit rather than on the primary care dyad alone. Not all elders have one consistent primary family caregiver, particularly elders with prolonged degenerative illnesses who may outlive available spouse caregivers.

Second, the research would suggest that practitioners are better advised to focus on how to support and enhance the quality of elder care and satisfaction with care based on the family unit's preferred level of involvement. The late 1970s practice literature on elder care took a more cheerleading or motivational approach. The goal of practice during this period was to encourage a potentially unwilling family to provide long-term care that was not available from public or private services (Brody, 1985). Today, practice wisdom suggests that there is little that can be done to encourage an unwilling family, regardless of gender, to provide long-term care (Finley, Roberts, & Banahan, 1988). The converse is equally true. It is exceedingly difficult to discourage a committed family, regardless of gender, from relinquishing its preferred level of involvement (Gwyther, 1990a).

Third, all the chapters in this book tend to describe family care in nonpathological terms. In this context, family caregiving is not a remediable disorder. Seasoned practitioners learn to accept family care as a normative, but potentially stressful, adaptive challenge (Brody, 1985). There is good evidence in the preceding chapters of persistent family solidarity based on values, preferences, reciprocity, obligation, or commitment.

Families are more likely to seek professional help if they are viewed by professionals as competent adults seeking personally relevant solutions to problems in living. This is in distinct contrast to the mental health services reimbursement regulations that require a family or individual diagnosis. Families are likely to be empowered to the extent they are treated as consumers who need information to make informed decisions, rather than as patients or clients who need "treatment."

Families may be in crisis when they seek clinical assistance, but effective crisis intervention builds on family strengths and well-practiced problem-solving or coping strategies rather than on diagnostic definitions of pathology. The consequences of labeling may include exacerbation of helplessness or hopelessness of family caregivers and exaggeration of family dependence on professionals. Reimbursement regulations tend to force the application of diagnostic labels to justify payment for professional services. If a clinician resists such diagnostic or pathologic labeling, he or she is more likely to enhance family capacity for effective coping and decision making. Further, the caregiving literature suggests that family adaptation and resilience are more common than defeat (George & Gwyther, 1986).

Although research findings document specific gender differences in behavior, attitudes, objective and subjective appraisal, and social support, these primarily cross-sectional findings do not tell clinicians much about what to expect over the course of an individual's or family's experience with long-term care. Elder care is a dynamic process in which context, events, and the meaning attached to these processes may be more significant than gender in determining practice goals and anticipated outcomes. For example, the meaning attached to the caregiving role may be particularly important:

> I keep reading doom and gloom and all this negative talk. The positive side is I've still got her and continue loving her and remember how many wonderful years we had together. I approach it just as I approached going to work before retiring to be with her. (Fulton, 1984)

Clinicians are often less constrained by limits of methodological rigor, and are more willing to apply research findings to fit their practice style. I view the preceding chapters about gender and family care in America a little like Garrison Keillor views his mythical Lake Wobegon. American family care may be at a place "where all the women are strong and stressed, all the men do better and less, and having a wife, many daughters, or sisters make your long term care odds above average" (Gwyther, 1990b). This would lead clinicians to two recommendations for families facing elder care: First, try to be born a man with lots of sisters, whether you become a caregiver or a care receiver; second, hold on to a long-term spouse, and have lots of daughters or sisters who remain in your hometown. Although these recommendations are obviously facetious, they highlight the major thesis of this chapter. Gender, in and of itself, does not provide much direction for practice, nor is it amenable to clinical tinkering. Yet gender is not irrelevant to clinical practice; rather, it is more relevant to certain phases of the clinical process than to others.

This chapter will highlight the use of gender research findings on elder care in three areas of clinical practice: the assessment of the individual and social context and the effects of gender on subjective perceptions of caregiver burden, gender-sensitive targeting of clinical support strategies, and professional interventions to overcome gender-specific barriers to the use of appropriate, timely informal and formal support.

Gender and Family Care

Spouses, when available, are the first-line primary caregivers to frail elders (Ikels, 1983), and male spouses of Alzheimer's patients may be the one group of male caregivers who have been studied in any depth (Fitting, Rabins, Lucas, & Eastham, 1986; George & Gwyther, 1986; Kaye & Applegate, 1990b). Dr. Smith, described in the following case study, illustrates many research findings on prototypical husband caregivers.[1]

Case Study: Dr. Smith

Dr. Smith cared for his wife, an Alzheimer's patient, in their home for more than 10 years. He took pride in her participation in clinical research trials and in his careful monitoring of her medication side effects. Over time, he reluctantly reduced his professional practice. The couple's extensive social life became constricted by Mrs. Smith's socially inappropriate behavior, but Dr. Smith continued to participate in professional and civic organizations with his two sons.

The Smiths had two sons and two daughters, all married and living within an hour's drive of the rural parental home. The daughter who had the most competing work and family demands was also the most actively involved and subjectively distressed by her mother's illness. Dr. Smith expected his daughters to call their mother three times a day, and to take her out at least three times a week. His sons had more resources, but they were less subjectively distressed and less involved in their mother's daily care. In contrast, the daughters and daughters-in-law called professionals regularly for support, participated actively in support groups, and worked with a social worker to convince Dr. Smith to try an adult day-care program for his wife at their church. Dr. Smith attended only one support group function, one honoring the "Male Caregiver of the Year," because the honoree was a well-known professional who also cared for his wife with only informal help from his daughters-in-law.

Dr. Smith approached care for his wife as he did care for his patients, in a problem-solving, good-humored, self-confident manner. He was disappointed in the inequitable division of responsibility among his daughters, but not in that between his daughters and his sons. He believed he was paying his wife back for a lifetime of support and nurturance, and he expected his children and the community to pay her back as well for her nurturing and volunteer leadership. He did not understand the necessity of payment for church-based adult day care, despite adequate income, because he believed his wife had "earned" her church's support. He refused to hire in-home help for personal care because "she had daughters for that." Nursing home placement was not an option because he "promised her he would never do that." By the time his wife became too impaired to attend day care, his daughters were physically and emotionally drained, feeling guilty, ineffective, and angry with their brothers.

Dr. Smith's daughters had much greater expectations of themselves than their father and their brothers had of themselves. Dr. Smith and his sons accepted their limits as family caregivers, and expressed no guilt or remorse. These men believed that they had lived up to values of family solidarity, and that Mrs. Smith's care should be a family responsibility.

Dr. Smith saw himself as a physician first, who, incidentally, cared for a sick wife. He did not identify himself as a "family caregiver." He expected his daughters to provide more personal care than his sons (Horowitz, 1985b; Zarit, Todd, & Zarit, 1986). He provided more concrete, instrumental help in managing his wife's money, medicines, and symptoms. He expressed little subjective burden, although he was objectively burdened by the loss of his practice and personal time. He was comfortable setting limits on his involvement (B. Miller, 1990). He did, however, express disappointment over his subjective perception of the adequacy of informal support. There was a mismatch between his perceived "earned right" to informal support and the availability and willingness of his preferred sources of support (i.e., his children and his church).

Dr. Smith's children further illustrate findings on adult sons and daughters as secondary caregivers. His daughters provided more intensive direct care, and they expressed more subjective distress and family conflict over the inequitable division of labor. The most overcommitted daughter was the most involved, and she felt guilty despite her intensive long-term contributions to her mother's care. The daughters and daughters-in-law were the information seekers and the links to both informal and formal services, and they were more comfortable with the use of formal help. The sons felt equally emotionally committed to their parents, but less constrained, and they provided more instrumental help with transportation and secondary support in accompanying their father to familiar, traditionally male activities. The men in this family perceived no inequities in informal responsibility.

Women, especially wives in recent second marriages, like Mrs. Jones, described in the next case study, express greater subjective burden in caregiving (Barusch, 1988; Brody, 1989; Fitting et al., 1986; George & Gwyther, 1986). Caregiving for a terminally ill spouse was not a new experience for Mrs. Jones, and she felt much more constrained and overwhelmed than Dr. Smith, despite the shorter duration of her husband's illness. The responses of Mrs. Jones's stepsons were also gender specific. They "expected" a female spouse to provide home care, despite their deeper emotional attachment to their father. Yet they appreciated the opportunity to provide "traditional male assistance" with financial and legal arrangements.

Case Study: Mrs. Jones

Mrs. Jones's second husband was dying of heart disease and he had been in and out of the hospital for a year. Mr. Jones required full nursing care. Mrs. Jones considered herself a fragile person who was incapable of providing such care despite available home health services. This was her second experience providing terminal care for a spouse, and she had vividly unpleasant memories of caring for first husband, an alcoholic with terminal cancer.

Mr. Jones had two sons who did not live nearby, but who were very committed to their father. They opposed nursing home placement for him, and they believed it was a wife's responsibility to provide terminal care for a husband in his own home with some outside help. Mrs. Jones was so frightened of assuming full-time care for Mr. Jones that she was willing to use her first husband's estate to pay privately for Mr. Jones's nursing home care.

A family meeting was held over a holiday weekend before Mr. Jones's final hospital discharge. The meeting was called by Mrs. Jones's daughter, Alice, an experienced home health nurse. Alice encouraged her mother to tell her stepsons how difficult it had been for her to care for Mr. Jones after his previous hospitalizations. Mrs. Jones expressed her fears, her sense of isolation, and her disappointment with the intensity of available home health care. Alice was a geriatric nurse, and she could interpret Mr. Jones's condition, prognosis, and care requirements to his sons. Alice encouraged her mother's stepsons to consider all reasonable options, except moving their father away from her mother. Alice reminded the sons that her mother was Mr. Jones's most available and most committed visitor and advocate. If this family meeting had not occurred before Mr. Jones's placement, the sons might have sabotaged Mrs. Jones's obviously painful decision.

This blended family came to an agreement on a common goal in just one family meeting facilitated by a family member who was also a geriatric nurse. Alice pointed out how Mrs. Jones and her stepsons were equally committed to assuring Mr. Jones's dignity, comfort, and self-esteem based on their common sustained interest in his well-being. All members of the family agreed to remind Mr. Jones repeatedly that he was not forgotten or abandoned.

Mr. Jones's sons, at Alice's suggestion, agreed to ask their father for power of attorney to use his assets for his care. This was a task that they considered appropriate for male children. By doing this, Mr. Jones's sons preserved their emotionally supportive relationship with their stepmother through their father's death and the family's bereavement. Further, their willingness to use their father's assets preserved Mrs. Jones's assets for her needs and/or her children's inheritance, a secondary gain that promoted positive blended family relationships as well.

Gender-Sensitive Assessment

An understanding of gender differences as predictors, enablers, or predisposing influences on behavior, subjective perceptions of burden, social expectations, and risks is helpful for assessment. Analysis of the effects of gender influences can provide direction for work with elder family care units in a number of ways.

First, gender may suggest potential sources of informal support, given the caveat that distance blurs gender differences in behavior, but not necessarily subjective distress. Dr. Smith looked to his daughters despite the advantaged position and proximity of his sons. Later in the course of his wife's illness, he expected the "church ladies" to deliver meals, but he did not expect similar concrete assistance from the men of the church. Mrs. Jones's daughter, Alice, was expected to provide secondary caregiving support despite the fact that Mr. Jones was not her father. Although Alice's proximity influenced her direct care for her stepfather, she was as subjectively distressed as Mr. Jones's more distant sons, because of the consequences of caregiving for her and her mother.

Second, gender-sensitive assessment may suggest potential specific dimensions of burden for both primary and secondary caregivers. For example, in studies of Alzheimer's caregivers at Duke University, women caregivers were more likely to report mental health symptoms and less satisfaction with the quantity and quality of personal time (George & Gwyther, 1986). Husband caregivers, however, were less likely to report subjective mental health symptoms and used less psychotropic medication (Clipp & George, 1990b). In contrast, these husbands voluntarily reported the use of alcohol as a coping response. Because the current cohort of older male caregivers may be at increased risk of cardiovascular disease, a clinician assessing a husband caregiver may inquire about diagnoses and medications as a proxy for physical health dimensions of burden. My own clinical experience suggests that husband caregivers, in particular, are more likely to endorse physical health than mental health symptoms in structured interviews. Husbands may also acknowledge less socially desirable coping strategies as the following suggests:

> I'm not stressed, and I don't need help with her. If I get fed up, I just tie her to the bed for the day and go fishing. (male caregiver respondent in a Duke University survey, 1983)

There are exceptions to every gender trend. Some clinicians believe that male caregivers are more likely to acknowledge decrements in financial well-being as a consequence of caregiving than are wife caregivers. The wife caregivers quoted below illustrate a prominent concern about objective financial burden:

I don't understand why people like me shouldn't be able to have some help every day. As always the problem is money. We just could not save enough to afford that kind of help—we raised three children and did not have much schooling. But we always paid plenty of taxes. (quoted in Gwyther & Ballard, 1988, p. 3)

I called the visiting nurse and she doesn't think even she could lift him. She told me I had burnout and they feel Carlo might have to go to a nursing home. He is only sixty-three. The doctor said he could live a normal longevity. Where do I get the heart to put him in one? Where do I get the money? Both situations are driving me crazy. (quoted in Strong, 1988, p. 263)

Adult children, especially daughters, report more subjective than objective dimensions of burden (George & Gwyther, 1986). It is painful to watch a formerly all-powerful parent deteriorate, or to watch a "well" parent caregiver decline in response to the demands of the other parent's illness. Sons may have strong subjective reactions to or cultural taboos about providing intimate personal care for a mother (see Chapter 5, this volume). Clinicians working with daughters as secondary caregivers might focus the assessment on subjective distress associated with the loss of a parent or subjective fears associated with the consequences of caregiving on the well parent.

Gender-Sensitive Targeting of Clinical Support

Gender may suggest the timing, selection, and interpretation of information most relevant to individual family caregivers. For example, my experience with husband caregivers for Alzheimer's patients suggests that they place greater emphasis initially on treatment options than on coping strategies. Males may cope with elder care initially through executive-style information gathering, and they often respond best to educational approaches. The assessment questions that address informational needs could focus on what the male caregiver has read, heard, or been told about Alzheimer's research or treatment options. Both husbands and sons may initially appear more eager to "leave no stone unturned" and are sometimes more likely to seek second opinions on significant diagnoses such as Alzheimer's.

A wise clinician assesses the "chief complaint," or what brings the caregiver to the clinic at this point. Often, the reasons stated vary by gender and/or relationship to the patient. Males are more likely to have questions about available instrumental assistance (i.e., help with meals, shopping, and laundry, or the availability of treatment options). Wife caregivers for Alzheimer's patients often, however, have initial questions about the behavioral, functional, mood, or personality changes in their husbands. These wives may need initial reassurance that their husbands' increased irritability may be a symptom of brain disease rather than a personal response to a well-meaning wife.

The acknowledgment of gender-specific concerns of caregiving families may guide the allocation of limited professional time for individual and family counseling. For example, early research at Duke indicates that husband caregivers may consider the problem-solving aspects of care more appropriate to their previous work or executive functions. They may not need professional guidance in investigating care options. On the other hand, female caregivers may initially express greater need to ventilate feelings, frustrations, and unmet expectations before they can organize care or develop effective coping strategies. Older women in more traditional gender-defined marital roles may be least likely to trust their decision making for cognitively impaired husbands. These women may respond best to support from male authority figures such as physicians.

Overcoming Gender-Specific Barriers

Gender research could provide some direction for how best to describe family support services in gender-sensitive terms. The language of family care is powerful. The term *caregiver* has feminine and potentially negative connotations for the oldest cohort of male caregivers, whose primary identity comes from work. If the clinical assessment of an executive male family caregiver suggests his preference for "organized" approaches, he may respond best to a description of a case manager as a "customer services representative." Older wife caregivers may view adult day care as demeaning to their formerly productive, competent husbands. They may, however, respond positively to the idea that a male participant can be helped to see himself as a "volunteer" at a "day center" rather than as an "adult day-care participant."

In a similar vein, female caregivers are more frequent users of family support hot lines or help lines, whereas male caregivers are more likely to seek "information and referral" services or to attend seminars about a wife's illness. Practice experience suggests that women are more likely to respond to such labels as "support group" and men are more likely to respond to such labels as "seminar" or "forum." The wise clinician will recognize the influence of gender in an assessment and label support services in gender-sensitive ways.

Practice Caveats for Use of Gender Considerations

Gender is only one elder-care variable and may not be the most salient one for individual practice with a family care unit. All husbands are not necessarily equal or interchangeable. Background information on a family's gender composition may be a necessary, but not sufficient, guide for establishing practice goals or measuring practice outcomes. If change is inevitable, change in the caregiving process, context, relationships, and events may be more salient for practice than static variables such as gender.

Heterogeneity among elder-care family units is no longer an issue. Clinical experience with one family caregiving dyad may or may not be relevant or transferable to the next elder-care situation encountered in practice. The implications for practice are obvious. Clinical practice with families must fit the family situation and process rather than forcing the family to fit a "model" of practice with family caregivers. Individualization of both individual and family practice is essential.

Persons with well-developed, effective palliative coping strategies, regardless of gender, report less subjective distress (Bearon & Koenig, 1990). Research at Duke University, for example, documents the effectiveness and pervasiveness of a strong religious faith in successful coping with late-life transitions and illness in rural southeastern Baptist-dominated areas. Clinicians and support group leaders frequently hear from successful survivors of caregiving who attribute their success to a sense of humor, the grace of God, good friends, and old-fashioned ingenuity. Strong social support and practical problem-solving skills are frequently associated with positive caregiving outcomes (Clipp & George, 1990a).

Subjective appraisal, or the meaning attached to a caregiving experience, can be a powerful predictor of outcome. Studies at Duke University have found that burden is more sensitive to subjective measures of adequacy and dependability of informal support than to objective levels of support (George & Gwyther, 1986). Dr. Smith, described in the first case study above, appreciated the opportunity to reciprocate his wife's devotion, but his burden was based on his subjective distress with the adequacy and dependability of his daughters' and church's secondary caregiving contributions. Objectively, he had more informal help than many husband caregivers, but his behavior, attitudes, and responses were based on his subjective appraisal of their adequacy vis-à-vis his gender-specific expectations.

Old family conflicts or dyadic conflicts often resurface around caregiving demands. These relational variables may affect preferred outcomes of care. One distant brother never forgave his "local" brother for the placement of their father in a nursing home during his final illness. When his mother became ill, this distant brother's goal was to make sure that she "was never abandoned" in the same way. Other family dynamics may influence values and preferred outcomes more than gender alone.

Another practice caveat in considering the role of gender is the evidence for both positive and negative outcomes of caregiving for both men and women. Younger wife caregivers are reported to be most subjectively distressed and objectively burdened by the off-time nature of their care demands. Moreover, some husbands relate similar feelings. One very committed and dedicated husband caregiver, when asked by a social worker what he had learned from caring for his wife that he wanted to share with future husbands facing caregiving, tearfully suggested, "Don't get married—it hurts too much" (quoted in Gwyther, 1990c).

Gender Implications for Intervention

It is likely that informal family care will continue to predominate in the long-term care provided to frail older persons. Formal services must continue to reach out actively to isolated frail elders without available family support who pose health and safety risks to themselves and others. For example, current estimates suggest that 20% of moderate to severe dementia patients live alone, and an estimated 10% have no family close by or at a distance (U.S. Congress, Office of Technology Assessment, 1990). These persons pose safety risks to themselves and others because of impaired judgment, disruptive behavior, or impaired decision making. Their passivity places them at even greater risk of neglect or exploitation than physically frail elders (U.S. Congress, Office of Technology Assessment, 1990).

For dependent elders with the potential for available family care, professional practice should focus on minimizing negative outcomes of care on caregivers and care receivers in four areas:

(1) increasing the effectiveness, quality, and satisfaction of the family with the care they are willing and able to offer;
(2) minimizing secondary disability in both caregivers and care receivers;
(3) filling gaps in available support services for families; and

(4) helping families achieve greater equity (not equality) in the division of responsibility within the kin network and between kin and public sources.

The reader will note that none of these goals directly relates to gender issues per se. However, these practice foci do target issues of subjective appraisal, equity, expectations, barriers, and potential sources of family conflict, all of which may be influenced by gender to some degree. For example, practice aimed at increasing the effectiveness and quality of family care must address traditional gender-specific definitions of *effectiveness* and *quality*. A 75-year-old wife caregiver's definition of quality care may mean nothing more than the personal attention she can offer. A 75-year-old husband caregiver's definition of effective care may include how quickly personal care tasks are completed. For male caregivers, minimizing secondary disability may mean professional attention to cardiovascular risks of caregiver stress; more likely secondary disability risks in female caregivers would be mental health symptoms, such as dysphoria.

Filling gaps in family support services may also be influenced by gender. Family support to an older wife caregiver may mean finding someone to assume responsibility for her husband's previous household repair role. Family support services for a male caregiver may mean encouraging him to eat out with his wife or to have meals delivered. Finally, helping families achieve greater equity in responsibility within the kin network may be most influenced by gender expectations. For example, one daughter-in-law felt oppressed by constant demanding telephone calls from her memory-impaired mother-in-law. Her mother-in-law's three sons all lived and worked nearby but delegated daily care to this homemaker daughter-in-law. The daughter-in-law's feelings of inequity were resolved with a family agreement that she would notify one of the sons whenever their mother wanted something.

Guidelines for Gender-Sensitive Interventions

Clinicians who work with families and impaired elders recognize that families reach out fleetingly and often before actually accepting help. Often, what a family wants first is some interpretation of the help available in terms of their unique situation. For clinicians, this implies an initial focus on family network strengths, expectations, and educational strategies geared toward filling in gaps or partial information, or correcting misconceptions that may adversely affect the family's interpretation of the help available. Sometimes, repetition and confirmation with secondary family caregivers are crucial.

Professional help with family conflict resolution may be the best use of available clinical time. The goals may be to enhance reciprocity among and between primary and secondary caregivers, to increase the emotional support available to the primary caregiver, and to assure a common understanding between primary and secondary caregivers. Gender issues may play a role, as they did with Mrs. Jones's family, discussed in the second case study above.

Sometimes, just knowledge of the availability of help is enough to change subjective family appraisals of the adequacy of support. A professional may help family members to say to each other that they will come when called or remain dependable and open to the primary caregiver's wishes, strengths, and limitations. For many female caregivers, this is enough to enhance their security and confidence in their ability to sustain preferred levels of involvement. For example, one married daughter who moved her mother in with her family to provide daily care told me, "I can manage just knowing I have an out. If Mom's care starts to affect my marriage or my relationship with my kids, my sisters are ready to take their turns."

The same can be said of professional availability. Women in particular, in my experience, seem to respond positively to the continuity of a trusted professional's availability on a family support hot line. These telephone relationships with anonymous caregivers over time can be quite therapeutic. Just the knowledge that a known voice is standing by if other questions or crises of confidence occur may be reassuring in itself. The medium is the message, and the power of the telephone in supporting female caregivers, particularly isolated women, should not be underestimated. Repetition of information often is necessary before women caregivers will reach out to others. Reassurance that they are not crazy or self-centered may empower them to seek additional support. The anonymity and privacy of a hot line offers additional benefits to women who believe they have not lived up to expectations or family values, or those who feel that they are betraying an impaired husband's confidence.

Women and men may have gender-specific criteria for acceptable helpers (Gwyther, 1990a). Matching people with acceptable helpers may enhance the family support process. One husband was particularly disturbed by his demented wife's delusions of infidelity on his part. He used the hot line for private help in understanding the source of her symptoms, and called several times to be reminded that many men in his situation have wishes to leave the situation that make them feel even more guilty in the face of such paranoid accusations. He finally agreed to see a counselor, but the female social worker on the hot line recognized that he would be more comfortable with a male, particularly a person who could "absolve his guilt." He was a deeply religious man, and he was successfully matched to a male pastoral counselor who could provide acceptable and religiously compatible explanations for his conflicted feelings.

Some women have strong feelings about other women providing personal care for their fathers or husbands. While there are limited numbers of available male aides, it is often worth the time of a professional to find a suitable match. Wives of Alzheimer's patients are particularly vulnerable to their husbands' misinterpretations of personal care from younger women. Some self-sacrificing wives feel displaced by their husbands' obvious enthusiasm for younger female helpers.

These gender-specific, idiosyncratic preferences should be acknowledged to the extent possible. Professionals should assume that the family unit is vulnerable and often in crisis at the time they first reach out for help. A successful experience is likely to encourage the use of other appropriate supports (Gwyther & Ballard, 1988). It is unrealistic to expect families in crisis to make major shifts in attitudes, beliefs, or expectations while they are feeling so threatened and vulnerable. Further, when family preferences are acknowledged, the family's feelings of control are enhanced. This is in keeping with the emphasis, discussed above, on treating the family as consumer versus patient and a nonpathological emphasis in practice.

The Future of Gender-Friendly Research and Care

The future of gender-friendly research in elder care awaits outcomes from five potentially promising areas of health services research. The first area includes studies of the efficacy and cost-effectiveness of various services specifically targeted to men or women as caregivers or care receivers. An example would be evaluations of demonstration programs for working women caregivers. A second promising area of inquiry is intervention research targeted to underserved or hard-to-reach male or female care receivers or caregivers. For example, older, poor, single black women as care receivers may need special support services. Male caregivers are also considered hard-to-reach research participants. A third potential area of inquiry is the role of gatekeepers to health care, such as physicians, or community gatekeepers, such as postal employees or pharmacists. It is unclear whether gatekeeper outreach strategies are more effective with women or with men; they are generally targeted to isolated elders, regardless of gender. A fourth promising area of research is that of gender-sensitive or gender-friendly adaptations or modifications of services or reimbursement systems. For example, support group strategies may need to be adapted or modified to become viable sources of support for male caregivers. Finally, new gender-sensitive designs could be evaluated in the context of demonstrations. For example, if isolated female caregivers find telephone support most accessible and acceptable, how can informal networks of telephone support be developed and sustained for long-term use?

Future clinical research with family caregivers should address successful models to support both males and females facing elder-care responsibilities. Demographic trends suggest that the focus of these interventions will not be as gender specific for future cohorts. Future cohorts of caregivers will face increasing conflicts and risks from combining work and family responsibilities, rather than from multiple family commitments currently faced by women in particular. Intervention research must address ways to help both men and women meet preferred obligations and commitments to family and work. To the extent we can dignify the equitable sharing of responsibility among family members and between family and public sources, we will better serve future cohorts of caregivers and care receivers. The future of gender-sensitive care strategies is immediately relevant, while we wait for the results of well-designed and -implemented health services research.

The timing and interpretation of information using essentially educational strategies is a critical first step. More practice attention should focus on the medium, the message, the timing, and the amount of information, particularly about the role of informal and formal support.

Individualized clinical work should target potential or real family conflicts, most often generated by inequities in shared responsibility, criticism of the primary caregiver, or different subjective appraisals of the need for, and availability of, help. The goal of professional interventions may be to empower families as consumers to use available informal and formal support in an appropriate, timely manner to meet preferred levels of commitment. Traditional gender-specific expectations and preferences die hard, and it may be more successful to honor these familiar and comforting traditions within families than to work for attitude or value changes among vulnerable families.

There is ample evidence that the buck stops with the family when it comes to emotional, physical, and financial responsibility for long-term care. If families are responsible, they should be afforded control and a mix of acceptable service options that can be activated as circumstances, contexts, and resources dictate. However, sometimes families appreciate concrete recommendations from professional authority figures such as physicians, who may temporarily relieve family ambivalence and conflict.

Practice wisdom suggests that we not "kill the goose that lays the golden eggs." Until we better understand the antecedents and consequences of deeply entrenched gender roles, beliefs, and expectations, and until we have adequate and gender-sensitive long-term care and family leave policies, we should support families in maintaining preferred levels of traditional gender-specific involvement. For practice, this means that we must look critically at what we offer both male and female caregivers, paying special attention to the timing, quality, and amount of information, and nontraditional service settings and methods. Further, we should consider the power of language to affect attitudes and behavior, and pay special attention to our labeling and marketing of family support services in gender-sensitive ways.

Note

1. I was the social worker for the family described in this case study; the Jones case study that follows is also drawn from my personal experience. Details have been changed in both cases to protect the families' identities.

References

Abel, E. K. (1986). Adult daughters and care for the elderly. *Feminist Studies, 12*, 479-497.

Abel, E. K. (1987). *Love is not enough: Family care of the frail elderly.* Washington, DC: American Public Health Association.

Abel, E. K. (1989). Family care of the frail elderly: Framing an agenda for change. *Women's Studies Quarterly, 1-2*, 75-86.

Abel, E. K. (1990a). Informal care for the disabled elderly: A critique of recent literature. *Research on Aging, 12*, 139-157.

Abel, E. K. (1990b). Family care of the frail elderly. In E. K. Abel & M. K. Nelson (Eds.), *Circles of care: Work and identity in women's lives* (pp. 65-91). Albany: State University of New York Press.

Abel, E. K., & Nelson, M. K. (1990). Circles of care: An introductory essay. In E. K. Abel & M. K. Nelson (Eds.), *Circles of care: Work and identity in women's lives* (pp. 1-34). Albany: State University of New York Press.

Abramovitz, M. (1988). *Regulating the lives of women: Social welfare policy from colonial times to the present.* Boston: South End.

Adams, B. N. (1968). *Kinship in an urban setting.* Chicago: Markham.

Adams, M. (1975). The compassion trap. In V. Gornick & B. Moron (Eds.), *Woman in sexist society* (pp. 555-578). New York: New American Library.

Adams, P. (1990). Children as contributions in kind: Social security and family policy. *Social Work, 35*, 492-498.

Albrecht, S. L., Bahr, H. M., & Chadwick, B. C. (1979). Changing family and sex roles: An assessment of age differences. *Journal of Marriage and the Family, 41*, 41-50.

Aldous, J. (1987). New views on the family life of the elderly and the near elderly. *Journal of Marriage and the Family, 49*, 227-234.

Aldous, J., Klaus, E., & Klein, D. M. (1985). The understanding heart: Aging parents and their favorite children. *Child Development, 56*, 303-316.

Alley, J. M. (1988). *Family caregiving: Family strains, coping response patterns, and caregiver burden.* Unpublished doctoral dissertation, Virginia Polytechnic Institute and State University.

Altergott, K., & Duncan, S. (1987, November). *Age, gender and activities of daily life.* Paper presented at the 40th Annual Meeting of the Gerontological Society of America, Washington, DC.

Alwin, D. F., Converse, P. E., & Martin, S. S. (1985). Living arrangements and social integration. *Journal of Marriage and the Family, 47*, 319-334.

Anderson, T. B. (1984). Widowhood as a life transition: Its impact on kinship ties. *Journal of Marriage and the Family, 46*, 105-114.

Anthony-Bergstone, C. R., Zarit, S. H., & Gatz, M. (1988). Symptoms of psychological distress among caregivers of dementia patients. *Psychology and Aging, 3*, 245-248.

Antonucci, T. C. (1990). Social supports and social relationships. In R. H. Binstock & L. K. George (Eds.), *Handbook of aging and the social sciences* (3rd ed.). San Diego, CA: Academic Press.

Antonucci, T. C., & Akiyama, H. (1987). Social networks in adult life and a preliminary examination of the convoy model. *Journal of Gerontology: Social Sciences, 42*, 519-527.

Araji, S. K. (1977). Husbands' and wives' attitude-behavior congruence on family roles. *Journal of Marriage and the Family, 39*, 309-320.

Archbold, P. G. (1983). The impact of parent-caring on women. *Family Relations, 32*, 39-45.

Arling, G., & McAuley, W. J. (1984). The family, public policy, and long-term care. In W. H. Quinn & G. A. Hughston (Eds.), *Independent aging: Family and social systems perspectives* (pp. 133-148). Rockville, MD: Aspen.

Aronson, J. (1985). Family care and the elderly: Underlying assumptions and their consequences. *Canadian Journal on Aging, 4*, 115-125.

Aronson, J. (1986). Care of the frail elderly: Whose responsibility? *Canadian Social Work Review, 3*, 45-84.

Atchley, R. (1988). *Social forces and aging.* Belmont, CA: Wadsworth.

Atkinson, M., & Glass, B. (1985). Marital age heterogamy and homogamy, 1900 to 1980. *Journal of Marriage and the Family, 47*, 685-691.

Avioli, P. S. (1989). The social support functions of siblings in later life. *American Behavioral Scientist, 33*, 45-57.

Axinn, J., & Stern, M. J. (1985). Age and dependency: Children and the aged in American social policy. *Milbank Memorial Fund Quarterly, 63*, 648-670.

Bahr, H. M. (1976). The kinship role. In F. I. Nye (Ed.), *Role structures and analysis of family* (pp. 61-79). Beverly Hills, CA: Sage.

Balbo, L. (1982). The servicing work of women and the capitalist state. *Political Power and Social Theory, 3*, 251-270.

Barnard, A., & Good, A. (1984). *Research practice in the study of kinship.* London: Academic Press.

Barney, J. L. (1977). The prerogative of choice in long-term care. *The Gerontologist, 17*, 309-314.

Barusch, A. (1988). Problems and coping strategies of elderly spouse caregivers. *The Gerontologist, 28*, 677-685.

Barusch, A., & Spaid, W. (1989). Gender differences in caregiving: Why do wives report greater burden? *The Gerontologist, 29*, 667-676.

Bass, D., & Noelker, L. (1987). The influence of family caregivers on elders' use of in-home services: An expanded conceptual framework. *Journal of Health and Social Behavior, 28*, 184-196.

Bearon, L., & Koenig, H. (1990). Religious cognitions and use of prayer in health and illness. *The Gerontologist, 29*, 114-119.

Becker, G. (1981). *A treatise on the family.* Cambridge, MA: Harvard University Press.

Bedford, V. H. (1989a). A comparison of thematic perceptions of sibling affiliation, conflict, and separation at two periods of adulthood. *International Journal of Aging and Human Development, 28*, 53-66.

Bedford, V. H. (1989b). Understanding the value of siblings in old age. *American Behavioral Scientist, 33*, 33-44.

Bem, S. L. (1979). Theory and measurement of androgyny: A reply to the Pedhazur-Tetenbaum and Locksley-Colten critiques. *Journal of Personality and Social Psychology, 37*, 1047-1054.

Berardo, D. H., Shehan, C. L., & Leslie, G. R. (1987). A residue of tradition: Jobs, careers, and spouses' time in housework. *Journal of Marriage and the Family, 49*, 381-390.

Berman, H. J. (1987). Adult children and their parents: Irredeemable obligation and irreplaceable loss. *Journal of Gerontological Social Work, 10*, 21-34.

Bernard, J. (1983). The good-provider role: Its rise and fall. In A. Skolnick & J. Skolnick (Eds.), *Family in transition* (4th ed., pp. 143-162). Boston: Little, Brown.

Bertghold, L. (1987). The impact of public policy on home health services for the elderly. *Pride Institute Journal of Long Term Home Health Care, 6*, 12-26.

Biegel, D. R., Schulz, B., Shore, B., & Morycz, R. (1989). *Economic support for family caregivers of the elderly: Tax policies and direct payment programs.* Cleveland, OH: Case Western Reserve University, School of Applied Social Sciences.

Binstock, R. H., & Shanas, E. (Eds.). (1985). *Handbook of aging and the social sciences* (2nd ed.). New York: Van Nostrand Reinhold.

Birkel, R. C., & Jones, C. J. (1989). A comparison of the caregiving networks of dependent elderly individuals who are lucid and those who are demented. *The Gerontologist, 29*, 114-119.

Blank, R. M. (1988). Women's paid work, household income and household well-being. In S. Rix (Ed.), *The American woman 1988-1989: A status report* (pp. 123-161). New York: W. W. Norton.

Blau, F. D., & Winkler, A. F. (1989). Women in the labor force: An overview. In J. Freedman (Ed.), *Women: A feminist perspective* (4th ed., pp. 265-286). Mountain View, CA: Mayfield.

Blau, Z. S. (1981). *Old age in a changing society* (2nd ed.). New York: Franklin Watts.

Blaxter, M. (1976). *The meaning of disability.* London: Heinemann.

Blieszner, R. S., & Mancini, J. A. (1987). Enduring ties: Older adults' parental role and responsibilities. *Family Relations, 36*, 176-180.

Blenkner, M. (1965). Social work and family relationships in later life with some thoughts on filial maturity. In E. Shanas & G. F. Streib (Eds.), *Social structure and the family: Generational relations* (pp. 46-59). Englewood Cliffs, NJ: Prentice-Hall.

Bohen, H. (1983). *Corporate employee policy affecting families and children: The United States and Europe.* New York: Aspen Institute for Humanistic Studies.

Bowlby, J. (1979). *The making and breaking of affectional bonds.* London: Tavistock.

Brady, E. M., & Noberini, M. R. (1987, August). *Sibling support in the context of a model of sibling solidarity.* Paper presented at the 95th Annual Meeting of the American Psychological Association, New York.

Branch, L. G., & Jette, A. M. (1983). Elders' use of informal long-term care assistance. *The Gerontologist, 23*, 51-56.

Briar, K., & Ryan, R. (1986). The anti-institution movement and women caregivers. *Affilia, 1*, 20-32.

Briggs, A., & Oliver, J. (1985). *Caring: Experiences of looking after disabled relatives.* London: Routledge & Kegan Paul.

Brocklehurst, J. C., Morris, P., Andrews, K., Richards, B., & Laycock, P. (1981). Social effects of stroke. *Social Science and Medicine, 15*, 35-39.

Brody, E. M. (1977). *Long-term care of older people: A practical guide.* New York: Human Services Press.

Brody, E. M. (1981). Women in the middle and family help to older people. *The Gerontologist, 21*, 471-480

Brody, E. M. (1984, November). *Women who help elderly mothers: Do work and parent care compete?* Paper presented at the 37th Annual Meeting of the Gerontological Society of America, San Antonio, TX.

Brody, E. M. (1985). Parent care as a normative family stress. *The Gerontologist, 25*, 19-29.

Brody, E. M. (1986). Filial care of the elderly and changing roles of women (and men). *Journal of Geriatric Psychology, 19*, 175-201.

Brody, E. M. (1989). The family at risk. In E. Light & B. D. Leibowitz (Eds.), *Alzheimer's disease treatment and family stress* (pp. 2-49) (DHHS Publication No. [ADM] 89-1569). Rockville, MD: U.S. Department of Health and Human Services.

Brody, E. M. (1990). *Women in the middle: Their parent-care years.* New York: Springer.

Brody, E. M., & Brody, S. J. (1989). The informal system of health care. In C. Eisdorfer, D. A. Kessler, & A. B. Spector (Eds.), *Caring for the elderly: Reshaping health policy* (pp. 259-277). Baltimore: Johns Hopkins University Press.

Brody, E. M., Dempsey, N. P., & Pruchno, R. A. (1990). Mental health of sons and daughters of the institutionalized aged. *The Gerontologist, 30*, 212-219.

Brody, E. M., Hoffman, C., Kleban, M. H., & Schoonover, C. B. (1989). Caregiving daughters and their local siblings: Perceptions, strain, and interactions. *The Gerontologist, 29*, 529-538.

Brody, E. M., Johnsen, P. T., & Fulcomer, M. C. (1984). What should adult children do for their elderly parents? Opinions and preferences of three generations of women. *Journal of Gerontology: Social Sciences, 39*, 736-746.

Brody, E. M., Johnsen, P. T., Fulcomer, M. C., & Lang, A. M. (1983). Women's changing roles and help to elderly parents: Attitudes of three generations of women. *Journal of Gerontology: Social Sciences, 38*, 597-607.

Brody, E. M., Kleban, M. H., Hoffman, C., & Schoonover, C. B. (1988). Adult daughters and parent care: A comparison of one-, two-, and three generation households. *Home Health Care Services Quarterly, 9*, 19-45.

Brody, E. M., Kleban, M. H., Johnsen, P. T., Hoffman, C. B., & Schoonover, C. B. (1987). Work status and parent care: A comparison of four groups of women. *The Gerontologist, 27*, 201-208.

Brody, E. M., & Noberini, M. R. (1987, August). *Sibling support in the context of a model sibling solidarity.* Paper presented at the 95th Annual Meeting of the American Psychological Association, New York.

Brody, E. M., & Schoonover, C. B. (1986). Patterns of parent-care when adult daughters work and when they do not. *The Gerontologist, 26*, 372-381.

Brubaker, T. H. (1985a). *Later life families.* Beverly Hills, CA: Sage.

Brubaker, T. H. (1985b). Responsibility for household tasks: A look at golden anniversary couples aged 75 years and older. In W. Peterson & J. Quadagno (Eds.), *Social bonds in later life* (pp. 27-36). Beverly Hills, CA: Sage.

Brubaker, T. H. (1990a). Continuity and change in later life families: Grandparenthood, couple relationships and family caregiving. *Gerontology Review, 3*, 24-40.

Brubaker, T. H. (1990b). Families in later life: A burgeoning research area. *Journal of Marriage and the Family, 52*, 959-981.

Brubaker, T. H., & Kinsel, B. (1988). Who is responsible for household tasks in long-term marriages of the young old elderly? In L. Ade-Ridder & C. Hennon (Eds.), *Lifestyles of the elderly: Diversity in relationships, health, and caregiving.* New York: Human Sciences Press.

Bulcroft, K., Van Leynseele, J., & Borgatta, E. F. (1989). Filial responsibility laws. *Research on Aging, 11*, 374-393.

Bulcroft, K., Van Leynseele, J., Hatch, L. R., & Borgatta, E. F. (1989, November). *Responsibility of relatives for old-age support: An analysis of state statutes.* Paper presented at the 51st Annual National Council of Family Relations Conference, New Orleans.

Bureau of National Affairs, Inc. (1986). *Work and the family: A changing dynamic.* Washington, DC: Author.

Callahan, D. (1988). Families as caregivers: The limits of morality. *Archives of Physical Medicine Rehabilitation, 69*, 323-328.

Cancian, F. M. (1986). The feminization of love. *Signs, 11*, 692-709.

Cantor, M. H. (1983). Strain among caregivers: A study of experience in the U.S. *The Gerontologist, 23*, 597-624.

Carmines, E. G., & Zeller, R. A. (1979). *Reliability and validity assessment.* Beverly Hills, CA: Sage.

Carriko, T., & Eisenberg, D. (1983). Informal resources for the elderly: Panacea or empty promises. *Journal of Gerontological Social Work, 6*, 39-47.

Caserta, M. S., Lund, D. A., Wright, S. D., & Redburn, D. E. (1987). Caregivers to dementia patients: The utilization of community services. *The Gerontologist, 27*, 209-214.

Chenoweth, B., & Spencer, B. (1986). Dementia: The experience of family caregivers. *The Gerontologist, 26*, 267-272.

Chodorow, N. (1978). *The reproduction of mothering: Psychoanalysis and the sociology of gender.* Berkeley: University of California Press.

Cicirelli, V. G. (1977). Relationship of siblings to the elderly person's feelings and concerns. *Journal of Gerontology: Social Sciences, 35*, 317-322.

Cicirelli, V. G. (1979, May). *Social services for the elderly in relation to the kin network* (Report to the National Retired Teachers Association). West Lafayette, IN: American Association of Retired Persons/Andrus Foundation.

Cicirelli, V. G. (1980). Sibling relationships in adulthood: A life-span perspective. In L. W. Poon (Ed.), *Aging in the 1980s: Psychological issues* (pp. 455-462). Washington, DC: American Psychological Association.

Cicirelli, V. G. (1981). *Helping elderly parents: Role of adult children.* Boston: Auburn House.

Cicirelli, V. G. (1982). Sibling influence throughout the life span. In M. E. Lamb & B. Sutton-Smith (Eds.), *Sibling relationships: Their nature and significance across the life span* (pp. 267-284). Hillsdale, NJ: Lawrence Erlbaum.

Cicirelli, V. G. (1983). Adult children's attachment and helping behavior to elderly parents: A path model. *Journal of Marriage and the Family, 45*, 815-824.

Cicirelli, V. G. (1984). Marital disruption and adult children's perception of their siblings' help to elderly parents. *Family Relations, 33*, 613-621.

Cicirelli, V. G. (1988). A measure of filial anxiety regarding anticipated care of elderly parents. *The Gerontologist, 28*, 478-482.

Cicirelli, V. G. (1989a). Feelings of attachment to siblings and well-being in later life. *Psychology and Aging, 4*, 211-216.

Cicirelli, V. G. (1989b). Helping relationships in later life: A reexamination. In J. A. Mancini (Ed.), *Aging parents and adult children* (pp. 167-175). Lexington, MA: Lexington.

Cicirelli, V. G. (1990a). [Fairness of siblings' caregiving participation]. Unpublished raw data.

Cicirelli, V. G. (1990b). Family support in relation to health problems of the elderly. In T. H. Brubaker (Ed.), *Family relationships in later life* (2nd ed., pp. 212-228). Newbury Park, CA: Sage.

Clark, N., & Rakowski, W. (1983). Family caregivers of older adults: Improving helping skills. *The Gerontologist, 23*, 637-642.

Clipp, E. C., & George, L. K. (1990a). Caregiver needs and patterns of social support. *Journal of Gerontology: Social Sciences, 45,* 102-111.

Clipp, E. C., & George, L. K. (1990b). Psychotropic drug use among caregivers of patients with dementia. *Journal of the American Geriatrics Society, 38*, 227-235.

Cole, J. (1986). Commonalities and differences. In J. Cole (Ed.), *American women: Lines that divide, ties that bind* (pp. 1-30). New York: Free Press.

Commonwealth Fund Commission. (1987). *Medicare's poor: Filling the pages in Medicare coverage for low income elderly Americans.* Baltimore: Author.

Comptroller General of the United States. (1977). *The well-being of older people in Cleveland, Ohio.* Washington, DC: Government Printing Office.

Condie, S. (1989). Older married couples. In S. Bahr & E. Peterson (Eds.), *Aging and the family* (pp. 143-158). Lexington, MA: Lexington.

Condran, J. G., & Bode, J. G. (1982). Rashomon, working wives, and family division of labor: Middletown, 1980. *Journal of Marriage and the Family, 44*, 421-425.

Connidis, I. A. (1989). Siblings as friends in later life. *American Behavioral Scientist, 33*, 81-93.

Coroni-Huntley, J., Foley, D., White, L., Suzman, R., Berkman, L., Evans, D., & Wallace, R. (1985). Epidemiology of disability in the oldest old: Methodologic issues and preliminary findings. *Milbank Memorial Fund Quarterly, 63*, 350-376.

Cott, N. (1977). *The bonds of womanhood: Woman's sphere in New England, 1780-1835.* New Haven, CT: Yale University Press.

Coulton, C. (1988). Prospective payment requires increased attention to quality of post-hospital care. *Social Work in Health Care, 13*, 19-31.

Coverman, S. (1985). Explaining husbands' participation in domestic labor. *Sociological Quarterly, 26*, 81-97.

Coverman, B., & Shelley, J. F. (1986). Change in men's housework and child-care time, 1965-1975. *Journal of Marriage and the Family, 48*, 413-422.

Coward, R. T. (1987). Factors associated with the configuration of the helping networks of noninstitutionalized elders. *Journal of Gerontological Social Work, 10*, 113-132.

Coward, R. T., & Brubaker, T. H. (1989, November). *The prevalence of men as caregivers.* Symposium conducted at the 51st Annual Meeting of the National Council on Family Relations, New Orleans.

Coward, R. T., Cutler, S. J., & Mullens, R. A. (1990). Residential differences in the helping networks of impaired elders. *Family Relations, 39*, 44-50.

Coward, R. T., Cutler, S. J., & Schmidt, F. E. (1989). Differences in the household composition of elders by age, gender, and area of residence. *The Gerontologist, 29*, 814-821.

Coward, R. T., & Dwyer, J. W. (1990). The association of gender, sibling network composition, and patterns of parent care by adult children. *Research on Aging, 12*, 158-181.

Crano, W. D., & Aronoff, J. (1978). A cross-cultural study of expressive and instrumental role complementarity in the family. *American Sociological Review, 43*, 463-471.

Crawford, M., & Maracek, J. (1989). Psychology reconstructs the female: 1968-1988. *Psychology of Women Quarterly, 13*, 147-165.

Creedon, M. A. (1987). *Issues for an aging America: Employees and elder-care.* Bridgeport, CT: Center for the Study of the Aging.

Crossman, L., London, C., & Barry, C. (1981). Older women caring for disabled spouses: A model for supportive services. *The Gerontologist, 21*, 464-470.

Cumming, E., & Henry, W. (1961). *Growing old.* New York: New American Library.

Dahlin, M. (1980). Perspectives on the family life of the elderly in 1900. *The Gerontologist, 20*, 99-107.

Daniels, A. K. (1987). Invisible work. *Social Problems, 34*, 403-415.

Davis, H., Priddy, J., & Tinklenberg, J. (1986). Support groups for male caregivers of Alzheimer's patients. *Clinical Gerontologist, 5*, 385-395.

Degler, C. (1980). *At odds: Women and the family in America from the Revolution to the present.* New York: Oxford University Press.

Deimling, G., & Bass, D. (1986). Symptoms of mental impairment among elderly adults and their effects on family caregivers. *Journal of Gerontology: Social Sciences, 41*, 778-785.

Denton, K., & Love, L. T. (1988). *Policy implications of corporate supports to elderly caregivers.* Final report submitted to the Gerontological Society of America 1988 Fellowship Program in Applied Gerontology.

Depner, C., & Ingersoll-Dayton, B. (1988). Supportive relationships in later life. *Psychology and Aging, 3*, 348-357.

Dexter, E. A. (1924). *Colonial women of affairs: A study of women in business and the professions in America before 1776.* Boston: Houghton Mifflin.

Diamond, L. M. (1985). *Financial support for family care: A review of current policies and programs* (Working Paper No. 23). Boston: Brandeis University, Policy Center on Aging.

di Leonardo, M. (1987). The female world of cards and holidays: Women, families and the work of kinship. *Signs, 12*, 440-453.

Dinkel, R. (1944). Attitudes of children toward supporting aged parents. *American Sociological Review, 9*, 370-379.

Doty, P. (1986). Family care of the elderly: The role of public policy. *Milbank Memorial Fund Quarterly, 64*, 34-75.

Doty, P., Liu, K., & Wiener, J. (1985). An overview of long term care. *Health Care Financing Review, 6*, 69-78.

Dressel, P. L., & Clark, A. (1990). A critical look at family care. *Journal of Marriage and the Family, 52*, 769-782.

Dura, J. R., & Kiecolt-Glaser, J. K. (1990). Sample bias in caregiving research. *Journal of Gerontology: Psychological Sciences, 45*, 200-204.

Dwyer, J. W., & Coward, R. T. (1991). A multivariate comparison of the involvement of adult sons versus daughters in the care of impaired parents. *Journal of Gerontology: Social Sciences, 46*, 259-269.

Dwyer, J. W., & Seccombe, K. (1991). Elder care as family labor: The influence of gender and family position. *Journal of Family Issues, 12*, 229-247.

Ehrenreich, B. (1983). *The hearts of men: American dreams and the flight for commitment.* Garden City, NY: Doubleday.

Ehrenreich, B., & English, D. (1979). *For her own good: 150 years of the experts' advice to women.* Garden City, NY: Anchor/Doubleday.

England, P., & Farkas, G. (1986). *Households, employment, and gender: A social, economic, and demographic view.* New York: Aldine.

English, J. (1979). What do children owe their parents? In O. O'Neill & W. Ruddick (Eds.), *Having children: Philosophical and legal reflections on parenthood* (pp. 351-356). New York: Oxford University Press.

Estes, C. L. (1989). Aging, health, and social policy. *Journal of Aging and Social Policy, 1*, 17-32.

Estes, C. L., & Arendell, T. (1986). *The unsettled future: Women and the economics of aging.* Paper presented at the conference Who Cares for the Elderly: Caregiving in Women's Lives, University of California, Los Angeles.

Estes, C. L., Newcomer, R., & Associates. (1983). *Fiscal austerity and aging.* Beverly Hills, CA: Sage.

Estes, C. L., Wood, J. B., & Lee, P. R. (1988). *Organizational and community responses to Medicare policy.* San Francisco: Institute for Health and Aging, University of California, San Francisco.

Evandrou, M., Arber, S., Dale, A., & Gilbert, G. N. (1986). Who cares for the elderly? Family care provision and receipt of statutory services. In C. Phillipson, M. Bernard, & P. Strang (Eds.), *Dependency and interdependency in old age: Theoretical perspectives and policy alternatives* (pp. 150-166). London: British Society of Gerontology.

Faulkner, A., & Micchelli, M. (1988). The aging, the aged, and the very old: Women the policy makers forget. *Women and Health, 14*, 5-19.

Felder, L. (1990). *When a loved one is ill.* New York: New American Library.

Fengler, A., & Goodrich, N. (1979). Wives of disabled elderly: The hidden patients. *The Gerontologist, 19*, 175-183.

Ferber, M. A. (1982). Women and work: Issues of the 1980s. *Signs, 8*, 273-295.

Filsinger, E. E. (1988). *Biosocial perspectives on the family.* Newbury Park, CA: Sage.

Finch, J. (1989). *Family obligations and social change.* Southampton, England: Camelot.

Finch, J., & Groves, D. (1983). Introduction. In J. Finch & D. Groves (Eds.), *A labour of love: Women, work, and caring* (pp. 1-10). London: Routledge & Kegan Paul.

Fine, M. (1985). Reflections on a feminist psychology of women: Paradoxes and prospects. *Psychology of Women Quarterly, 9*, 167-183.

Finley, N. J. (1989). Theories of family labor as applied to gender differences in caregiving for elderly parents. *Journal of Marriage and the Family, 51*, 79-86.

Finley, N. J., Roberts, M. D., & Banahan, B. F. (1988). Motivators and inhibitors of attitudes of filial obligation toward aging parents. *The Gerontologist, 28*, 73-78.

Fischer, D. H. (1978). *Growing old in America.* New York: Oxford University Press.

Fischer, L. R. (1983). Mothers and mothers-in-law. *Journal of Marriage and the Family, 45*, 187-192.

Fischer, L. R. (1985). Elderly parents and the caregiving role: An asymmetrical transition. In W. A. Peterson & J. Quadagno (Eds.), *Social bonds in later life* (pp. 105-114). Beverly Hills: Sage.

Fischer, L. R., & Eustis, N. N. (1988). DRGs and family care for the elderly: A case study. *The Gerontologist, 28*, 383-389.

Fischer, L. R., & Hoffman, C. (1984). Who cares for the elderly: The dilemma of family support. In M. Lewis & J. Miller (Eds.), *Research in social problems and public policy: A research annual* (Vol. 3, pp. 169-215). Greenwich, CT: JAI.

Fisher, B., & Tronto, J. (1990). Toward a feminist theory of caring. In E. K. Abel & M. K. Nelson (Eds.), *Circles of care: Work and identity in women's lives* (pp. 35-62). Albany: State University of New York Press.

Fisher, C. B., Reid, J. D., & Melendez, M. (1989). Conflict in families and friendships of later life. *Family Relations, 38*, 83-89.

Fitting, M., & Rabins, P. (1985). Men and women: Do they care differently? *Generations, 10*, 23-26.

Fitting, M., Rabins, P., Lucas, M. J., & Eastham, J. (1986). Caregivers for dementia patients: A comparison of husbands and wives. *The Gerontologist, 26*, 248-252.

Fox, J. R. (1967). *Kinship and marriage*. Baltimore: Penguin.

Fox, M. F., & Hesse-Biber, S. (1984). *Women at work*. Palo Alto, CA: Mayfield.

Fradkin, L., & Liberti, M. (1987). Caregiving. In P. B. Doress & D. L. Siegal (Eds.), *Ourselves growing older* (pp. 198-212). New York: Simon & Schuster.

Friedl, E. (1975). *Women and men: An anthropologist's view.* New York: Reinhold.

Fulton, G. (1984). [Letter to the editor]. *The Caregiver* (Newsletter of the Duke Family Support Program, Duke Center for Aging).

Galinsky, E. (1986). Family life and corporate policies. In M. Yogman & T. B. Brazelton (Eds.), *In support of families* (pp. 109-145). Cambridge, MA: Harvard University Press.

Gallagher, D., Lovett, S., & Zeiss, A. (1988). Interventions with caregivers of frail older persons. In M. Ory & K. Bond (Eds.), *Aging and health care: Social science and policy perspectives* (pp. 167-189). New York: Tavistock.

Gallagher, D., Rose, J., Rivera, P., Lovett, S., & Thompson, L. (1989). Prevalence of depression in family caregivers. *The Gerontologist, 29*, 449-456.

George, L. K., & Gwyther, L. P. (1986). Caregiver well-being: A multidimensional examination of family caregivers of demented adults. *The Gerontologist, 26*, 253-259.

Gibeau, J. L., & Anastas, J. W. (1987). *Breadwinners and caregivers: Supporting workers who care for elderly family members.* Washington, DC: National Association of Area Agencies on Aging.

Gibeau, J. L., & Anastas, J. W. (1989). Breadwinners and caregivers: Interviews with working women. *Journal of Gerontological Social Work, 14*, 19-40.

Gibson, R. (1986). Outlook for the black family. In A. Pifer & L. Bronte (Eds.), *Our aging society: Paradox and promise* (pp. 181-187). New York: W. W. Norton.

Gilligan, C. (1982). *In a different voice: Psychological theory and women's development.* Cambridge, MA: Harvard University Press.

Glazer, N. Y. (1990). The home as workshop: Women as amateur nurses and medical providers. *Gender and Society, 4*, 479-499.

Goetting, A. (1986). The development tasks of siblingship over the life cycle. *Journal of Marriage and the Family, 48*, 703-714.

Gold, D. T. (1986). *Sibling relationships in retrospect: A study of reminiscence in old age.* Unpublished doctoral dissertation, Evanston University.

Gold, D. T. (1987). Siblings in old age: Something special. *Canadian Journal on Aging, 6*, 211-227.

Gold, D. T. (1989a). Generational solidarity. *American Behavioral Scientist, 33*, 19-32.

Gold, D. T. (1989b). Sibling relationships in old age: A typology. *International Journal of Aging and Human Development, 28*, 53-66.

Goldscheider, F. K. (1990). The aging of the gender revolution. *Research on Aging, 12*, 531-545.

Gordon, C., Gaitz, C. M., & Scott, J. (1976). Leisure and lives: Personal expressivity across the life span. In R. H. Binstock & E. Shanas (Eds.), *Handbook on aging and the social sciences* (pp. 310-341). New York: Van Nostrand Reinhold.

Graham, H. (1983). Caring: A labour of love. In J. Finch & D. Groves (Eds.), *A labour of love: Women, work, and caring* (pp. 13-30). London: Routledge & Kegan Paul.

Guberman, N. (1988). The family, women and caring: Who cares for the carers? *New Feminist Research, 17*, 37-41.

Gubrium, J. F. (1988). Family responsibility and caregiving in the qualitative analysis of the Alzheimer's disease experience. *Journal of Marriage and the Family, 50*, 197-207.

Gubrium, J. F., & Buckholdt, D. R. (1982). Fictive family: Everyday usage, analytic, and human services considerations. *American Anthropologist, 84,* 878-884.

Guttman, D. L. (1987). *Reclaimed powers: Toward a new psychology of men and women in later life.* New York: Basic Books.

Gwyther, L. P. (1990a). Clinician and family: A partnership for support. In N. L. Mace (Ed.), *Dementia care: Patient, family, community* (pp. 193-230). Baltimore: Johns Hopkins University Press.

Gwyther, L. P. (1990b, November). *Gender and family care of the elderly.* Paper presented at the 43rd Annual Meeting of the Gerontological Society of America, Boston.

Gwyther, L. P. (1990c). Letting go: Separation-individuation in the wife of an Alzheimer's patient. *The Gerontologist, 30,* 698-702.

Gwyther, L. P., & Ballard, E. (1988). *In-home respite care: Guidelines for programs serving family caregivers for memory-impaired adults.* Durham, NC: Duke Center for Aging.

Gwyther, L. P., & George, L. K. (1986). Caregivers for dementia patients: Complex determinants of well-being and burden. *The Gerontologist, 26,* 245-247.

Haber, C. (1983). *Beyond sixty-five: The dilemma of old age in America's past.* New York: Cambridge University Press.

Hagestad, G. O. (1982). Parent and child: Generations in the family. In T. M. Field, A. Huston, H. C. Quay, L. Troll, & G. E. Finley (Eds.), *Review of human development* (pp. 485-499). New York: Wiley Interscience.

Hagestad, G. O. (1987). Parent-child relations in later life: Trends and gaps in past research. In J. B. Lancaster, J. Altman, A. S. Rossi, & L. R. Sherrod (Eds.), *Parenting across the lifespan: Biosocial dimensions* (pp. 405-433). New York: Aldine de Gruyter.

Hamon, R. R., & Blieszner, R. (1990). Filial responsibility expectations among adult child-older parent pairs. *Journal of Gerontology: Psychological Sciences, 45,* 110-112.

Hampton Roads Alzheimer's Association. (1990). [Journal excerpt from an anonymous wife caregiver]. *Hampton Roads Alzheimer's Association Newsletter* (Virginia Beach, VA).

Hanson, S. L., Sauer, W. J., & Seelbach, W. C. (1983). Racial and cohort variations in filial responsibility norms. *The Gerontologist, 23,* 626-663.

Harrington, C., Estes, C., Lee, P., & Newcomer, R. (1986). Effects of state Medicare policies on the aged. *The Gerontologist, 26,* 437-444.

Louis Harris & Associates, Inc. (1981). *Families at work.* Minneapolis: General Mills.

Hartman, H. (1980). The family as locus of gender, class, and political struggle: The example of housework. *Signs, 6,* 366-394.

Hartman, H. (1988). Achieving economic equity for women. In M. Raskin & C. Harman (Eds.), *Winning America: Ideas and leadership for the 1990s* (pp. 95-105). Boston: South End/Institute for Policy Studies.

Haug, M. (1985). Home care for the elderly: Who benefits? *American Journal of Public Health, 25,* 127-128.

Hayden, D. (1981). *The grand domestic revolution: A history of feminist designs for American homes, neighborhoods, and cities.* Cambridge: MIT Press.

Health Care Financing Administration. (1981). *Long term care: Background and future directions* (DHHS Publication No. HCFA 81-20047). Washington, DC: Government Printing Office.

Hefner, R., Rebecca, M., & Oleshansky, B. (1975). Development of sex-role transcendence. *Human Development, 18,* 143-158.

Hertz, R. (1988). *More equal than others: Women and men in dual-career marriages.* Berkeley: University of California Press.

Hess, B., & Soldo, B. (1985). Husband and wife networks. In W. J. Sauer & R. T. Coward (Eds.), *Social support networks and the care of the elderly* (pp. 67-92). New York: Springer.

Hess, B. B., & Waring, J. M. (1978a). Changing patterns of aging and family bonds in later life. *Family Coordinator, 27,* 303-314.

Hess, B. B., & Waring, J. M. (1978b). Parent and child in later life: Rethinking the relationship. In R. M. Lerner & G. B. Spanier (Eds.), *Child influences on marital and family interaction* (pp. 241-273). New York: Academic Press.

Hiller, D. A., & Philliber, W. J. (1986). The division of labor in contemporary marriage. *Social Problems, 33,* 191-201.

Hirshorn, B., & Montgomery, R. J. V. (in press). Close kin support for U.S. elderly over 60: Who's in need, who responds. *Research on Aging.*

Hochschild, A. (1989). *The second shift: Working parents and the revolution at home.* New York: Viking/Penguin.

Hokenstad, M., & Johansson, L. (1990). Caregiving for the elderly in Sweden: Program challenges and policy initiatives. In D. E. Biegel & A. Blum (Eds.), *Aging and caregiving: Theory, research, and policy* (pp. 254-269). Newbury Park, CA: Sage.

Holter, H. (1985). *Patriarchy in a welfare state.* Bergen: University of Bergen Press.

Homans, G. C. (1974). *Social behavior: Its elementary forms.* New York: Harcourt Brace Jovanovich.

Hooyman, N. (1989). *Women, caregiving and equity: A feminist perspective.* Invited presentation at the annual program meeting of the Council on Social Work Education.

Hooyman, N. (1990). Women as caregivers to the elderly. In D. E. Biegel & A. Blum (Eds.), *Aging and caregiving: Theory, research, and policy* (pp. 221-241). Newbury Park, CA: Sage.

Hooyman, N., & Lustbader, W. (1986). *Taking care: Supporting older people and their families.* New York: Free Press.

Horowitz, A. (1985a). Family caregiving to the frail elderly. *Annual Review of Gerontology and Geriatrics, 5,* 194-246.

Horowitz, A. (1985b). Sons and daughters as caregivers to older parents: Differences in role performance and consequences. *The Gerontologist, 25,* 612-617.

Horowitz, A. (1989, November). *Methodological issues in the study of gender and caregiving.* Paper presented at the 42nd Annual Meeting of the Gerontological Society of America, Minneapolis.

Horowitz, A., & Dobrof, R. (1982). *The role of families in providing long-term care to the frail and chronically ill elderly living in the community* (Final Report, Health Care Financing Administration Grant No. 18-P-97541/20-02). Unpublished manuscript.

Horowitz, A., & Shindleman, L. W. (1983). Reciprocity and affection: Past influences on current caregiving. *Journal of Gerontological Social Work, 5,* 5-20.

Horowitz, A., Silverstone, B. M., & Reinhardt, J. (1991). A conceptual and empirical exploration of personal autonomy issues within family caregiving relationships. *The Gerontologist, 31,* 23-31.

Houser, B. B., & Berkman, S. L. (1984). Aging parent/mature child relationships. *Journal of Marriage and the Family, 46,* 295-299.

Houser, B. B., Berkman, S. L., & Bardsley, P. (1985). Sex and birth order differences in filial behavior. *Sex Roles, 13,* 641-651.

Howard, J. A., Blumstein, P., & Schwartz, P. (1986). Sex, power, and influence tactics in intimate relationships. *Journal of Personality and Social Psychology, 51,* 102-109.

Huber, J. (1990). Macro-micro links in gender stratification. *American Sociological Review, 55,* 1-10.

Ikels, C. (1983). The process of caretaker selection. *Research on Aging, 5,* 491-509.

Jackson, J. (1989). Race, ethnicity and psychological theory and research. *Journal of Gerontology: Psychological Sciences, 44,* 1-2.

Jackson, R. M. (1989). The reproduction of parenting. *American Sociological Review, 54,* 215-232.

Jarrett, W. H. (1985). Caregiving within kinship systems: Is affection really necessary? *The Gerontologist, 25,* 5-10.

Johnson, C. L. (1983). Dyadic family relations and social support. *The Gerontologist, 23,* 377-383.

Johnson, C. L. (1988). Relationships among family members and friends in later life. In R. Milardo (Ed.), *Families and social networks* (pp. 168-189). Newbury Park, CA: Sage.

Johnson, C. L., & Catalano, D. J. (1981). Childless elderly and their family supports. *The Gerontologist, 21,* 610-618.

Johnson, C. L., & Catalano, D. J. (1983). A longitudinal study of family supports to the impaired elderly. *The Gerontologist, 23,* 612-618.

Jones, D. A., & Vetter, N. J. (1984). A survey of those who care for the elderly at home: Their problems and their needs. *Social Science and Medicine, 19,* 511-514.

Justice, D. (1988). *State long-term care reform: Development of community care systems in six states.* Washington, DC: Center for Policy Research, National Governor's Association.

Kahana, E., & Midlarsky, E. (1983). Helping by the elderly: Conception and empirical considerations. *Interdisciplinary Topics in Gerontology, 17,* 10-24.

Kamerman, S. B., & Kahn, A. J. (1981). *Child care, family benefits, and working parents: A study in comparative policy.* New York: Columbia University Press.

Kane, R. (1989). The home care crisis of the nineties. *The Gerontologist, 29,* 24-31.

Kane, R., Ouslander, J. G., & Abrass, I. B. (1989). *Essentials of clinical geriatrics.* New York: McGraw-Hill.

Kaye, L. W., & Applegate, J. S. (1989). *Unsung heroes? A national analysis and intensive local study of males and the elder caregiving experience* (Final Report to the AARP Andrus Foundation). Bryn Mawr, PA: Bryn Mawr College, Graduate School of Social Work and Social Research.

Kaye, L. W., & Applegate, J. S. (1990a). *Men as caregivers to the elderly: Understanding and aiding unrecognized family support.* Lexington, MA: Lexington.

Kaye, L. W., & Applegate, J. S. (1990b). Men as elder caregivers: A response to changing families. *American Journal of Orthopsychiatry, 50,* 86-95.

Keith, J. (1990). Age in social and cultural context: Anthropological perspectives. In R. H. Binstock & L. K. George (Eds.), *Handbook of aging and the social sciences* (3rd ed., pp. 91-111). San Diego, CA: Academic Press.

Keith, P. M., & Schafer, R. B. (1986). Housework, disagreement, and depression among younger and older couples. *American Behavioral Scientist, 29,* 405-422.

Kirp, D. L., Yudof, M. G., & Franks, M. S. (1986). *Gender justice.* Chicago: University of Chicago Press.

Kivett, V. R. (1985). Consanguinity and kin level: Their relative importance to the helping networks of older adults. *Journal of Gerontology: Social Sciences, 40,* 228-234.

Kivett, V. R. (1988). Older rural fathers and sons: Patterns of association and helping. *Family Relations, 37,* 62-67.

Kivett, V. R., & Atkinson, M. P. (1984). Filial expectations, association, and helping as a function of number of children among older rural-transition parents. *Journal of Gerontology: Social Sciences, 39,* 499-503.

Kleban, M. H., Brody, E. M., Schoonover, C. B., & Hoffman, C. (1989). Family help to the elderly: Perceptions of sons-in-law regarding parent care. *Journal of Marriage and the Family, 51*, 303-312.

Kline, C. (1975). The socialization process of women. *The Gerontologist, 15*, 486-492.

Land, H., & Rose, N. (1985). Compulsory altruism for some or an altruistic state for all? In P. Bean (Ed.), *In defense of welfare* (pp. 74-96). London: Tavistock.

Lang, A. M., & Brody, E. M. (1983). Characteristics of middle-aged daughters and help to their elderly mothers. *Journal of Marriage and the Family, 45*, 193-202.

Lastrucci, C. L. (1967). *The scientific approach.* Cambridge, MA: Schenkman.

Lave, J. (1985). Cost-containment policies in long-term care. *Inquiry, 22*, 7-23.

Lee, G. R. (1980). Kinship in the seventies: A decade review of research and theory. *Journal of Marriage and the Family, 42*, 923-934.

Lee, G. R. (1982). *Family structure and interaction: A comparative analysis* (2nd ed.). Minneapolis: University of Minnesota Press.

Lee, G. R. (1985a). Kinship and social support of the elderly: The case of the United States. *Aging and Society, 5*, 19-38.

Lee, G. R. (1985b). Theoretical perspectives on social networks. In W. J. Sauer & R. T. Coward (Eds.), *Social support networks and the care of the elderly* (pp. 21-37). New York: Springer.

Lee, G. R. (1988). Kinship ties among older persons: The residence factor. In R. Marotz-Baden, C. B. Hennon, & T. H. Brubaker (Eds.), *Families in rural America.* Saint Paul, MN: National Council on Family Relations.

Lee, G. R., Dwyer, J. W., & Coward, R. T. (1990). Residential location and proximity to children among impaired elderly parents. *Rural Sociology, 55*, 579-589.

Lee, G. R., & Ihinger-Tallman, M. (1980). Sibling interactions and morale. *Research on Aging, 2*, 367-391.

Leigh, G. K. (1982). Kinship interaction over the family life span. *Journal of Marriage and the Family, 44*, 197-208.

Lein, L. (1979). Male participation in home life: Impact of social supports and breadwinner responsibility on the allocation of tasks. *Family Coordinator, 28*, 489-495.

Leonard, E. A., Drinker, S. H., & Holden, M. Y. (1962). *The American women in colonial and revolutionary times, 1565-1800.* Philadelphia: University of Pennsylvania Press.

Lewin & Associates. (1987). *An evaluation of Medi-Cal program's system for establishing reimbursement rates for nursing homes.* Report submitted to the Office of the Auditor General, State of California.

Lewis, J., & Meredith, B. (1988). *Daughters who care: Daughters caring for mothers at home.* London: Routledge & Kegan Paul.

Lewis, R. A. (1990). The adult child and older parents. In T. H. Brubaker (Ed.), *Family relationships in later life* (2nd ed., pp. 68-85). Newbury Park, CA: Sage.

Lingsom, S. (1989). Filial responsibility in the welfare state. *Journal of Applied Gerontology, 8*, 18-35.

Linville, P. (1987). Self-complexity as a cognitive buffer against stress-related illness and depression. *Journal of Personality and Social Psychology, 52*, 663-676.

Litwak, E. (1965). Extended kin relations in an industrial democratic society. In E. Shanas & G. F. Streib (Eds.), *Social structure and the family* (pp. 290-323). Englewood Cliffs, NJ: Prentice-Hall.

Litwak, E. (1985). *Helping the elderly: The complementary roles of informal networks and formal systems.* New York: Guilford.

Litwak, E., & Kulis, S. (1987). Technology, proximity, and measures of kin support. *Journal of Marriage and the Family, 49*, 649-661.

Liu, K., Manton, K. G., & Liu, B. M. (1985). Home care expenses for the elderly. *Health Care Financing Review, 7*, 51-58.

Loevinger, J. (1977). *Ego development.* San Francisco: Jossey-Bass.

Lopata, H. Z. (1979). *Women as widows: Support systems.* New York: Elsevier.

Lopata, H. Z. (1987). Women's family roles in life course perspective. In B. B. Hess & M. M. Ferree (Eds.), *Analyzing gender* (pp. 381-407). Newbury Park, CA: Sage.

Lund, D. A., Pett, M. A., & Caserta, M. S. (1988). Institutionalizing dementia victims: Some caregiver considerations. *Journal of Gerontological Social Work, 11*, 119-135.

MacDonald, B. (1988). *Caregiving.* Paper presented at Working Conference on Older Women, University of Utah, Salt Lake City.

Macken, C. L. (1986). A profile of functionally impaired elderly persons living in the community. *Health Care Financing Review, 7*, 33-49.

Magnus, M. (1988). Eldercare: Corporate awareness, but little action. *Personnel Journal, 67*, 19-23.

Mancini, J. A. (Ed.). (1989a). *Aging parents and adult children.* Lexington, MA: Lexington.

Mancini, J. A. (1989b). Family gerontology and the study of parent-child relationships. In J. A. Mancini (Ed.), *Aging parents and adult children* (pp. 3-13). Lexington, MA: Lexington.

Mancini, J. A., & Blieszner, R. S. (1989). Aging parents and adult children: Research themes in intergenerational relations. *Journal of Marriage and the Family, 51*, 275-290.

Manton, K., & Soldo, B. (1985). Dynamics of health changes in the oldest old: New perspectives and evidence. *Milbank Memorial Fund Quarterly, 63*, 206-285.

Markides, K. S., Boldt, J. S., & Ray, L. A. (1986). Sources of helping and intergenerational solidarity: A three-generations study of Mexican Americans. *Journal of Gerontology: Social Sciences, 41*, 506-511.

Marshall, V. W., Rosenthal, C. J., & Daciuk, J. (1987). Older parents' expectations for filial support. *Social Justice Review, 1*, 405-424.

Martin, T. C., & Bumpass, L. L. (1989). Recent trends in marital disruption. *Demography, 26*, 37-51.

Matthews, S. H. (1987). Provision of care to old parents: Division of responsibility among adult children. *Research on Aging, 6*, 45-60.

Matthews, S. H. (1988, October). *Gender and the division of filial responsibility.* Paper presented at the conference Gender Roles through the Life Course, Ball State University, Muncie, IN.

Matthews, S. H., Delaney, P. J., & Adamek, M. E. (1989). Male kinship ties: Bonds between adult brothers. *American Behavioral Scientist, 33*, 58-69.

Matthews, S. H., & Rosner, T. T. (1988). Shared filial responsibility: The family as the primary caregiver. *Journal of Marriage and the Family, 50*, 185-195.

Matthews, S. H., & Sprey, J. (1989). Older family systems: Intra- and intergenerational relations. In J. A. Mancini (Ed.), *Aging parents and adult children* (pp. 63-77). Lexington, MA: Lexington.

Matthews, S. H., Werkner, J. E., & Delaney, P. J. (1989). Relative contributions of help by employed and nonemployed sisters to their elderly parents. *Journal of Gerontology: Social Sciences, 44*, 36-44.

McAdoo, H. (1986). Societal stress: The black family. In J. Cole (Ed.), *All American women: Lines that divide, ties that bind* (pp. 187-197). New York: Free Press.

McGhee, J. L. (1985). The effects of siblings on the life satisfaction of the rural elderly. *Journal of Marriage and the Family, 47*, 85-91.

McHale, S. M., & Huston, T. L. (1984). Men and women as parents: Sex role orientations, employment, and parental roles. *Child Development, 55*, 1349-1361.

McNeely, R. L., & Fogarty, B. A. (1988). Balancing parenthood and employment: Factors affecting company receptiveness to family-related innovations in the workplace. *Family Relations, 37*, 189-195.

Mechanic, D. (1987). Challenges in long-term care policy. *Health Affairs, 6*, 22-36.

Meissner, M. (1977). Sexual division of labor and inequality: Labor and leisure. In M. Stephenson (Ed.), *Women in Canada* (pp. 163-180). Toronto: Women's Educational Press.

Menaghan, E. G., & Parcel, T. L. (1990). Parental employment and family life: Research in the 1980s. *Journal of Marriage and the Family, 52*, 1079-1098.

Mercier, J. M., Paulson, L., & Morris, E. W. (1989). Proximity as a mediating influence on the perceived aging parent-adult child relationship. *The Gerontologist, 29*, 785-791.

Merton, R. K. (1968). *Social theory and social structure*. New York: Free Press.

Miller B. (1987). Gender and control among spouses of the cognitively impaired: A research note. *The Gerontologist, 27*, 447-453.

Miller, B. (1989). Adult children's perceptions of caregiver stress and satisfaction. *Journal of Applied Gerontology, 8*, 275-293.

Miller, B. (1990). Gender differences in spouse management of the caregiver role. In E. K. Abel & M. K. Nelson (Eds.), *Circles of care: Work and identity in women's lives* (pp. 92-104). Albany: State University of New York Press.

Miller, B., & Montgomery, A. (1990). Family caregivers and limitations in social activities. *Research on Aging, 12*, 72-93.

Miller, M. K. (1991). Editorial comments. *Journal of Rural Health, 7*, 7-8.

Minkler, M., & Stone, R. (1985). The feminization of poverty and older women. *The Gerontologist, 25*, 351-357.

Moen, P., & Dempster-McClain, D. I. (1987). Employed parents: Role strains, work time, and preferences for working less. *Journal of Marriage and the Family, 49*, 579-590.

Montgomery, R. J. V., & Borgatta, E. F. (1985). *Family Support Project* (Administration on Aging Grant No. 90AM0046). Seattle: University of Washington, Institute on Aging/Long-term Care Center.

Montgomery, R. J. V., & Borgatta, E. F. (1989). The effects of alternative support strategies on family caregiving. *The Gerontologist, 29*, 457-464.

Montgomery, R. J. V., & Datwyler, M. M. (1990). Women and men in the caregiving role. *Generations, 14*, 34-38.

Montgomery, R. J. V., Gonyea, J. G., & Hooyman, N. R. (1985). Caregiving and the experience of subjective and objective burden. *Family Relations, 34*, 19-26.

Montgomery, R. J. V., & Hatch, L. R. (1977, November). *Caregiving career lines*. Paper presented at the 30th Annual Scientific Meeting of the Gerontological Society of America, Chicago.

Montgomery, R. J. V., & Kamo, Y. (1989). Parent care by sons and daughters. In J. A. Mancini (Ed.), *Aging parents and adult children* (pp. 213-230). Lexington, MA: Lexington.

Montgomery, R. J. V., Kosloski, K., & Borgatta, E. F. (1988-1989). The influence of cognitive impairment on service use and caregiver response. *Journal of Applied Social Sciences, 13*, 142-169.

Montgomery, R. J. V., & Prothero, J. (Eds.). (1986). *Developing respite services for the elderly*. Seattle: University of Washington Press.

Morgan, D. (1989). Adjusting to widowhood: Do social networks really make it easier? *The Gerontologist, 29*, 191-207.

Moroney, R. (1980). *Families, social services and social policy: The issue of shared responsibility.* Rockville, MD: National Institute of Mental Health.

Morycz, R. K. (1985). Caregiving strain and the desire to institutionalize family members with Alzheimer's disease. *Research on Aging, 7,* 329-361.

Moss, M. S., Lawton, M. P., Dean, J., Goodman, M., & Schneider, J. (1987, November). *Satisfaction and burden in caring for impaired elderly persons.* Paper presented at the 40th Annual Meeting of the Gerontological Society of America, Washington, DC.

Moss, M. S., Moss, S. Z., & Moles, E. L. (1985). The quality of relationships between elderly parents and their out-of-town children. *The Gerontologist, 25,* 134-140.

National Center for Health Statistics. (1990). *Longitudinal study on aging, version 3.* Springfield, VA: National Technical Information Service.

National Research Council. (1988). *The aging population in the twenty-first century.* Washington, DC: National Academy Press.

Neale, A. V. (1987). Widows in a Florida retirement community. In H. Lopata (Ed.), *Widows* (Vol. 2, pp. 71-94). Durham, NC: Duke University Press.

Neighbors, H., & Jackson, J. S. (1984). The use of informal and formal help: Four patterns of illness behavior in the black community. *American Journal of Community Psychology, 12,* 629-644.

Neugarten, B. (Ed.). (1968). *Middle age and aging.* Chicago: University of Chicago Press.

Neugarten, B., & Gutmann, D. (1968). Age-sex roles and personality in middle age: A TAT study. In B. Neugarten (Ed.), *Middle age and aging* (pp. 58-76). Chicago: University of Chicago Press.

Noddings, N. (1984). *Caring: A feminine approach to ethics and moral education.* Berkeley: University of California Press.

Noelker, L. S. (1990). Family caregivers: A valuable but vulnerable resource. In Z. Harel, P. Ehrlich, & R. Hubbard (Eds.), *The vulnerable aged: People, services, and policies* (pp. 189-204). New York: Springer.

Noelker, L. S., & Poulshock, S. W. (1982). *The effects on families of caring for impaired elderly in residence.* Washington, DC: U.S. Department of Health and Human Services, Administration on Aging.

Noelker, L. S., & Townsend, A. L. (1987). Perceived caregiving effectiveness: The impact of parental impairment, community resources, and caregiver characteristics. In T. H. Brubaker (Ed.), *Aging, health, and family: Long-term care* (pp. 58-79). Newbury Park, CA: Sage.

Noelker, L. S., & Wallace, R. W. (1985). The organization of family care for the impaired elderly. *Journal of Family Issues, 6,* 23-44.

Norris, J. (Ed.). (1988). *Daughters of the elderly: Building partnerships in caregiving.* Bloomington: Indiana University Press.

Norton, M. B. (1980). *Liberty's daughter: The revolutionary experience of American women, 1750-1800.* Boston: Little, Brown.

Norton, A. J., & Moorman, J. E. (1987). Current trends in marriage and divorce among American women. *Journal of Marriage and the Family, 49,* 3-14.

Nye, F. I. (1979). Choice, exchange, and the family. In W. R. Burr, R. Hill, F. I. Nye, & I. L. Reiss (Eds.), *Contemporary theories about the family* (Vol. 2, pp. 1-41). New York: Free Press.

O'Bryant, S. L. (1988). Sibling support and older widows' well-being. *Journal of Marriage and the Family, 50,* 173-183.

O'Bryant, S. L., & Morgan, L. A. (1990). Recent widows' kin support and orientations to self-sufficiency. *The Gerontologist, 30,* 391-398.

Ogburn, W. F. (1923). *Social change.* New York: Viking.

Older Women's League. (1986). *Report on the status of midlife and older women.* Washington, DC: Author.

Older Women's League. (1989). *Failing America's caregivers.* Washington, DC: Author.

Oliver, J. (1983). The caring wife. In J. Finch & D. Groves (Eds.), *A labour of love: Women, work, and caring* (pp. 72-89). London: Routledge & Kegan Paul.

Olsen, R. (1986). Integrating formal and informal social care in the utilization of social support networks. *British Journal of Social Work, 16*(Suppl.), 15-22.

Ory, M. G., Williams, T. R., Emi, N., Lebowitz, B., Rabins, P., Salloway, J., Sluss-Radbaugh, T., Wolf, E., & Zarit, S. (1985). Families, informal supports and Alzheimer's disease. *Research on Aging, 7,* 623-645.

Osterbusch, S., Keigher, S., Miller, B., & Linsk, N. (1987). Community care policies and gender justice. *International Journal of Health Services, 17,* 217-232.

Ostrander, S. (1984). *Women of the upper class.* Philadelphia: Temple University Press.

Palmore, E. (1974). *Normal aging II.* Durham, NC: Duke University Press.

Paringer, L. (1983). *The forgotten costs of long-term care.* Washington, DC: Urban Institute.

Parron, E. M., & Troll, L. E. (1978). Golden wedding couples: Effects of retirement on intimacy in long-lasting marriages. *Alternative Lifestyles, 1,* 447-464.

Parsons, T. (1944). The social structure of the family. In R. N. Anshen (Ed.), *The family: Its function and destiny* (pp. 173-201). New York: Harper.

Parsons, T., & Bales, R. F. (Eds.). (1955). *Family, socialization, and interaction process.* Glencoe, IL: Free Press.

Pateman, C. (1988). The patriarchal welfare state. In A. Gutmann (Ed.), *Democracy and the welfare state.* Princeton, NJ: Princeton University Press.

Pegels, C. (1988). Demographics of older Americans. In C. Pegels (Ed.), *Health care and the older citizen* (pp. 19-27). Rockville, MD: Aspen.

Pilisuk, M., & Parks, S. H. (1988). Caregiving: Where families need help. *Social Work, 33,* 436-440.

Pleck, J. H. (1985). *Working wives/working husbands.* Beverly Hills, CA: Sage.

Polansky, E. (1985). *A feminist analysis of hospital discharge planning: Women as caregivers of disabled family members.* Paper presented at the annual program meeting of the Council on Social Work Education, Washington, DC.

Poulshock, S. W., & Deimling, G. (1984). Families caring for elders in residence: Issues in the measurement of burden. *Journal of Gerontology: Social Sciences, 39,* 230-239.

Pratt, C. C., & Kethley, A. J. (1988). Aging and family caregiving in the future: Implications for education and policy. *Educational Gerontology, 14,* 567-576.

Pratt, C. C., Schmall, V., Wright, S., & Cleland, M. (1985). Burden and coping strategies of caregivers to Alzheimer's patients. *Family Relations, 34,* 27-33.

Preston, S. 1984. Children and the elderly in the United States. *Scientific American, 250,* 44-49.

Pruchno, R. A., Kleban, M. H., Michaels, J. E., & Dempsey, N. P. (1990). Mental and physical health of caregiving spouses: Development of a causal model. *Journal of Gerontology: Psychological Sciences, 45,* 192-199.

Pruchno, R. A., & Potashnik, S. L. (1989). Caregiving spouses: Physical and mental perspectives. *Journal of the American Geriatrics Society, 37,* 697-705.

Pruchno, R. A., & Resch, N. (1989). Husbands and wives as caregivers: Antecedents of depression and burden. *The Gerontologist, 29,* 159-165.

Quinn, W. (1983). Personal and family adjustment in later life. *Journal of Marriage and the Family, 45,* 57-73.

Raabe, P. H., & Gessner, J. C. (1988). Employer family-supportive policies: Diverse variations on the theme. *Family Relations, 37*, 196-202.

Reiss, I. L., & Lee, G. R. (1988). *Family systems in America* (4th ed.). New York: Holt, Rinehart & Winston.

Retirement Advisors, Inc. (1986). *Eldercare in the workplace: Corporate, employee, and retirement implications.* New York: Author.

Rexroat, C., & Shehan, C. (1987). The family life cycle and spouses' time in housework. *Journal of Marriage and Family, 49*, 735-750.

Riegel, K.F. (1976). The dialectics of human development. *American Psychologist, 31*, 679-700.

Riley, M. A. (1986). Overview and highlights of a sociological perspective. In A. B. Sorensen, F. E. Weinert, & L. Sherrod (Eds.), *Human development and the life course* (pp. 153-175). Hillsdale, NJ: Lawrence Erlbaum.

Rimmer, L. (1983). The economics of work and caring. In J. Finch & D. Groves (Eds.), *A labour of love: Women, work, and caring* (pp. 131-147). London: Routledge & Kegan Paul.

Risman, B. (1987). Intimate relationships from a microstructural perspective: Men who mother. *Gender and Society, 1*, 6-32.

Risman, B., & Schwartz, P. (Eds.). (1989). *Gender in intimate relationships: A microstructural approach.* Belmont, CA: Wadsworth.

Rivlin, A. M., & Wiener, J. M. (1988). *Caring for the disabled elderly: Who will pay?* Washington, DC: Brookings Institution.

Robinson, B., & Thurnher, M. (1979). Taking care of aged parents: A family circle transition. *The Gerontologist, 19*, 586-593.

Roff, L. L., & Klemmack, D. L. (1986). Norms for employed daughters' and sons' behavior toward frail older parents. *Sex Roles, 14*, 363-368.

Rosenthal, C. J. (1985). Kinkeeping in the familial division of labor. *Journal of Marriage and Family, 47*, 965-974.

Rosenthal, R., & Rosnow, R. (1975). *The volunteer subject.* New York: John Wiley.

Rosenwaike, I. (1985). A demographic portrait of the oldest old. *Milbank Memorial Fund Quarterly, 63*, 187-205.

Ross, C. E. (1987). The division of labor at home. *Social Forces, 65*, 816-833.

Ross, H. G., & Milgram, J. I. (1982). Important variables in sibling relationships: A qualitative study. In M. E. Lamb & B. Sutton-Smith (Eds.), *Sibling relationships: Their nature and significance over the life span* (pp. 225-249). Hillsdale, NJ: Lawrence Erlbaum.

Rossi, A. S. (1977). A biosocial perspective on parenting. *Daedalus, 106*, 1-30.

Rossi, A. S. (1984). Gender and parenthood. *American Sociological Review, 49*, 1-19.

Rossi, A. S., & Rossi, P. H. (1990). *Of human bonding: Parent-child relations across the life course.* New York: Aldine de Gruyter.

Ruddick, S. (1989). *Maternal thinking: Towards a politics of peace.* Boston: Beacon.

Sangl, J. (1985). The family support system of the elderly. In R. J. Vogel & H. C. Palmer (Eds.), *Long-term care: Perspectives from research and demonstration* (pp. 307-336). Rockville, MD: Aspen.

Sankar, A., Newcomer, R., & Wood, J. (1986). Prospective payment: Systematic effects on the provision of community care for the elderly. *Home Health Care Services Quarterly, 7*, 93-117.

Satariano, W. A., Minkler, M. A., & Langhauser, C. (1984). The significance of an ill spouse for assessing health differences in an elderly population. *Journal of the American Geriatrics Society, 32*, 187-190.

Sauer, W., & Coward, R. T. (Eds.). (1985). *Social support networks and the care of the elderly: Theory, research, and practice.* New York: Springer.

Sauer, W., Seelbach, W., & Hanson, S. (1981). Rural-urban and cohort differences in filial responsibility norms. *Journal of Minority Aging, 5,* 299-305.

Scanlon, W. J. (1988). A perspective on long-term care for the elderly. *Health Care Financing Review* (Annual Suppl.), 7-15.

Scharlach, A. (1987). Role strain in mother-daughter relationships in later life. *The Gerontologist, 27,* 627-631.

Scharlach, A., & Boyd, S. (1989). Caregiving and employment: Results of an employee survey. *The Gerontologist, 29,* 382-387.

Schlesinger, M. R., Tobin, S. S., & Kulys, R. (1981). The responsible child and parental well-being. *Journal of Gerontological Social Work, 3,* 3-16.

Schoonover, C. B., Brody, E. M., Hoffman, C., & Kleban, M. H. (1988). Parent care and geographically distant children. *Research on Aging, 10,* 472-492.

Schorr, A. L. (1960). *Filial responsibility in the modern American family.* (DHEW Publication). Washington, DC: Government Printing Office.

Schorr, A. L. (1968). *Explorations in social policy.* New York: Basic Books.

Schorr, A. L. (1980). *. . . thy father and thy mother . . . : A second look at filial responsibility and family policy* (DHHS Publication No. 13-11953). Washington, DC: Government Printing Office.

Schrimper, R. A., & Clark, R. L. (1985). Health expenditures and elderly adults. *Journal of Gerontology: Social Sciences, 40,* 235-243.

Schulz, J. (1988). *The economics of aging* (4th ed.). Belmont, CA: Wadsworth.

Schulz, R., Visintainer, P., & Williamson, G. M. (1990). Psychiatric and physical morbidity effects of caregiving. *Journal of Gerontology: Psychological Sciences, 45,* 181-191.

Scott, J. P. (1983). Siblings and other kin. In T. H. Brubaker (Ed.), *Family relationships in later life* (pp. 47-62). Beverly Hills, CA: Sage.

Seccombe, K., & Beeghley, L. (n.d.). *Gender and medical benefits.* Working paper.

Seelbach, W. C. (1977). Gender differences in expectations for filial responsibility. *The Gerontologist, 17,* 421-425.

Seelbach, W. C. (1978). Correlates of aged parents' filial responsibility expectations and realizations. *Family Coordinator, 27,* 341-350.

Seelbach, W. C. (1981). Filial responsibility among aged parents: A racial comparison. *Journal of Minority Aging, 5,* 286-292.

Seelbach, W. C. (1984). Filial responsibility and the care of aging family members. In W. H. Quinn & G. A. Hughston (Eds.), *Independent aging: Family and social systems perspectives* (pp. 92-105). Rockville, MD: Aspen.

Seelbach, W. C., & Sauer, W. J. (1977). Filial responsibility expectations and morale among aged parents. *The Gerontologist, 17,* 492-499.

Shanas, E. (1979a). The family as a social support system in old age. *The Gerontologist, 19,* 169-174.

Shanas, E. (1979b). The social myth as hypothesis: The case of family relations of old people. *The Gerontologist, 19,* 3-9.

Shanas, E. (1980). Older people and their families: The new pioneers. *Journal of Marriage and the Family, 42,* 9-15.

Shank, S. E. (1988). Women and the labor market: The link grows stronger. *Monthly Labor Review, 3,* 3-8.

Shelton, B. A. (1990). The distribution of household tasks: Does wife's employment status make a difference? *Journal of Family Issues, 11*, 115-135.

Shenk, D. (1987). *Someone to lend a helping hand: The lives of rural older women in central Minnesota.* St. Cloud: Central Minnesota Council on Aging.

Silliman, R., & Sternberg, J. (1988). Family caregiving: Impact of patient functioning and underlying causes of dependency. *The Gerontologist, 28*, 377-381.

Silverman, P. (1987). Widowhood as the next stage in the life course. In H. Lopata (Ed.), *Widows* (Vol. 2, pp. 171-190). Durham, NC: Duke University Press.

Sinnott, J. D. (1986). *Sex roles and aging: Theory and research from a systems perspective.* Basel, Switzerland: Karger.

Slocum, W. L., & Nye, F. I. (1976). Provider and housekeeper roles. In F. I. Nye (Ed.), *Role structure and analysis in the family* (pp. 81-99). Beverly Hills, CA: Sage.

Smuts, R. W. (1959). *Women and work in America.* New York: Columbia University Press.

Snyder, B., & Keefe, K. (1985). The unmet needs of family caregivers for frail and disabled adults. *Social Work in Health Care, 10*, 1-14.

Soldo, B. J., & Agree, E. M. (1988). America's elderly. *Population Bulletin, 43*, 1-53.

Soldo, B. J., & Manton, K. G. (1985). Health status and service needs of the oldest old: Current patterns and future trends. *Milbank Memorial Fund Quarterly, 63*, 286-319.

Soldo, B., & Myllyluoma, J. (1983). Caregivers who live with dependent elderly. *The Gerontologist, 23*, 605-611.

Sommers, T., & Shields, L. (1987). *Women take care: The consequences of caregiving in today's society.* Gainesville, FL: Triad.

Spitze, G. (1988). Women's employment and family relations: A review. *Journal of Marriage and the Family, 50*, 595-618.

Spitze, G., & Logan, J. (1989). Gender differences in family support: Is there a payoff? *The Gerontologist, 29*, 108-113.

Spitze, G., & Logan, J. (1990a). More evidence on women (and men) in the middle. *Research on Aging, 12*, 182-198.

Spitze, G., & Logan, J. (1990b). Sons, daughters, and intergenerational social support. *Journal of Marriage and the Family, 52*, 420-430.

Stafford, P. B. (1988). Caregiving and men's issues. In J. Norris (Ed.), *Daughters of the elderly: Building partnerships in caregiving* (pp. 179-184). Bloomington: Indiana University Press.

Stahl, S. M., & Feller, J. R. (1990). Old equals sick: An ontogenic fallacy. In S. M. Stahl (Ed.), *The legacy of longevity* (pp. 21-34). Newbury, CA: Sage.

Stephens, S. A., & Christianson, J. B. (1986). *Informal care of the elderly.* Lexington, MA: Lexington.

Stinchcombe, A. L. (1987). *Constructing social theories.* Chicago: University of Chicago Press.

Stoller, E. P. (1983). Parental caregiving by adult children. *Journal of Marriage and the Family, 45*, 851-858.

Stoller, E. P. (1985). Exchange patterns in the informal support networks of the elderly: The impact of reciprocity on morale. *Journal of Marriage and the Family, 47*, 335-348.

Stoller, E. P. (1990). Males as helpers: The roles of sons, relatives, and friends. *The Gerontologist, 30*, 228-235.

Stoller, E. P., & Earl, L. L. (1983). Help with activities of everyday life: Sources of support for the noninstitutionalized elderly. *The Gerontologist, 23*, 64-70.

Stoller, E. P., & Pugliesi, K. L. (1989). Other roles of caregivers: Competing responsibilities or supportive resources. *Journal of Gerontology: Social Sciences, 44*, 231-238.

Stoller, E. P., Pugliesi, K. L., & Gilbert, M. (1988). *Informal support and networks of the rural elderly: A panel study*. Technical report to the National Institute on Aging, Washington, DC.

Stone, R., Cafferata, G. L., & Sangl, J. (1987). Caregivers of the frail elderly: A national profile. *The Gerontologist, 27*, 616-626.

Stone, R., & Short, P. F. (1990). The competing demands of employment and informal caregiving to disabled elders. *Medical Care, 28*, 513-526.

Streib, G. F. (1965). Intergenerational relations: Perspectives of the two generations on the older parent. *Journal of Marriage and the Family, 27*, 469-476.

Streib, G. F., & Beck, R. W. (1980). Older families: A decade review. *Journal of Marriage and the Family, 42*, 937-956.

Strong, M. (1988). *Mainstay*. New York: Penguin.

Suggs, P. K. (1989). Predictors of association among older siblings: A black/white comparison. *American Behavioral Scientist, 33*, 70-80.

Suitor, J. J., & Pillemer, K. (1990). Transition to the status of family caregiver: A new framework for studying social support and well-being. In S. M. Stahl (Ed.), *The legacy of longevity* (pp. 310-320). Newbury Park, CA: Sage.

Sussman, M. B. (1965). Relationship of adult children to their parents in the United States. In E. Shanas & G. F. Streib (Eds.), *Social structure and the family* (pp. 62-92). Englewood Cliffs, NJ: Prentice-Hall.

Sweetser, D. A. (1984). Love and work: Intergenerational household composition in the U.S. in 1900. *Journal of Marriage and the Family, 46*, 289-293.

Szinovacz, M. (1989). Retirement couples and household work. In S. J. Bahr & E. Peterson (Eds.), *Aging and the family* (pp. 33-58). Lexington, MA: Lexington.

Targ, D. (1989). Feminist family sociology: Some reflections. *Sociological Focus, 22*, 151-160.

Tennstedt, S., McKinlay, J., & Sullivan, L. (1989). Informal care for frail elders: The role of secondary caregivers. *The Gerontologist, 29*, 677-683.

Thoits, P. (1983). Multiple identities and psychological well-being. *American Sociological Review, 48*, 174-187.

Thompson, L. (1989). Contextual and relational morality: Intergenerational responsibility in later life. In J. A. Mancini (Ed.), *Aging parents and adult children* (pp. 259-282). Lexington, MA: Lexington.

Thompson, L. (1990, November). *Feminist methodology for family studies*. Paper presented at the annual meeting of the National Council on Family Relations, Seattle, WA.

Thompson, L., & Walker, A. J. (1984). Mothers and daughters: Aid patterns and attachment. *Journal of Marriage and the Family, 46*, 313-322.

Thompson, L., & Walker, A. J. (1989). Gender in families: Women and men in marriage, work, and parenthood. *Journal of Marriage and the Family, 51*, 845-871.

Thornton, A. (1989). Changing attitudes toward family issues in the United States. *Journal of Marriage and the Family, 51*, 873-893.

Titmuss, R. M. (1968). *Commoners and welfare*. London: Allen & Unwin.

Tonti, M. (1988). Relationships among adult siblings who care for their aged parents. In M. D. Kahn & K. G. Lewis (Eds.), *Siblings in therapy: Life span and clinical issues* (pp. 417-434). New York: W. W. Norton.

Torrey, B. B. (1985). Sharing increasing costs on declining income: The visible dilemma of the invisible aged. *Milbank Memorial Fund Quarterly, 63*, 377-394.

Toseland, R. W., & Rossiter, C. M. (1989). Group interventions to support family caregivers: A review and analysis. *The Gerontologist, 29*, 438-448.

Townsend, P. (1957). *The family life of old people: An inquiry in East London.* Glencoe, IL: Free Press.

Townsend, A. L., & Poulshock, S. W. (1986). Intergenerational perspectives on elders' support networks. *Journal of Gerontology: Social Sciences, 41*, 101-109.

Travelers Companies. (1985). *The Travelers employee caregiver survey.* Hartford, CT: Author.

Treas, J. (1977). Family support systems for the aged: Some social and demographic considerations. *The Gerontologist, 17*, 486-491.

Troll, L. E. (1971). The family in later life: A decade review. *Journal of Marriage and the Family, 33*, 263-290.

Troll, L. E. (1987). Mother-daughter relationships through the life span. In S. Oskamp (Ed.), *Applied social psychology annual: Vol. 7. Family processes and problems: Social psychological aspects* (pp. 284-305). Newbury Park, CA: Sage.

Troll, L. E., Miller, S., & Atchley, R. (1979). *Families in later life.* Belmont, CA: Wadsworth.

Turner, J. H. (1982). *The structure of sociological theory* (3rd ed.). Homewood, IL: Dorsey.

Uhlenberg, P. (1980). Death and the family. *Journal of Family History, 5*, 313-320.

Ungerson, C. (1983). Why do women care? In J. Finch & D. Groves (Eds.), *A labour of love: Women, work, and caring* (pp. 31-49). London: Routledge & Kegan Paul.

Ungerson, C. (1987). *Policy is personal: Sex, gender, and informal care.* London: Tavistock.

U.S. Bureau of the Census. (1975). *Historical statistics of the United States, colonial times to 1970, bicentennial edition, part 2.* Washington, DC: Government Printing Office.

U.S. Bureau of the Census. (1989). *Projections of the population of the United States by age, sex, and race* (Current Population Reports, Series P-25, No. 1018). Washington, DC: Government Printing Office.

U.S. Bureau of the Census. (1990). *Statistical abstract of the United States, 1990* (110th ed.). Washington, DC: Government Printing Office.

U.S. Congress, Office of Technology Assessment. (1990). *Confused minds, burdened families: Finding help for people with Alzheimer's and other dementias* (Publication No. OTA-BA-403). Washington, DC: Government Printing Office.

U.S. Department of Health and Human Services. (1984). *1982 national long-term care survey/national survey of informal caregivers: Methods and procedures.* Washington, DC: Government Printing Office.

U.S. Department of Health and Human Services. (1989). *National long-term care survey, 1982-1984.* Washington, DC: U.S. Department of Commerce.

U.S. Department of Labor. (1985). *Handbook of labor statistics.* Washington, DC: Government Printing Office.

U.S. Department of Labor. (1986). *Facts on U.S. working women* (Fact Sheet No. 86-4). Washington, DC: Government Printing Office.

U.S. Department of Labor. (1987). *Half of mothers with children one year old or under are in the labor force in March 1987* (News Release No. 87-345). Washington, DC: Government Printing Office.

U.S. Department of Labor. (1988, January). *Employment and earnings.* Washington, DC: Government Printing Office.

U.S. House of Representatives, Committee on Energy and Commerce. (1986). *Long-term care service for the elderly.* Washington, DC: Government Printing Office.

U.S. House of Representatives, Select Committee on Aging. (1987). *Exploding the myths: Caregiving in America* (100th Congress, 1st session, Comm. Pub. No. 99-611). Washington, DC: Government Printing Office.

U.S. Senate, Special Committee on Aging. (1987). *Developments in aging, 1986*. Washington, DC: Government Printing Office.

U.S. Senate, Special Committee on Aging. (1988a). *Developments in aging, 1987* (Vol. 1). Washington, DC: Government Printing Office.

U.S. Senate, Special Committee on Aging. (1988b). *Developments in aging, 1987* (Vol. 3). Washington, DC: Government Printing Office.

U.S. Senate, Special Committee on Aging. (1990). *Developments in aging, 1989*. Washington, DC: Government Printing Office.

Vera, H., Berardo, D., & Berardo, F. (1985). Age heterogamy in marriage. *Journal of Marriage and the Family, 47*, 553-566.

Vaux, A. (1985). Variations in social support associated with gender, ethnicity, and age. *Journal of Social Issues, 41*, 89-110.

Verbrugge, L. M. (1983). Multiple roles and physical health of women and men. *Journal of Health and Social Behavior, 24*, 16-30.

Verbrugge, L. M. (1989). Gender, aging, and health. In K. S. Markides (Ed.), *Aging and health* (pp. 23-78). Newbury Park, CA: Sage.

Waerness, K. (1985). *Informal and formal care in old age: What is wrong with the new ideology of community care in the Scandinavian welfare state today?* Paper presented at the Conference on Gender Divisions and Policies for Community Care, University of Kent, Canterbury, England.

Wagner, D. L., Creedon, M. E., Sasala, J., & Neal, M. B. (1989, September). *Employers and elder care: Designing effective responses for the workplace.* Paper prepared for Workplace Responses to Eldercare Teleconference, Center for the Study of Aging, University of Bridgeport, CT.

Wake, S. B., & Sporakowski, M. J. (1972). An intergenerational comparison of attitudes towards supporting aged parents. *Journal of Marriage and the Family, 34*, 42-48.

Walker, A. J. (1983). Care for elderly people: A conflict between women and the state. In J. Finch & D. Groves (Eds.), *A labour of love: Women, work, and caring* (pp. 106-128). London: Routledge & Kegan Paul.

Walker, A. J. (1985). From welfare state to caring society? The promise of informal support networks. In J. Jonker, R. Leaper, & J. Yoder (Eds.), *Support networks in a caring community* (pp. 41-58). Lancaster, England: Martins Nijhoff.

Walker, A. J., Pratt, C. C., Shin, H. Y., & Jones, L. L. (1989). Why daughters care: Perspectives of mothers and daughters in a caregiving situation. In J. A. Mancini (Ed.), *Aging parents and adult children* (pp. 199-212). Lexington, MA: Lexington.

Walker, A. J., Pratt, C. C., Shin, H. Y., & Jones, L. L. (1990). Motive for parental caregiving and relationship quality. *Family Relations, 39*, 51-56.

Walker, A. J., Shin, H., & Bird, J. N. (1990). Perceptions of relationship change and caregiver satisfaction. *Family Relations, 39*, 147-152.

Walker, A. J., Shin, H., Jones, L. L., & Pratt, C. C. (1987, November). *Mothers' and daughters' reasons for daughters' caregiving.* Paper presented at the 49th Annual Meeting of the National Council on Family Relations, Atlanta, GA.

Walker, A. J., & Thompson, L. (1983). Intimacy and intergenerational aid and contact among daughters and mothers. *Journal of Marriage and the Family, 45*, 841-849.

Ward, R. A., Sherman, S. R., & La Gory, M. (1984). Informal networks and knowledge of services for older persons. *Journal of Gerontology: Social Sciences, 39*, 216-223.

Warshaw, L. J., Barr, J. K., Rayman, I., Schachter, J., & Lucas, T. G. (1986). *Employer support for employee caregivers.* New York: New York Business Group on Health.

Weitzman, L. J. (1985). *The divorce revolution.* New York: Free Press.

Wenger, G. C. (1984). *The supportive network: Coping with old age.* London: George Allen & Unwin.

Wiener, J. M., Hanley, R. J., Clark, R., & Van Nostrand, J. F. (1990). Measuring the activities of daily living: Comparisons across national surveys. *Journal of Gerontology: Social Sciences, 45,* 229-237.

Wiesenfeld, A. R., Whitman, P. B., & Malatesta, C. Z. (1984). Individual differences among adult women in sensitivity to infants: Evidence in support of an empathy concept. *Journal of Personality and Social Psychology, 46,* 118-124.

Wisensale, S. K. (1990). Approaches to family policy in state government: A report on five states. *Family Relations, 39,* 136-140.

Wisensale, S. K., & Allison, M. D. (1988). An analysis of 1987 family leave legislation: Implications for caregivers of the elderly. *The Gerontologist, 28,* 779-785.

Wisensale, S. K., & Allison, M. D. (1989). Family leave legislation: State and federal initiatives. *Family Relations, 38,* 182-189.

Woehrer, C. E. (1982). The influence of ethnic families on intergenerational relationships and later life transitions. *Annals of the American Academy of Political and Social Science, 464,* 65-78.

Wood, J. B., Fox, P. J., Estes, C. L., Lee, P. R., & Mahoney, C. W. (1986). *Public policy, the private nonprofit sector and the delivery of community-based long term care services for the elderly: Final report, executive summary.* San Francisco: University of California, Institute for Health and Aging.

Wright, F. (1983). Single careers: Employment, housework, and caring. In D. Finch (Ed.), *A labour of love: Women, working, and caring* (pp. 89-105). London: Routledge & Kegan Paul.

Young, R., & Kahana, E. (1989). Specifying caregiver outcomes: Gender and relationship aspects of caregiving strain. *The Gerontologist, 29,* 660-666.

Zarit, S. H. (1989). Do we need another stress and caregiving study? *The Gerontologist, 29,* 660-666.

Zarit, S. H., Reever, K. E., & Bach-Peterson, J. (1980). Relatives of the impaired elderly: Correlates of feelings of burden. *The Gerontologist, 20,* 649-655.

Zarit, S. H., Todd, P., & Zarit, J. (1986). Subjective burden of husbands and wives as caregivers: A longitudinal study. *The Gerontologist, 26,* 260-266.

Zarit, S. H., & Toseland, R. W. (1989). Current and future directions in family caregiving research. *The Gerontologist, 29,* 481-483.

Zelditch, M., Jr. (1955). Role differentiation in the nuclear family: A comparative study. In T. Parsons & R. F. Bales (Eds.), *Family, socialization, and interaction process.* Glencoe, IL: Free Press.

Zimmerman, S. L., & Owens, P. (1989). Comparing the family policies of three states: A content analysis. *Family Relations, 38,* 190-195.

Zuzanek, J. (1987, November). *Till leisure us part . . .* Paper presented at the 40th Annual Meeting of the Gerontological Society of America, Washington, DC.

Author Index

243

Subject Index

Abandonment, 169
Activity of daily living (ADL):
  aging and, 21
  caregiving definitions, 11-13
  daughter's roles, 80
  gender-related cultural taboos, 75
  measure variability for, 154
  NLTCS samples and, 23
Adult child caregivers:
  Alzheimer's patient case study, 206-207
  attitudes towards aging, 96
  burden and stress, 75-77, 94-95, 116, 210
  caregiving definitions of, 11-12
  cohort membership, 117
  daughter dominance, 26, 28, 29, 31, 33,
    67-68, 80, 87, 100, 120-121
  developmental crisis for, 106
  division of labor, 114-115, 122-123
  dyadic relationship quality, 78
  employment, 71-72, 76, 77, 81-82, 111
  expectations, 107-110
  fairness perceptions, 92-93
  family size and, 15
  gender interactions, 139-140, 153-154
  kinship roles, 124-125
  marital status of, 88, 171
  mental health effects, 145
  motivations of, 125-127
  NLTCS results, 24-25
  parent demographics and, 26-32, 129

  parent impairment level and, 91-92
  prevalence of, 65, 67, 80
  primary caregiver hierarchy, 14
  roles of, 69, 77-78, 106, 109, 114-116
  satisfaction, 79
  self-identification, 35-36
  siblings of, 86-89
  support for, 69-70
  types of tasks, 68-69
  See also Filial responsibility; Parent
    care; Sibling caregivers
Affection, 11, 36-37
  burden and, 75
  filial responsibility and, 36-37, 66-67,
    113
  importance for care receivers, 109
  parent-child relationships, 78, 126-127
  See also Attachment
Age and aging:
  ADL impairment and, 21
  caregiver characteristics versus, 26-29
  cultural influences, 158
  denial of, 96
  gender covariance, 159-160
  sex roles and, 55, 100
  spouse caregivers, 63
  stratification, 39-40
Aged Services Project, 110
Alzheimer's patients, 205-207, 210-211
Anger, 51

247

256   Gender, Families, and Elder Care

About the Editors

Jeffrey W. Dwyer, Ph.D., is Associate Professor in the College of Nursing and Associate Research Scientist in the Center for Health Policy Research at the University of Florida. He received his doctorate from the Department of Sociology at the University of Florida and formerly was a postdoctorate fellow in the Center for Health Policy Research. In 1990 he was selected as the Graduate Faculty Teacher of the Year in the UF College of Nursing. His research has appeared in a number of noted publications, including *The Gerontologist, Research on Aging, Family Relations, New England Journal of Medicine, Academic Medicine,* and the *Journal of Health and Social Behavior.* He was also one of the guest editors for the 1990 "decade review" issue of the *Journal of Rural Health.* In addition to teaching a graduate course in health policy, he pursues research interests in the areas of family caregiving, health and aging, the impact of social structure on health outcomes, health policy, and the education of health professionals.

Raymond T. Coward, M.S.W., Ph.D., is Associate Director of the Center for Health Policy Research at the University of Florida Health Science Center, and Professor in the Department of Medicine. He is also a Faculty Associate with the UF Center for Gerontological Studies; the Geriatric Research, Education and Clinical Center of the Department of Veterans Affairs Medical Center; the UF Geriatric Education Center; and, the Claude Denson Pepper Center for Research on Oral Health and Aging. He served as editor of the *Journal of Rural Health*, an official publication of the National Rural Health Association, from 1985 through 1990. He is the author or editor

257

of eight books, including several related to aging issues, such as *The Elderly in Rural Society* and *Social Support Networks and Care of the Elderly*. In 1991, he received a Distinguished Alumni award from Purdue University, and in 1989 he was named the University Scholar in the Social Sciences by the Graduate College of the University of Vermont. In addition, he received the Distinguished Research Award from the American Rural Health Association in 1981 and was named the John K. Friesen Visiting Lecturer in Gerontology at Simon Fraser University (Burnaby, British Columbia) in 1989. He is a member of the honor societies of Phi Kappa Phi and Sigma Xi. His primary research interests are the development, delivery, and evaluation of health and human services for elders and their families. He has served as an expert witness and consultant to state and federal agencies and legislative bodies and has lectured internationally at universities and professional societies in Canada, Poland, Hong Kong, the Philippines, and Mexico, and in 1988 was a guest of the Institute of Sociology of the Hungarian Academy of Sciences.

About the Contributors

Rosemary Blieszner, Ph.D., is Associate Professor in the Department of Family and Child Development and Associate Director of the Center for Gerontology at Virginia Polytechnic Institute and State University. She received her Ph.D. from the Pennsylvania State University in human development/family studies, with a concentration in adult development and aging. Her research focuses on family and friend relationships and life events in adulthood and old age, with emphases on relationship processes over time and the contributions of close relationships to psychological well-being. She is coeditor, with Rebecca G. Adams, of *Older Adult Friendship: Structure and Process*, and her work has appeared in the *Journal of Marriage and the Family, Family Relations,* the *Journals of Gerontology, The Gerontologist,* and the *Journal of Social and Personal Relationships.*

Victor G. Cicirelli, Ph.D., is Professor of Developmental and Aging Psychology in the Department of Psychological Sciences at Purdue University. He holds doctorates from the University of Michigan and Michigan State University. He has been a postdoctoral fellow at both the Institute for Cognitive Learning of the University of Wisconsin and the Andrus Gerontology Center of the University of Southern California. In the spring of 1991, he held a visiting scientist fellowship at the Max Planck Institute in Berlin. In addition to his teaching activities in gerontological psychology, his research interests include parent-child relationships in later life, sibling relationships, and family support of the elderly. He is the author of *Helping Elderly Parents: Role of Adult Children* and *Respect for Autonomy and*

Paternalism: When Adult Children Help Elderly Parents, as well as numerous articles and book chapters.

Lisa P. Gwyther, M.S.W., A.C.S.W., is Assistant Professor in the Division of Psychiatric Social Work, Department of Psychiatry, at Duke University Medical Center. She directs the Duke Center for Aging's Family Support Program and the Information Transfer and Community Education Core of the Joseph and Kathleen Bryan Alzheimer's Disease Research Center at Duke. She received her M.S.W. from Case Western Reserve University. She is editor of the "Practice Concepts" section of *The Gerontologist* and the author of numerous articles, manuals, and a book on caregiving and Alzheimer's disease. She is a member of the Department of Health and Human Services Advisory Panel on Alzheimer's Disease and a subcommittee chair for the national Alzheimer's Association.

Raeann R. Hamon, Ph.D., is Assistant Professor of Family Studies at Messiah College. She received her M.S. and Ph.D. from the Department of Family and Child Development and a graduate certificate in gerontology at Virginia Polytechnic Institute and State University. She teaches courses in family theory, marriage and the family, interpersonal relations, and gerontology. Her research interests include families in later life, intergenerational relationships, and the effects of adult children's divorce on aging parents.

Nancy R. Hooyman, Ph.D., is Professor and Dean of the School of Social Work at the University of Washington. Her Ph.D. is in sociology and social work from the University of Michigan. Nationally recognized for her scholarship in aging, issues related to caregiving of dependents, feminist social work practice, and administration and community organization, she has coauthored or edited five books, among them *Social Gerontology: A Multidisciplinary Perspective* (two editions) and *Taking Care: Supporting Older People and Their Families* (two editions). She has published more than 50 articles and chapters related to gerontology and women's issues. She is a frequently requested speaker, and has given more than 70 academic presentations nationally and internationally. She has served as chair of the Council on Social Work Education (CSWE) Commission on the Role and Status of Women in Social Work Education, is currently a member of the Aging Subcommittee of the National Association of Social Workers Commission on Family and Primary Associations, is a board member of the CSWE, and has served on a number of national committees related to social work education, gerontology, and women's issues.

Claydell Horne, M.S.N., is a doctoral candidate in the College of Nursing and a Graduate Research Assistant in the Center for Health Policy Research at the University of Florida in Gainesville. Her professional experience includes teaching adult health and gerontological nursing. Her current research interests include family caregiving and patient education.

Amy Horowitz, D.S.W., is the Associate Executive Director for Research and Evaluation at the Lighthouse Inc. and an Adjunct Associate Professor at Fordham University Graduate School of Social Services. She received her M.S.W. at Fordham University and her D.S.W. at Columbia University. Her research interests include family caregiving, relationships between formal and informal care systems, and adaptation to chronic disability. Among her numerous publications is the much-cited "Family Caregiving to the Frail Elderly," which appeared in the *Annual Review of Gerontology and Geriatrics* in 1985. Her most recent publication is a forthcoming article in *The Gerontologist* titled "A Conceptual and Empirical Exploration of Personal Autonomy Issues within Family Caregiving Relationships."

Gary R. Lee, Ph.D., received his doctorate from the University of Minnesota in 1973. He is currently Professor of Sociology at the University of Florida. His research interests involve both family sociology and the sociology of aging, and concentrate particularly on the intersection of those two fields. He is the author of *Family Structure and Interaction: A Comparative Analysis* and *Family Systems in America* (with Ira L. Reiss). He is also coeditor (with Raymond T. Coward) of *The Elderly in Rural Society: Every Fourth Elder.* His recent research has involved marital happiness in later life and rural-urban differences in the availability of adult children as caregivers for the frail elderly.

Rhonda J. V. Montgomery, Ph.D., is the Director of the Institute of Gerontology and Associate Professor of Sociology at Wayne State University in Detroit, Michigan. She is also the editor of *Research on Aging.* For the last 10 years, her research has focused on public policy and family relations among older adults. She has conducted several studies of families providing care to the elderly aimed at assessing the feasibility, costs, and benefits of alternative programs for supporting these families in their caregiving efforts. Currently she is studying the utility, design, and delivery of respite services for families caring for persons with Alzheimer's disease.

Karen Seccombe, M.S.W., Ph.D., is Assistant Professor in the Department of Sociology at the University of Florida. She received her Ph.D. from Washington State University, and was a postdoctoral fellow in the Institute on Aging at the University of Washington. Her research interests include social inequality, with a particular focus on gender stratification, manifested within the family and health care systems. She is currently investigating the antecedents and consequences of employer-sponsored medical insurance coverage among workers in the United States. In addition, she teaches courses in medical sociology and poverty.

Eleanor Palo Stoller, Ph.D., is Professor of Sociology and Coordinator of Women's Studies at the State University of New York at Plattsburgh. She received her Ph.D. from Washington University (St. Louis). Her research on lay care and informal networks of community-based elderly has been funded by the National Institute on Aging and the Administration on Aging. Her research has appeared in a number of prestigious publications, including the *Journal of Marriage and the Family*, *The Gerontologist*, the *Journals of Gerontology*, *Journal of Health and Social Behavior*, *Research on Aging*, *Medical Care*, and *Health and Aging*.

Alexis J. Walker, Ph.D., is Associate Professor of Human Development and Family Science at Oregon State University. She received her Ph.D. in human development and family studies from the Pennsylvania State University. Her research interests include family caregiving, gender and families, and inter-generational relationships. She recently guest edited a special issue of the *Journal of Family Issues* titled "Gender and Unpaid Work." She is on the editorial boards of *Family Relations*, the *Journal of Marriage and the Family*, and the *Psychology of Women Quarterly*.